King Charles II

~

ANTONIA FRASER

Volume Two

PHOENIX

This edition produced for The Book People Ltd,
Hall Wood Avenue, Haydock, St Helens WA11 9UL

First published in Great Britain in 1979
by Weidenfeld & Nicolson Ltd
First published in paperback in 1993
by Mandarin Paperbacks

Paperback edition published in 2002
by Phoenix,
an imprint of Orion Books Ltd,
Orion House, 5 Upper St Martin's Lane,
London WC2H 9EA

A CIP catalogue record for this book is available from the British Library.

ISBN 978 1 4072 1529 7

Printed and bound in Great Britain by
Clays Ltd, St Ives plc

The Orion Publishing Group's policy is to use papers that are natural, renewable
and recyclable products and made from wood grown in sustainable forests. The
logging and manufacturing processed are expected to conform to the environmental
regulations of the country of origin.

www.orionbooks.co.uk

Contents

PART FOUR

The Monarchy in Danger

'The Monarchy itself is in great Danger, as well as His
Majesty's person....'
JAMES DUKE OF YORK to William of Orange, 1679

CHAPTER NINETEEN

Subsisting Together?

'Affairs are at present here in such a state as to make
one believe that a King and a Parliament can no longer
subsist together; that they [the King and the Duke of
York] must now think only of the war against the
Dutch, using the means which they now have, without
further recourse to Parliament.'

James Duke of York, July 1671

The position of Charles II in the two years following the
Secret Treaty of Dover of 1670 would have struck any
cognizant observer as ironical, even humorous. On the
one hand, the English King was committed by the treaty to a
war against Holland as soon as was convenient – and the French
King was committed to participate in the action. For such a war
Charles II would need an ample additional 'supply' from his
Parliament. Quite apart from the troops promised, this was
especially true if his beloved Navy was to acquit itself with glory.
The new French subsidy was nothing like sufficient for a land
and sea campaign.

On the other hand, the very existence of this treaty was
unknown to the English Parliament as a whole: of those ministers
who were in the secret, only the most intimate knew the whole
truth. In the next few years many members of both Houses
would begin to guess from the pro-French drift of the King's
actions that something of the sort had taken place. But the
ability to make foreign treaties, like that to make peace and war,
remained within the most closely guarded enclave of the royal
prerogative.

One result of this secrecy was that Members of Parliament
remained extremely suspicious about the use the King might

make of the supplies they voted. Just as the King feared in the recesses of his mind the return of revolution, or something approaching it, Parliament feared the arrival of absolutism. In February 1673, after the start of the Third Dutch War, Charles II castigated Parliament for 'a jealousy ... that is maliciously spread abroad', so weak and frivolous that he would not have mentioned it, but for the fact that it had gained ground with some 'well-minded people': and that is, 'that the forces I have raised in this war were designed to control law and property'.[1]

But the fact was that the King's growing disgust with Parliament, the cynical if understandable determination he showed to circumvent it where possible, contributed to this paranoia on its part. Equally, the King's own wariness about the attacks on his prerogative – where would it all end? With another 1642? With another 1649? – was fed by the obstreperous nature of Parliament from 1671 onwards. Neither side trusted the other. And there was a good deal to be said for both points of view.

The behaviour of the Parliament called by the King in February 1671 did nothing to smooth the situation. Back in the early 1660s, how lovingly the King had spoken of Parliaments: with genuine emotion he had declared that neither King nor Parliament could function without the other. By July 1671, in contrast, the Duke of York was doubting whether Parliament could contribute anything at all to the current royal project. 'Affairs are at present here in such a state,' he wrote, 'as to make one believe that a King and a Parliament can no longer subsist together; that they [that is, the King and the Duke of York] must now think only of the war against the Dutch, using the means which they now have, without further recourse to Parliament.'[2]

This session of Parliament ended in April, when the King prorogued it once more; Parliament did not meet again till February 1673. The most significant effect of this session was to demonstrate the new amity of the royal brothers. The Roos divorce case had come and gone. A precedent had been set up that a man could gain a divorce by Act of Parliament. The King had not availed himself of it. Succession-watchers – who comprised most members of the Court and many Members of

Parliament – considered that the Duke of York's position was in consequence much strengthened.

The trouble was that the King still needed money to make his promised war, and his finances were in their familiar critical state. By adjourning Parliament, he had forfeited certain valuable revenues not yet voted to him. This was the background to the desperate new remedy proposed – probably by Clifford – known as the Stop of the Exchequer. This measure put a violent end to the system started in 1667 by which direct assignments of revenue were issued by the Treasury in return for loans to the government. These paper orders or tallies were registered in the Treasury Book in order to be paid off in order of issue by funds on their way to the Exchequer. Now the King announced that in future monies would go directly to the Exchequer, regardless of these tallies.

Much later the King would say of the Stop to Lord Bruce: 'It was a false step.' It was certainly a colossal psychological mistake. Marvell expressed the national mood of indignation when he called it 'the Robbery at the Exchequer'. Many of those ruined were the weak, those traditionally at the mercy of the mighty. There was another side to it, equally psychologically damaging, the destruction of the strong. Evelyn referred to the Stop in poignant and angry terms as 'an action which not only lost the hearts of his subjects, and ruined many widows and orphans, whose stocks were lent him, but the reputation of his Exchequer forever'. Two banking businesses never recovered. Edward Backwell, for example, he who had persistently put his trust in a prince's credit, held nearly three hundred thousand pounds' worth of paper orders, many incurred in the interests of paying off William of Orange, and as a result he could never lend on a large scale again.[3] The fatal impression was created that it was too dangerous to lend money to the English monarchy.

While it is not possible to quarrel with the King's own estimate of the Stop – it was a false step – one can also sympathize with the circumstances which drove him to it. The goldsmiths were reluctant to lend: the interest they charged – between eight and ten per cent – was not inordinate in an age when fifteen, even twenty per cent was known and they themselves were probably having to pay six per cent. Loans were difficult to obtain.[4] The real culprit was the current English banking system, or rather the lack of it. The problems were not properly solved before the reign of William III, when not only was the Bank of England founded (the happy Dutch already had a national bank), but the concept of a 'perpetual fund' was developed; while William's Parliament – unlike that of Charles II – was willing to underwrite the debts of the State.

The unpopularity and distrust incurred over the Stop did not assist the King in the promulgation of his next measure, done without the support of Parliament. This was the Declaration of Indulgence, given out by the King on 15 March 1672.[5] Its terms made it quite clear that it rested solely upon the powers of the King. Charles II had long wished to do something for both types of religious extremist contained within his kingdom, dissenters and Catholics. It will be remembered that back in 1662 he had issued a declaration granting toleration to both sets of believers.

Then he attempted – in vain – to get the declaration ratified by the authority of Parliament. Now he made no such attempt. The King himself in the new Declaration referred bitterly to the 'sad experience' of the past twelve years and how there was 'very little fruit' from it. Now therefore he felt himself obliged to make use of 'that supreme power in ecclesiastical matters which is not only inherent in us, but hath been declared and recognized to be so by several statutes and Acts of Parliament ...'. Resting on this power, he proposed to suspend all the penal laws against nonconformists and Catholics. Nonconformists should further be allowed public places of worship by licence; the Catholics would be allowed to worship in their own way privately in their homes.

The words were bold, the sentiments admirable. The measure was taken 'for the quieting the minds of our good subjects ... for inviting strangers in this conjuncture to come and live under us' – the language being reminiscent of that of another exponent of toleration, Oliver Cromwell, who declared himself as 'loving strangers', hoping that they would live in England's midst. Like

Cromwell, Charles II was to be unsuccessful in swaying the spirit of the times.

The trouble was that it was by no means generally agreed that the King possessed any such 'supreme power in ecclesiastical matters'. The attempt of Charles II to exercise such a power without seeking Parliamentary ratification, while Parliament was not even in session, provoked several types of fear. The Stop of the Exchequer had scarcely prepared the way for the popularity of the King's personal policies. Now the Declaration of Indulgence, by appearing to favour Catholics (for so it was inevitably interpreted by the anti-Popish lobby), confirmed suspicions already aroused by the rumoured conversion of the Duke of York.

Even so, the King might have spiritedly carried through the Declaration of Indulgence, were it not for the demands of the Dutch War. Without money voted by Parliament, he would not be able to carry out that provision of the Secret Treaty of Dover most precious to him. Seen from that angle, the timing of the Declaration of Indulgence, a few days off from another declaration – that of war against Holland – was too spirited altogether. There was a rancorous outcry, not only from Westminster but from far beyond its purlieus. 'It is incredible how much excitement the measure causes all over the country,' wrote the Venetian Ambassador. Neither all the criticism, nor all the support, came from predictable quarters. The judges, for instance, disapproved of the measure because they considered the King was claiming powers he did not possess – this despite the fact that since 1668 they had generally held their offices *durante bene placito* (at the King's good pleasure) rather than *quamdiu se bene gesserit* (so long as they behaved themselves).[6] Lord Ashley, on the other hand, approved of it because he believed that it was widening the basis of the Church of England.[7] Shortly afterwards he was created Earl of Shaftesbury, as part of a general distribution of honours to members of the Cabal on the eve of the war, by which name he will in future be known. Arlington also received an earldom, Clifford a barony, and Lauderdale a dukedom.

There was another crucial element in the treatment of the

Declaration within Parliament. And that was the ability of the King's ministers to provide some sort of Court bloc. Lately Clifford's and Arlington's right-hand man, Sir Joseph Williamson, had apparently been more successful in this respect, although the fact that by February 1671 well over two hundred seats had changed hands since the original election of the Cavalier Parliament in 1661 meant that the composition of the body was more mysterious than the Court managers supposed.

Williamson, another government official of the King's own generation, had begun his career in the office of Sir Edward Nicholas. He transferred to the service of Arlington when the latter succeeded Nicholas as Secretary of State. Williamson entered Parliament himself in 1669, after various attempts; in 1672 he became Clerk of the Council, and was knighted. Possessing exceptional diligence, he also acted as editor of the *London Gazette*, the official publication of the government, which had grown out of a news-sheet disseminated in Oxford at the time of the Court's residence there in 1665. He was, then, like Arlington, an able and devoted servant of the Crown.

But the abortive affair of the Declaration of Indulgence would demonstrate that, for all the work of Williamson, Arlington and Clifford, the King might have his way in small things, but he still could not push through any measure to which Parliament was opposed. His 'supreme power in ecclesiastical matters' was a hollow boast.

There were a series of ostensible excuses for making war on Holland. The official line was given by Charles II in March 1672, when he wrote of England (to his brother) as 'having received many wrongs and indignities from the States General of the United Provinces'. Wrongs were suffered in Surinam, over the East India trade and the English fisheries; indignities were also suffered by the King's Majesty in a series of Dutch satirical pamphlets and medallions. English tactics leading up to the war were however more frankly summed up by Arlington: 'Our business is to break with them and yet to lay the breach at their door.'[8]

Charles' unwavering personal view was given by the Venetian

Ambassador: 'The King is convinced that the hatred of the Dutch for England is hereditary, that it increased because of trade and became implacable owing to the pretensions of the United Provinces.' As to the place of France in the awkward triangle which had existed for the last five years between the three countries, the King told the Council, 'The French will have us or Holland always with them and if we take them not, Holland will have them.'[9]

These were familiar arguments: later Shaftesbury would cry out for the destruction of the Dutch, quoting the famous phrase of the Roman senator, on another hereditary feud between two peoples: '*Delenda est Carthago*'. With more convictions than Shaftesbury, because he had held the view much longer, Charles II believed in the need to crush, or at any rate curb, the United Provinces at sea, in the various corners of the growing English empire and wherever else their 'pretensions' might prickle the English. This, plus a French alliance, was the foreign policy he had worked out for himself. Under the circumstances, a dreadful insult endured by the English yacht *Merlin* at the hands of the Dutch was largely irrelevant – and almost wholly manufactured. All the same, the mixture was not quite as before. On the Dutch side, there was a new and explosive element present. This was their recently appointed General, William of Orange.

It is time to return to this solemn youth, last heard of visiting England in 1670 and attempting to get his engaging uncle to pay his debts to the House of Orange. William too was busy working out the proper direction of his foreign policy. In February 1672 he was made Captain General and Admiral General of the Dutch forces in the field. But, faced as he was with the hordes of France only an inadequate land-mass away, he could hardly afford the luxury of treating England as a foe. Besides, the natural link between England and Holland, from the Orangists' point of view, was one of warm family alliance rather than enmity.

The Orangists naively believed that William's new office would sway his uncle of England in his approach to Holland. They could not understand that Charles' debonair approach to William concealed a genuine inability to understand his nephew's

9

point of view. The insensitivity which Charles continued to show in his letters to William throughout 1672 is striking in such a normally diplomatic man. In April Charles suggested that although 'our interests seem to be a little differing at this present' – a blithe way of alluding to a state of war between their respective countries – he had still done William a considerable service; for had war not broken out, William would never have become General of the Dutch forces!

In July Charles was confident that if William would only follow his advice, 'I make little doubt by the blessing of God of establishing you in the power there [that is, in Holland] which your forefathers always aimed at.' Charles was presumably taking the line to himself that the terms of the Secret Treaty of Dover stood to carve a hereditary principality out of the United Provinces for his nephew. Equally obtuse were Charles' attempts later in the year to make a humiliating peace with Holland via William: 'Such a one as in the bad condition of your affairs will be much better for you and that poor people than any war can be....'[10] To Charles II's amazement, William did not answer.

This insensitivity is striking. It is also surprising. One is obliged to conclude that it sprang from Charles II's own peculiar and deep-seated attitude to family relationships. Towards the end of the seventies these relationships – with his brother, his wife – were tested in a crucible and survived. In the mean time, because Charles II felt warmly towards his family, he obviously expected his relatives to feel the same. In the case of his sister Mary, his expectations had been fulfilled. In the case of her son William, they were to be grievously disappointed.

As William told Buckingham and Arlington, on a joint mission to Holland in 1673 in search of a satisfactory peace – satisfactory to England, that is – 'he liked better the condition of Stadtholder they [the Dutch] had given him ... he believed himself obliged in conscience and honour not to prefer his interest before his obligation.'[11] For the next few years William, all unaware of the Secret Treaty of Dover, would see his obligation as the task of detaching England from France. First however he had to win his spurs in his own country, by saving it from extinction.

When war was declared on 17 March, the total forces of

French and English far outnumbered those of the Dutch, both by land and by sea. Only in naval guns – 4,500 to the allies' 6,000 – did the Dutch approach any kind of equality. Charles II was confident that the spoils of war would include not only those Dutch territories specified in the Secret Treaty, but also some rich naval prizes calculated to swell his depleted Treasury. Since the conduct of the war at sea was left to the English, Charles construed it as his 'obligation', as William would have put it, to interfere himself whenever possible. He paid two visits to the Nore off Chatham, where the Duke of York was once more installed in charge of the fleet; at the end of June he was accompanied by Queen Catharine and Shaftesbury, as Lord Chancellor; at the start of September he took Prince Rupert, Shaftesbury and other members of the Council.

At the beginning of May Charles also wrote James a long letter in his own handwriting, beginning, 'I was this day in our meeting for the business of the fleet, and amongst other things I thought it not amiss to give you this hint. . . .'[12] The hint was the inadvisability of fighting with the Dutch alone: the Duke ought to wait until he had joined up with the French squadron. But at the first proper battle of the war, neither French nor English – nor, by implication, the English commander the Duke of York – covered themselves with glory.

On 7 June, lying in Southwold Bay, off the East Anglian coast between Yarmouth and Lowestoft, the combined squadrons were surprised by the great Dutch Admiral De Ruyter. In the ensuing action both sides endured vast losses. On the English side, the Duke of York had to abandon two successive flagships, the *Prince* and *St Michael*. Lord Sandwich was killed; his body, drifting anonymously in the sea, was only recognized by the George it still wore, the insignia of the Garter. De Ruyter was now limited by lack of funds to using guerrilla tactics. Yet this he did brilliantly, using his superior knowledge of the shoals and islands off the Dutch coast to pounce and harass, then disappear.

It was on land that the Dutch situation seemed most desperate. How could the unfortunate Dutch hope to hold off the great swoop of the French forces through the southern and eastern provinces? The answer was the dramatic and totally unexpected response of a small nation to the aggression of a great power. The Dutch opened their dykes, flooding the land in the face of the oncoming invader. Shortly afterwards William received supreme civilian as well as military command.

The French had been held off, but that was all: the crisis remained. There was no prophet to foresee that 8 July 1672, the date on which William III became Stadholder, had ushered in a new era in Europe.

In August Johann De Witt and his brother were murdered by 'the people' – as Charles II described the killers in one of his missives to William – for being 'the authors and occasion of the war'. William kept himself coldly aloof from the crime. It is extremely unlikely that he participated, as his enemies suggested.[13] Nevertheless, the assassins went unpunished, and later he paid one of them a pension. Admittedly, it was granted for quite a different reason, but the implication that William was not sorry to see Johann De Witt out of the way was easily drawn.

In England, in contrast to fierce and fighting Holland, reactions to the war were desultory. By June, many of the English were talking openly of peace. Even her forces were not immune from this general malaise. In August Sir Charles Lyttelton wrote back from his ship, 'I never saw people so intolerably weary as they are all of being at sea, not only land men and volunteers, but the seamen themselves.'[14] In general, the autumn of 1672 was not a golden time for good King Charles. William, as we have seen, did not acknowledge his uncle's vulpine overtures for peace. Then Charles had a growing problem with the Catholicism of the Duke of York: much publicity was given to the fact that the Duke had not taken Anglican Communion at Easter. A smashing naval victory under the Duke's command might have given him some further mileage in the popular esteem; instead, he was faced with the responsibility for South-wold Bay.

The Duke of York was not the only prominent Catholic who had newly swum into the public gaze. The King's latest mistress, that well-born French girl who had caught his eye in his sister's train at Dover, Louise de Kéroüalle, was also a Catholic. Out of the Queen's discreetly conducted but acknowledged Catholicism, the conversion of Barbara Duchess of Cleveland, the suspected Catholicism of Clifford and even Arlington, it was possible for the imaginative to weave a positive web of Popery around the King.

Under the circumstances, it cannot be denied that the choice of a new Catholic mistress was unfortunate – assuming that any political criterion at all was to be used in such matters. It was additionally unfortunate that Louise was French. Thus in her beguiling person she managed to combine the two attributes most likely to worry the English paranoiacs.

On the surface, there was some substance to these fears. There is evidence that Louis XIV did indeed view Louise as his secret French weapon. Madame cannot be accused of forwarding the plot, having frowned on her brother's proposed abduction of Louise at Dover. But her death freed the girl to accept an invitation probably phrased in the first instance by Buckingham.[15] But, as ever, the wayward Duke showed a reluctance to carry through his own settled plans. He allowed Louise to wait in vain at a French port for his yacht to convey her across the Channel. It was an unwise piece of neglect. As a result of her suffering, Louise arrived in England the friend of Arlington, who treated her with greater courtesy; it was not until later that the firm alliance of Buckingham and Louise became a feature of the scene at Court.

Louise arrived at Court a virgin. Such was her mixture of romance, propriety and ambition, that she may actually have convinced herself that the King intended to marry her before she allowed him to seduce her. She certainly spoke of the Queen's health to the Ambassador, Colbert de Croissy, as though it was likely to deteriorate violently at any moment; then she would marry the King. With similar wishful thinking, Louise later reckoned on making her son, the little Duke of Richmond, the King's heir at a time when the prospect of a half-French, wholly Catholic bastard succeeding was remote indeed. Where marriage was concerned, Louise never even enjoyed the putative chance of Frances Stewart. If Queen Catharine had died in the 1670s, the King would surely have headed for some rich princess, with a European alliance as an additional dowry. Louise, while retaining the pretensions of a lady, as Nelly angrily protested, suffered the vicissitudes of an older profession: she is reported to have caught the pox from the King, who gave her a pearl necklace to make her better.[16]

In other ways Louise did not suffer quite so much. Her baby face, with the fat cheeks that led the King to nickname her Fubbs (for chubby), stares innocently out of her lovely portrait by Gascar, surrounded by a halo of dark curls. One small round breast is revealed: altogether, she resembles a fat little pigeon, or the soft white dove beneath her hand. Though she was described by a contemporary as 'wondrous handsome', we should probably term her merely pretty – and wondrous appealing.[17]

There is no trace in the portraits of Louise's slight cast, which caused Nelly to christen her 'Squintabella' at first sight; so perhaps jealous Nell exaggerated. But there is shrewdness in the expression of her almond-shaped eyes, dark and watchful in the childish face. Louise was nearly twenty-one when she caught the King's eye in Madame's train; it was surprising that such a beautiful girl remained unmarried: 'la Belle Bretonne' she was called at the French Court, where the manners were politer than Nell Gwynn's. The explanation lay in her parents' poverty: Louise had no dowry. As a result, she imported into her role as *maitresse en titre* a nice sense of the importance of money. It was respectable French Louise who saw to it that her pension was tied to the profitable wine excise, where reckless English Barbara settled for a much less stable source of income.[18] When the dukedoms were being handed out to the royal bastards, Louise saw to it that her son gained precedence over Barbara's by the stratagem of getting Danby to sign the relevant document at midnight on the given date.

Tears and hysterics, as well as respectability, were part of Louise's stock-in-trade; it was not for nothing that Nelly chose to nickname her the 'weeping willow' when bored by 'Squintabella'. Louise had correctly summed up Charles as a man who would be made uncomfortable, then guilty, by such things. Later she would swoon and threaten suicide in order to avoid losing his favour. In one sense she overplayed her hand. The Duchess of Monmouth relates the story of the King being told – not for the first time – that Louise was dying: 'God's fish!' he answered. 'I don't believe a word of all this; she's better than you or I are, and she wants something that makes her play her pranks over this. She has served me so often so, that I am as sure of what I say as if I was part of her.'[19] Yet he never did quite get rid of her.... Louise would survive the determined broadsides of that magnificent fighting ship, Hortense Mancini, Duchess of Mazarin, and come to safe harbour as the resident mistress at the time of Charles' death.

Sir John Reresby, a vigilant observer of such matters, described Louise as 'the most absolute of all the King's mistresses'. She was certainly the most disliked by the populace. None of the ballads of the time were particularly tasteful – Barbara was generally depicted as insatiable in her sexual appetites – but the language addressed to Louise was notably intemperate:

> Portsmouth, the incestuous Punk,*
> Made our most gracious Sovereign drunk,
> And drunk she made him give that Buss
> That all the Kingdom's bound to curse...

So ran a fragrant piece, of 1673, entitled 'The Royal Buss Rock'. The most playful piece of satire – if such an innocent adjective may be used – was that dialogue which, taking advantage of the King's notorious weakness for his dogs, made Louise and Nelly into two pampered pets, named Snappy and Tutty. Even so, there was a social sneer: Snappy (Louise) was made to criticize Tutty (Nell) for her low breeding and suggest that she return to her 'dunghill'.[20]

Louise's rise was rapid. Her seduction by the King – if one may use the word for an event so obviously planned on both sides – seems to have taken place in October 1671 at Euston

---

* In its original sense of harlot; the secondary meaning of rotten, revived in the present day, came later.

Hall, Arlington's splendid new county house near Newmarket. The scene, as reported, had dramatic overtones which must have pleased Louise's histrionic nature, while its erotic ones pleased everyone else. For there was a 'mock marriage', at which 'the Fair Lady Whore' (Evelyn's phrase for Louise) 'was bedded one of these nights and the stocking flung, after the manner of a married bride'. By July 1672 her ascendancy was great enough for a large new coach for 'Madame Carwell', as her incomprehensible Breton name was anglicized, to feature in the royal expenses.[21] In the same year, roughly nine months after the 'marriage' at Euston Hall, she gave birth to her only child; this boy was, incidentally, to be the last of the acknowledged royal bastards. In February 1673 Louise was created Duchess of Portsmouth, Countess of Fareham and Lady Petersfield – while Nelly still languished as Mrs Gwynn.

As befitted her position as she interpreted it, the new Duchess kept increasing state in the large area over which she held sway in Whitehall – she finally acquired a total of twenty-four rooms and sixteen garrets. Evelyn described her appartments as having 'ten times the richness and the glory' of the Queen's.[22] He also paints an inviting picture of Louise having her hair combed by her maids in bed, while the King and his gallants stood around. Three times her rooms were redecorated (amazing luxury). Her acquisitions included French tapestries specially woven at her command, such diversities as Japanese cabinets, clocks, silver, great vases of wrought plate and ornamental screens, as well as paintings originally belonging to the Queen.

'What contentment can there be in the riches and splendour of this world, purchased with vice and dishonour?' enquired Evelyn in elegant disgust. The answer was that Louise Duchess of Portsmouth found a great deal of contentment in such things; riches and splendour, after all, were visible to the naked eye, which was more than could be said for vice and dishonour.

For all this, Louis xiv did not really succeed in planting a Trojan horse in the person of the desirable Duchess. The reason for the failure lay in the character of Charles ii. The varied intrigues which led to the establishment of Louise, the whole process of dangling this nubile beauty before a famously susceptible King, all presupposed that Charles' political sympathies followed his amorous inclinations. In the cool light of history, one cannot view the King in quite such a romantic light. As with Madame, so with Louise: it seems more likely that the reverse was true. Charles chose a confidante whose views or tastes accorded with his own, rather, than tailoring his to fit those of the lady.

Oddly enough, Louise's strongest card with the King appears to have been the aura of charming domesticity which she cast around her. In the end, it was this traditional attribute of a French mistress down the ages which delighted Charles II: the ability to provide agreeable surroundings and good food (Louise was famous for her table) as much as her physical appeal. Mercenary as she may have been, haughty to her social inferiors, at times tiresomely hysterical, Louise possessed an excellent instinct where men were concerned. She was clever enough to spot that Charles II was reaching an age where a settled and comfortable salon possessed at least as much attraction as a voluptuous bedroom. It was in this manner that Louise's French blood won Charles II, rather than in any more Machiavellian sense of political alignment.

Nevertheless, the murmurs against Popery in high places grew from the spring of 1672 onwards. Charles might in fact be immune from petticoat persuasion; but it was too much to expect his raucous popular critics to believe such a paradoxical fact about a King of such evident 'amorous complexion'. The rise of Louise, for all the private ease it granted, coincidental with the conversion of the Duke of York, and the disappointing course of the war, increased the problems the King had to face by the autumn of 1672.

To the north, the outlook was not much brighter. Lauderdale had promised his sovereign a citadel in Scotland. But in June 1672 the Scottish Parliament demonstrated that its sympathies lay – perhaps not surprisingly – with the Protestant Dutch, with whom the Scots did a great deal of trade, rather than with the Catholic French. Lauderdale's appeal to this body for much-needed money to prosecute the Dutch War was therefore not a success. Moreover, the coarse and tactless streak in the man had been enhanced with age: Lauderdale no longer managed his Scottish opponents with the same wiliness that he had displayed in the 1660s, while his foul-mouthed manner gained him additional enemies.

Nevertheless, the old warhorse remained sufficiently canny to see the most obvious dangers of his situation. In England, Shaftesbury was his particular enemy. In Scotland, the Duke of Hamilton led a rising faction against his policies. Lauderdale could see for himself that the patronage of the King was vital to his survival. Therefore his management of Scotland was dedicated to giving Charles II what he wanted.

At least the King was quite clear what that was. He continued to regard Scotland as a useful reservoir of money and men, and that was about all. His letter to Lauderdale of August 1672, which he himself admitted to be both overdue and over-brief, concentrated on the needs for an invasion of the United Provinces. If the first attempt of the English to land were to succeed, he would want additional troops at hand to back them up: 'therefore if it were possible to have two thousand men ready in Scotland upon such an occasion ...'.[23] In the event, there was no invasion, so that the crisis was not reached. All the same, the tide of revolt against Lauderdale's vice-regal rule was rising in Scotland, with the King quite unaware of the danger.

It was as well for Charles II, concentrating on the needs of an 'important necessary and expensive war', as he would later call it to Parliament, that Ireland was in one of her rare periods of quiescence. The Irish Army was, like the country, poor, and not much reliance could be placed on reinforcements from that source.* Sir William Petty analysed the situation in the island in 1672: 800,000 Papists, 200,000 English and 100,000 Scots. It was not a prescription for future happiness. Yet after the horrors of Cromwell's campaign and the subsequent wave of settlement

---

* Although in some respects it was in advance of the English Army. Kilmainham Hospital provided the model for Chelsea Hospital for veteran and wounded soldiers.

(following on so many waves of settlement), Ireland in the 1670s temporarily resembled Gibbon's description of Abyssinia: 'the world forgetting by the world forgot' – even if it would hardly be allowed to sleep for a thousand years. In November 1670 the *Dublin Gazette* actually ceased to appear on the wonderful – for Ireland – grounds that 'there was no news'.[24]

The country's condition was ameliorated still further when the Earl of Essex succeeded the corrupt Lords Berkeley and Robartes as Lord Lieutenant in 1672. Essex was much esteemed by his contemporaries for his upright character as well as his love of learning, and of libraries in particular. He was the son of a war hero – always a passport to respect. His father Arthur Capel, who had been in Cornwall with Charles II (when Prince of Wales), was executed in 1649 shortly after Charles I. Charles II, having the death of a beloved father in common, paid young Capel special attention; he was created Earl of Essex at the Restoration.

In Ireland, Essex's determination to stamp out English corruption was symbolized by his fight against the rapacity of Barbara Duchess of Cleveland. Barbara may well have received £10,000 from Berkeley as the price of his office. She was certainly granted Phoenix Park in Dublin, as well as some deliciously fertile lands round it, by the King. He showed by the gift his total lack of knowledge of the geography of the town as well as his indifference to Irish affairs. Essex was furious. 'I will not have the least concurrence with it,' he announced.[25] He was undeniably influenced by the fact that Phoenix Park was the only place where the Lord Lieutenant could walk or ride in comfort, Dublin Castle being hideously uncomfortable. Yet by Essex's action Phoenix Park was saved for future generations (remaining to this day one of the largest public parks in the world).

The cancellation of the Declaration of Indulgence was a blow to Irish Catholics, as it had been to English: Essex was instructed to 'suppress the insolency of the Irish Papists', this insolency having among its component parts 'convents, seminaries, friaries, nunneries and Popish schools'. But Essex, like all the wisest rulers of Ireland during this period (and like Charles II himself), distinguished between Catholic gentlemen and Catholic rebels. He pointed out that there were several hundred thousand Catholics in the country and that to 'suppress' them – the word was frequently used – he would need an army of over fifteen thousand, regularly paid....[26] As it was, not all the titular Catholic bishops left the country according to the new proclamation; the lesser clergy were often left in peace.

The existence of the ordinary people as a whole was not enviable; but the harsh choice of the next centuries, emigration or misery at home, had not yet reached them. Catholic laymen, although virtually excluded from Parliament, were able to practise most other professions. Essex's main domestic problem was one he shared with the Irish people as a whole – the failure of law and order (the rise of those brigands known locally as Tories brought the word into the vocabulary of the English people).

Charles II, however, unfussed by Irish Tories, continued to regard Ireland as a fertile pasture to be milked. Now that his original generous desire to establish a state of indemnity in Ireland had lapsed with time and fierce pressures at home, revenues were treated as rewards (Barbara's grant came into that category). His personal participation was limited to the odd occasions when he intervened over harsh treatment to an individual with regard to land.

If Ireland gave out little hard news, by the end of 1672 there was plenty of news in London. The *London Gazette* would shortly be reporting the recall of Parliament. Failing to secure his peace with William of Orange, Charles II was left with the impossibility of sailing his fleet the following spring without money to hand. The royal expenses display the nature of the preparations. Hay, two whole loads of it, was ordered for stuffing the seats, sacks and benches in the Parliamentary chambers. Two pairs of tongs – 'handsome and serviceable' – were acquired, as was a pillow of down for the Lord Chancellor. Candlesticks had to be got and that ever-present expense of the time, close-stools (nine of them). Green baize was to be employed in quantity, so that the seats in the House of Commons could be 'new repaired'. More green baize was to be used for window curtains for 'H.M.'s service'.[27]

The fact was that this session of February 1673 contained a crucial appeal by the King for money for his 'important, necessary and expensive war', and an equally crucial rejection of that appeal by both Commons and Lords. Where Charles spoke emotionally of his ships, and the contest into which he dared to say that he had been 'forced', the Commons clamoured furiously to have the Declaration of Indulgence of the previous year withdrawn. Only Parliament, they reiterated, could suspend the penal laws. The King first prevaricated; then equivocated. Referring to 'his power in ecclesiastics', he assured the Commons that he never had any thoughts of using it otherwise than as it had been 'entrusted' to him, for the peace and establishment of the Church of England, and 'the ease of all his subjects in general'. He had no thought, he declared, of 'avoiding or precluding the advice of Parliament'.[28]

Wriggle as the King might, he could not avoid the tight hold of the Parliamentary pincers in which the demands of his war had placed him. He tried in vain to appeal to the House of Lords, whose relations with the Commons were at the time sufficiently acrimonious for him to hope for better things from their assembly. He continued to put the most comforting gloss on what he had done: 'My Lords and Gentlemen: if there be any scruple remaining with you concerning the suspension of penal laws, I here faithfully promise you that what hath been done in that particular shall not for the future be drawn either into consequence or example.' But the Lords would not support him. In the end the King was obliged to withdraw the Declaration in return for an assessment of £70,000 a month for three years.

It was a galling defeat.

There was worse to come. Immediately after their triumph the Commons pressed through a Test Act. This measure was as divisive as Charles' Declaration of Indulgence had been potentially healing. Every holder of office had to take public communion in the Church of England. Furthermore, various oaths of allegiance were framed, as well as a declaration concerning the doctrine of transubstantiation; together they formed a test, in the truest sense of the word, which it was impossible for an sincere Catholic to pass. Once again, the King found himself in no position to combat the challenge.

Bowing his head before the storm, a familiar posture, he gave his assent to the Test Act on 29 March. The consequences were felt at once. The Duke of York and Thomas Clifford both failed to take Anglican communion at Easter. The Duke laid down his post as Lord High Admiral in June. Clifford also resigned as Lord Treasurer – to die shortly afterwards. The King took refuge in one of those pieces of 'raillery'. He was heard to say that he would purge his Court of all Catholics except his barber 'whom he meant to keep in despite of all their bills, for he was so well accustomed to his hand'. The joke was a pointed one: if a Catholic could be trusted with a razor so near the royal person, his co-religionists could hardly be the cut-throats of popular imagination.[29]

How prescient had proved the words of the Duke of York two years before! In the summer of 1673 it was even more difficult to see how a King and a Parliament could 'subsist together' for very long. Inevitably, the King prorogued Parliament once more. He was alleged to have observed that he would rather be a poor King than no King....[30] But the long war of attrition between King and Parliament was in fact gathering new momentum.

CHAPTER TWENTY

The Knot in the Comb

~

'This knot will again return to the teeth of the comb
and never disentangle itself unless the King take courage
to combat the licence of Parliament.'
The Venetian Ambassador, 1674

It was the presumed connection of Catholicism with royal
absolutism which dominated the politics of the next few
years. The installation of a young French Catholic mistress
might be shrugged off with a worldly air, although the rumour
that Charles II and Louise were secretly married by a Catholic
rite showed how far suspicion could desert sense – a Catholic
rite was the last thing which could have united the King and
his mistress during the lifetime of Catharine of Braganza.
The genuine marriage plans of the Duke of York to a
Catholic princess were quite a different matter. Anne Duchess
of York died in March 1671 and thereafter James looked
around for a new wife. These plans followed a joint venture
with the French of increasing unpopularity. Meanwhile the
absolutist French government across the water aroused fears
that the King himself might be contemplating something
similar.

Charles II strenuously denied the connection of Catholicism
and absolutism, for the good reason that the two were not
connected in his own mind. The rise of Catholicism in England
was in fact a chimera. Like many popular scares, statistics show
that it had no foundation. The numbers of Catholics in the
country were actually declining, as they had been declining

throughout the century and would continue to do.* They were a persecuted and depressed body, given an artificial appearance of strength and spirit by three factors. First, like immigrants in our own day, they tended to group together, so that they could share a priest without too much loss of security. Wolverhampton, for example, was termed 'a little Rome'. Secondly, there was a link in the popular imagination between Catholicism and the Army. This had some basis in the original Royalist armies, where Catholics from Ireland and elsewhere found employment. And Catholics continued to serve in the Army (although officers were excluded by the Test Act), particularly in campaigns and outposts abroad. The standing army of Charles II was always subject to keen and worried scrutiny: the association of the Catholics and the Army made for a vicious circle of apprehension.[2]

Thirdly, as has been stressed, the characters boldly lit up on the public stage of the Court were beginning to have a Catholic air. Or, as Evelyn put it, the 'fopperies of the Papists' were now coming out in the open.[3] To the suspicious country, the Court appeared to be going rapidly Catholic – a disastrous state of affairs.

The King continued to view these matters from quite a different angle. Since Worcester, he had seen the poorer Catholics in their true light as essentially loyal, if unhappy, creatures. It was a point of view he had twice tried to impose on the law of the land by repealing the penal laws, without success. When he drew up the Army at Blackheath in the autumn of 1673, it was a gesture widely interpreted as menacing towards the capital. But no evidence has ever been found that Charles II intended to parody in such a way the actions (and mistakes) of his predecessor Cromwell – let alone use his standing army as a Popish instrument.[4] He made nothing of the Catholic air of the Court: he breathed it with enjoyment, but to him it did not reek of absolutism. Because this connection between Catholicism and

---

* Obviously the numbers of members of a proscribed religion are hard to estimate: they have been put as low as sixty thousand – just over one per cent of the population.[1]

absolutism did not exist, he seemed unable to grasp that it played a part in the suspicions of Parliament. To the extent that he was unwilling to check his brother's Catholic marriage plans, Charles set up an intricate tangle for himself in the autumn of 1673.

The political scene was further complicated by the mounting intrigues of William of Orange, to bring about that separate peace with England, cutting off France, on which he had set his heart. His plan was to concentrate on the manifestly weak link in the chain of the King's pro-French foreign policy – the House of Commons. Various agents were employed, principal amongst them Peter Du Moulin. A code language evolved in which, for example, the King was known as 'Mr Young', the Duke of York 'Mr Cook' and the Catholics 'the Stone-Chandlers'. It was Du Moulin, a man of devious yet lucid intelligence, who had first pointed out to the Dutch prince that England was setting her compass in the direction of France. In his report on the subject, he had underestimated the personal control of Charles II over the nation's affairs. Nevertheless, his original plan of sowing dissension amongst the various members of the Cabal, while at the same time emphasizing the threat of France to the House of Commons, could hardly be said to have failed.[5]

Even if he had misunderstood the wide powers remaining with the King – and who did understand the disposition of power between King and Parliament at this point? – it was perfectly true that by the summer of 1673 the King's ministers were in demonstrable disarray. Dutch money was also dispensed with a generosity not usually associated with a country described by an English statesman later as 'offering too little and taking too much'. Perhaps most of it was spent on satirical pamphlets and other pieces of sordid but carefully aimed abuse, rather than on paying the English MPs on a large scale. Nevertheless, the presence of Dutch *largesse* on any scale provides a sardonic counterpart to the King's own reception of French subsidies. It was an age when political purses somehow existed on a very different level from political principles.

The Catholic marriage project of the Duke of York was an open invitation to the Dutch-inspired satirists to spread their calculated venom. In his search for a bride, one of the Duke's aims was to provide himself with a male heir whose claims to the succession would supersede those of his two surviving daughters Mary and Anne, now eleven and eight respectively. But the Duke, who was showing himself almost as convincing a womanizer as his brother, also paid a particular attention to his future wife's appearance: as he approached forty, his taste ran to young and beautiful girls.

It was ironic that James's first choice, the widowed Susan Lady Belasyse, was actually a Protestant: and he selected her for the good reason that he was much in love with her. Charles made short work of the project. James, he said, had made a fool of himself once and was not to be allowed to do so again. He had in mind a foreign princess who would bring some prestige and power in her train, even some money, rather than a mere Englishwoman. As for love, it was Charles who dismissed the whole notion of marrying with that in mind – one could get used to anyone's face in a week, he remarked.[6] Charles' witticism that his brother's mistresses were so plain that they must have been imposed on him by his confessors as a penance is sometimes quoted as evidence of James' general boorishness – there is something very unattractive about having a positive taste for plain women. Anne Hyde was undoubtedly plain, but perhaps this early experience gave James a good fright. For Lely made of James' post-Restoration mistress Lady Chesterfield a doe-like creature with nothing plain about her. The evidence of this quest for a bride is also very much to the contrary: it is Charles who concentrates on the worldly position of the lady, James who anxiously queries her physical attributes.[7]

A taste for pretty girls was really James' only vice: unless you took into account that sinister rigidity, increasing with the years, remarked on earlier. Gradually the brave, bluff Duke of York was being moulded by circumstances and age into the future James II. His appearance had altered markedly from the slender, thoughtful youth he was in exile. By the mid-1660s he had become 'all fat and ruddy and lusty' from the sun and air aboard ship.[8] James' character had also expanded, strengthened and hardened. His courage was turned in another direction. Buckingham's clever saying of the King and the Duke, that Charles could see things if he would and James would see things if he could, contained a kernel of truth, as such aphorisms often do, albeit simplified. The trouble was that the things James *did* see were the need for 'Papistry' and 'arbitrary government' – matters with which most English people were quite out of sympathy.

Having adopted his Catholicism 'with full deliberation', he could not imagine himself abandoning it, 'though I were sure it would restore me into the good opinion and esteem of the nation which I once had', as he told Laurence Hyde (Clarendon's son) in 1681. His great-grandmother, Mary Queen of Scots, had made the same kind of proud declaration when urged to embrace the Protestant religion to please Queen Elizabeth: 'Constancy becometh all folks well, and none better than princes, ... and specially in matters of religion.'[9] However admirable, it was a very different spirit from that of Henri Quatre – and Charles II.

His religion was only one aspect of his development. James had also acquired a youthful conviction of the rightness of absolutist government from his years in the French Army – here, if anywhere, was the connection of Catholicism and absolutism feared by his brother's Parliamentary critics. It is sometimes forgotten, in stressing French influences of all sorts on Charles II, from the political to the literary, that he was expelled from the country in 1654. In no sense did he return from *France* to England in 1660. James, on the other hand, both spent more of his exile in direct touch with French influences and had happier memories of the experience.

The Duke of York was also, understandably, a stern advocate of the legitimate succession. In 1675 he made a significant remark to the French Ambassador: Queen Elizabeth, he said, had been as much of a usurper as Cromwell. This alluded to Elizabeth's birth, which by Catholic standards was illegitimate, and left Mary Queen of Scots as the proper sovereign of England by her legitimate Tudor descent. The Duke of York clearly intended the same standards to prevail a hundred years later. On another occasion Admiral Tromp told him not to worry about his lack of a son, since England had been well ruled by women. James replied tartly that the reign of Queen Elizabeth had been 'the worst reign since the Conquest'.[10] He referred here as much to the growth of Parliamentary liberty as to her bastard birth. As the Duke of York fired off on the subject of Elizabeth the disaster, the English people were busy celebrating her Accession Day with increasing Protestant fervour. It was a symbolic contrast.

Over his impending marriage, the Duke of York certainly displayed all the resolution for which one alternately admires and condemns him. The King's choice had been an Austrian archduchess; but she was wrested from James' grasp when the Emperor, finding himself unexpectedly a widower, promptly made the archduchess his own. The plain Princess of Neuburg was banned by James – to Charles' amazement – and Charles himself banned a Princess of Württemberg, either because he continued to dislike princesses of 'cold Northern countries' or for the more rational reason that she had a trouble-making mother.

There was a certain haste over the enquiries, because James at least was determined to marry before the autumn, when Parliament was due to reconvene. He was under no illusion as to what their reactions would be to the kind of Catholic match he now had in mind. When word came of the availability of *two* Princesses of Modena, the fifteen-year-old Mary Beatrice and her thirty-year-old aunt, James' marital pulse raced – particularly when he learnt that these pious Catholic ladies would be backed up by substantial payments from Louis XIV. For Modena lay within the French interest: Mary Beatrice's mother had been a niece of Cardinal Mazarin. In the end, reports of Mary Beatrice's beauty – 'her hair black as jet' and her graceful figure – as well as her tender age, inclined the Duke of York towards her. The proxy marriage was performed on 20 September with Lord Peterborough acting the part of the groom.[11]

When the news was made public, the uproar was immense. It became the violent concern of Parliament to fend off this marriage with 'the daughter of the Pope', as Mary Beatrice was unkindly termed, before it could actually be consummated.

Shaftesbury in particular was vociferous in his opposition. In any case, this strange, warped and talented politician was veering towards more public opposition to the King, and his days as Lord Chancellor were clearly numbered. Admittedly, he had voted for the Declaration of Indulgence, but he had also, like Arlington, voted for the Test Act. Like Arlington, he was on increasingly hostile terms with the Duke of York as a result, and by the autumn was reported to be unable to sit at the same Council Table with him. At the same time, the balance of power in the King's inner councils altered.

In June 1673 Thomas Osborne was made Lord High Treasurer: he was also created Lord Latimer, and the next year Earl of Danby (by which name he will in future be designated). Danby's contemporaries did not bother their heads with jealousy, cynically supposing that in view of the state of the economy the post of Lord High Treasurer was calculated to ruin anyone.[12] But the rise of Danby, a firm Anglican, a supporter of the Triple Alliance, and a man obstinately determined to put the King's finances on a better footing, was in fact the most hopeful thing which had happened to Charles II, domestically, for several years, although its full effects would not be felt immediately.

The angry chaos provoked by the news of the Duke of York's match remained. Charles, as so often before when under pressure, took refuge in delay. On the one hand, he withdrew his offer of the public chapel of St James to Mary Beatrice: she would have to make do with a private one. The Queen was made to claim the St James' chapel in order to gloss over the affront. On the other hand, Charles put off the summoning of Parliament for a crucial week, hoping that in the meantime Mary Beatrice would arrive in the country and the marriage would be duly consummated before any further protests could be heard.

London was already awash with ugly rumours. The notion that the King might divorce the Queen – and thus at a stroke defeat the Duke of York's Popish plans – was once more publicly discussed.[13] More talk was heard on the subject of the King's favourite son, the Duke of Monmouth. The 'Revolting Darling', as a popular ballad described him – flattery was intended – was now twenty-three; his marriage to Anne, the heiress of Buccleuch, had presented him with a solid base of money and estates. The Catholicism of his youth (he had been educated at one point at the Oratory in Paris at the orders of Henrietta Maria) was a thing of the past; Monmouth had been quick to see the advantages of a Protestant position.

Delay for Charles II did not mean irresolution, nor the desertion of the Duke of York. It was Parliament the King hoped to outwit, not his brother. Shaftesbury in particular was showing his hand in a way which was ominous in such an adroit politician. He was sympathetic to the Dutch, rather than actually working with them. But his marked hostility to the Duke of York made it unlikely that the King could preserve both men within the same regime, even if he wanted to. Shaftesbury showed his hand even more publicly when he suggested in Council that the King should divorce Catharine and marry a Protestant. In addition, Charles suspected Shaftesbury of stirring up trouble for Lauderdale in Scotland. He was probably wrong. But even if this particular charge was unjust, Charles had had enough of Shaftesbury.

To know Shaftesbury and his 'slippery humour' was not necessarily to love him. He has been immortalized as Dryden's Achitophel:

> Restless, unfixed in principles and place,
> In power unpleas'd, impatient of disgrace....

While Charles II did not match Dryden in venom, he did not subscribe to the view that Shaftesbury's various changes in 'principles and place' sprang from a deep concern for the common weal. As Clarendon expressed it, 'Few men knew Lord Ashley [Shaftesbury] better than the King himself did, and had a worse opinion of his integrity.' Charles for once did not trouble to hide his opinion. On one occasion at the theatre, observing the swarthy appearance of the Murderers in *Macbeth*, he enquired rhetorically, 'Pray, what is the meaning that we never see a Rogue in a Play, but, Godsfish! they always clap him on a black Periwig? When, it is well known one of the greatest Rogues in England always wears a fair one ...' – an allusion to Shaftesbury's florid looks, as well as, no doubt, to the King's own dark ones.[14]

In general, the estimates of Shaftesbury's own contemporaries are much less favourable than those of a later age, influenced by the success of his principles – or at least some of them. The younger Whigs came to consider him a dangerous opportunist.[15] King Charles II was to be counted amongst those who had reason to remember his conduct under the Commonwealth and on the eve of the Restoration. As men today cannot altogether elude the stigma of a bad war record, Shaftesbury's 'integrity' was suspect in his own day for historical reasons.

It was a nerve-racking time for the King. Outwardly, he remained steady. But for once his inner confidence seems to have been shaken, since he took the unusual step of consulting the eminent astrologer, Elias Ashmole, on the subject of the House of Commons. Very likely the step was taken at the suggestion of Clifford, who was interested in astrology and in touch with Ashmole. Nevertheless, King Charles in better days showed praiseworthy disregard for the superstition which obsessed so many of his contemporaries. In exile he had joked about Lord Bristol: he hoped 'the stars' would permit Bristol to stay in Brussels till he got there; and then, if 'Taurus be as successful to him as Aries has been … I hope he will think a little more of terrestrial things.' He made the point that a comet visible in 1664 interested him for scientific reasons and not for its 'prophecies' (although, if it portended anything, he joked, he hoped it might be an English victory). When a 'prophet' or fortune-teller came to the Court, Charles told Madame that he gave little credit to 'such kind of cattle'. He added even more definitely, 'The less you do it the better, for if they could tell anything 'tis inconvenient to know one's fortune beforehand, whether good or bad.'[16]

It is a valuable indication of the atmosphere of tension in late October 1673 that Charles II should have gone against his own instincts to the extent of letting Ashmole set a chart. In so doing, Ashmole combined the time of the King's address to the House of Commons following the short prorogation with that of his nativity. The ensuing predictions should justly have sent the King back to his original sceptical position. Ashmole was infinitely calming, as prophets are wont to be with princes, even those as merciful as Charles II. He foresaw 'a notable harmony and unity between the King and Parliament' within a few days; that the King would be able to dispose of and control the House of Commons, which 'in all things, shall please him'.[17]

In fact, Parliament when it did meet proved itself horribly vociferous on the subject of Popery, royal absolutism and royal money. The King saw no other course but to prorogue it once more till after Christmas.*

It was in November that the King finally got rid of Shaftesbury. Although he continued to sit on one council, that of Trade and Plantations, till the following March, he was dismissed as Chancellor. When Mary Beatrice finally arrived at Dover towards the end of the month, the atmosphere was still so strained that hardly anyone dared make the ride out to meet her. Yet Charles II had in the end demonstrably preferred the interests of his brother's marriage to those of 'harmony and unity', in Ashmole's optimistic phrase, with Parliament. The politicians, including Shaftesbury, who would stir up the powerful movement to exclude James from the succession five years later, should perhaps have remembered the fact.

January 1674 inexorably brought another session of Parliament. Its inception, as usual, was due to the acute royal need for money, and in an effort to secure it, Charles now found it in himself to give Parliament a personal assurance: 'There is no other treaty with France, either before or since, not already printed, which shall not be made known.' It is true that he fumbled with his notes as he spoke; but that was probably due to nervousness not shame: he remained a diffident speaker, probably the effect of the lurking family stammer not otherwise evident in his speech.[19] The straight lie did not however save him. Both Houses of Parliament voted for a separate peace with the Dutch, a culmination, amongst other things, of the secret intrigues of William of Orange.

---

* Ashmole was consulted once more, in January 1674; he also continued to follow the King's astrological progress in the future, although there is no proof that he did so with the King's approval other than the fact that it was in theory treason to cast the sovereign's horoscope without authorization.[18]

Once more Charles II took cover. Abandoning the policy which had secretly obsessed him for the last five years, he gave Parliament another assurance on 11 February: he hoped for 'a speedy, honourable, and I hope, lasting peace with the Dutch'.[20] And his ally, Louis XIV, still bent on securing those lowland dominions on which he had set his heart? The Treaty of Westminster with the Dutch was such a clear public repudiation of the Treaty of Dover that one might imagine Charles II would have had some difficulty in justifying it to the betrayed French King. But Charles, that redoubtable diplomat, who had concluded the Triple Alliance while secretly negotiating with France, was equal to the task. He convinced Louis XIV that he was obliged to adopt this course by lack of money. A year later he would be able to form another secret alliance with Louis XIV, seamed together by further French subsidies.

Yet the interests of the two Kings had diverged. While Louis XIV was determined to make his life 'a battle and a march', in the words of Schiller's Wallenstein, Charles II had perceived at last the impossibility of combining an aggressive foreign policy and a docile Parliament. That did not however leave him without a European role. Between William of Orange and Louis XIV it was surely practical for a man who was the uncle of one and the first cousin of the other to act as mediator. For the next few years Charles would confine his foreign relationships, perforce, to compromise and negotiation. And since Louis XIV remained rich, while Charles remained poor, his role might bring him financial benefits.

At home, the King speedily prorogued Parliament once more. The seats of the MPs, covered in their new green baize and stuffed with their newly bought hay, were emptied once again. Before this could happen however Parliament also witnessed the final disintegration of the Cabal. Buckingham overreached himself in his criticism of the royal policies. Rash as ever, he appealed in person to the House of Commons, without seeking the permission of the King, or indeed that of the body to which he himself belonged, the House of Lords. He was stripped of his offices, the ultimate humiliation occurring when he was made to surrender his patent as Master of the Horse to that popinjay

Monmouth (but the King had to pay Buckingham compensation).

With Shaftesbury and Buckingham out of the way, only Lauderdale and Arlington remained of the original five who had formed the acronym of the Cabal, and Arlington's star had been eclipsed by that of Danby. Lauderdale was fully occupied trying to hold down Scotland to the royal will – as interpreted by himself. The fact that Shaftesbury would now go to all intents and purposes into opposition (to use the modern phrase), forming the nucleus of the future Whig party, showed how shallow had been the surface unity of the Cabal. Only the common aim of carrying through the King's policies had brought them together. Now this task was left to Danby alone.

The Venetian Ambassador gives an interesting portrait of Charles as he appeared to a foreign observer in 1674. 'The King lives from day to day,' he wrote disapprovingly, but 'This knot will again return to the teeth of the comb and never disentangle itself unless the King takes courage to combat the licence of Parliament.' Unfortunately, he was not likely to do so. The Ambassador continued, 'The King is intent on enjoying life, has no heirs and always hesitates to raise a finger for fear of a relapse into the miseries and perplexities of youth.'[21]

The last part of this analysis certainly rings true: a relapse – not only for himself but for the monarchy as a whole – into the aptly termed 'miseries and perplexities' of his youth was exactly what Charles II did fear. Whether he enjoyed life in this confused period may be doubted. Still more it may be doubted whether his best course was to tug valiantly at the Knot in the Comb represented by the licence of Parliament. Courage was one thing, cunning another. Courage would lead to a confrontation which he might well lose. Cunning suggested skirting round the whole subject of the licence of Parliament, until Danby had established the monarchy on a more solid basis, both economically and politically.

In the economic sphere at least, Danby scored an early success. He raised the royal revenues considerably, an increase which joined with a natural upswing in trade in the early seventies to provide new affluence. Danby also took retrenchment extremely seriously and, under his guidance, some kind of austerity was once more introduced into the conduct of the royal household and finances. He aimed at disbanding the new regiments of the Army, for instance, and ended by saving £97,000 by cutting the Army to its normal peacetime complement of six thousand men. The Navy alone was costing £1,500 a *day* at the date when Danby became Lord Treasurer: this kind of disbursement Danby realized was simply not within the King's power to keep up, if he was to be left with any resources of his own.[22]

Some of Danby's expedients have an odd air to modern economists. For example, he added to the annual rent received from the farming of the Excise the sum which farmers would have normally dispensed in pensions, and undertook that the King would pay them himself, where they were justified. The idea, a laudable one, was to increase the King's cash flow. The result was to add a whole new list of financial dependents to the monarchy, already cursed with far too many. But in an age when the practice of economics was barely understood – remember that desperate, unhappy measure the Stop and the equally desperate situation it sought to cure – Danby passed for a genius because he actually brought about a positive improvement. Expenditure on the Household, Wardrobe, Chamber and Privy Purse, which had risen to over £250,000 a year, from an average of £185,000 between 1660 and 1669, was brought down sharply in 1675.[23]

The trouble was that it was impossible to divorce the economics of the period from the politics – and the Court intrigues. Unquestionably the King's expenditure on his mistresses, not perceptibly extravagant by the standards of the time in the 1660s, had moved into a more lavish sphere. And it would expand still further as the 1670s wore on. Where women were concerned, the King was weak, not only in the bed-chamber, at the sight of their tears, but in the counting-house. Louise Duchess of Portsmouth, as has been seen, regarded a large income as one of the unalterable prerequisites of a royal mistress; Nelly Gwynn was equally mercenary, if not equally successful; Barbara Duchess of Cleveland – mother of five children by the

King – was still on his payroll; Hortense Duchesse de Mazarin would prove another expensive luxury.

The economic demands of Louise Duchess of Portsmouth – what has been aptly termed 'harem finance' – did the King far more real damage than her alleged Catholic influence. For Danby, good husbandman as he might be, flinched from quarrelling with the reigning mistress. The result was that the annual household expenditure rose once again after 1675 to £210,000. There were other 'extraordinary' expenses for the ladies – of vast, if ultimately unknowable, proportions, since much of this was found from French money: the Secret Service account. Where knowable expenditure is concerned, it has been pointed out that the Treasury records in the 1670s show *permanent* grants of more than £45,000 a year to Barbara, Louise and their children alone.[24]

The controversy concerning the extravagance of Charles II persists – did he contribute to his own problems or was he kept permanently short by Parliament? Whatever the force of the latter view, it is surely impossible to acquit the King altogether of extravagance, or rather weakness, where his mistresses were concerned, in the last ten years of his reign. A King must keep state, ceremonies are demanded by the populace which then criticizes the cost of them, and so forth – all these arguments have been advanced in Chapter 12, discussing his Restoration. In those days Goethe might have been quoted on the subject: '*Ein Mächtiger, der für die Seinen nicht/Zu sorgen weiss, wird von dem Volke selbst/Getadelt*' ('A man of power, who cannot look after the interests of his own favourites, will be blamed even by the people'). The mood changed as the reign progressed. Such a saying would not have been applied to the immoral panoply of Charles II's later Court by a nation grown less joyous. It was a difference in degree, but it was a significant difference.

The spending on the royal bastards should not have appeared so irksome: it has been correctly pointed out that the monies laid out on the various dukelings and little ladies was a tithe of what a proper legitimate royal brood would have consumed.[25] The King himself was not personally extravagant. He was not lavish over matters like dress; where food and drink were concerned he was positively abstemious. But the planting of trees round his palaces, afforestation generally, was an expensive pastime. The renovation of Windsor, begun in 1674, also cost a pretty penny. The concentration on Windsor – it was the only palace easy to fortify – symbolized the new type of monarchy evolving in the last decade of the King's reign: embattled but at the same time loftier and more magnificent than the institution restored in 1660. It is here that one can imagine the King as described by Thomas Otway in a long memorial poem: 'Windsor Castle is a Monument to our Late Sovereign King Charles II':

> Then in his Mind the beauteous Model laid,
> Of that Majestic pile, where oft, his Care
> A while forgot, he might for Ease repair:
> A Seat for sweet Retirement, Health, and Love....

But Windsor was also

> Britain's Olympus, where, like awful Jove
> He pleas'd could sit, and his Regards bestow
> On the vain, busy, swarming World below.

In 1675 commenced the building of St Paul's, another Olympus, another symbolic act, since the great new cathedral would come to embrace the ceremonies of state under its powerful dome.

This same summer of 1674 two pathetic little skeletons, believed not implausibly to be those of the vanished 'striplings' Edward V and the Duke of York, were turned up by workmen at the Tower of London. The point is debatable and, as with all evidence pertaining to the controversial life of Richard III, keenly debated. Here we are only concerned with the reaction of Charles II. The find was reported to him by Sir Thomas Chicheley, Master of the Ordnance. The King's immediate instinct was to command a more reverent burial for these pathetic relics: they were transferred to Westminster Abbey and Sir Christopher Wren was ordered to design a marble urn to encase them. Admittedly, the Royal Warrant, signed by Arlington the following February, hedged its bets by referring to 'a white

Marble Coffin for the supposed bodies of the two Princes ...'. Nevertheless, here, in the Abbey, they lie to this day, with a Latin inscription commemorating the action of the *Rex Clementissimus* – the most merciful King Charles the Second. Moreover, the English inscription beneath declares, in bolder terms than the Royal Warrant, that the bones 'were deposited here by command of King Charles ii, in the firm belief that they were the Bones of King Edward v and Richard Duke of York'.[26]

Whatever the rights and wrongs of the boys' death, it was a gesture towards the concept of legitimate monarchy – as represented by the youthful Edward v, in contrast to his usurping uncle *Richardus Perfidus*, as the Latin inscription had it. The same instinct led to the glorification of the tomb of Charles i at about the same time, another monarch whose life was brought to an unnatural end. Less sceptical perhaps than his minister Arlington in his attitude to the 'supposed' remains, Charles ii was reaching down for his royal roots.

For the first time, in 1674 the Court spent four months at Windsor during the summer. Within the picturesque fortress both King and Queen had new apartments created by Hugh May. Grinling Gibbons and Antonio Verrio were employed by May to adorn them; May was inspired by the patronage of the King. Charles showed throughout his life a love of the arts quite natural in a boy educated at that legendary, cultured Court of the 1630s who could remember going by barge with his father to visit the studio of Van Dyck. His predilection has however been understandably overshadowed by the supreme artistic taste of King Charles i. Charles ii did all that he could to reacquire his father's great art collection (it has been mentioned that he secured some pictures from the Dutch on the eve of his Restoration) although some masterpieces proved irrecoverable. Of his cabinet of treasures and curiosities, he spoke wistfully that it was not to be compared with his father's, thirty years before. Charles ii may well have been responsible for the collection of drawings by Leonardo da Vinci at Windsor, either by purchase, or by receiving them as gifts.[27]

As he enjoyed the company of writers, so Charles II appreciated that of artists generally; he sent for a doctor from Paris to treat the history painter, Robert Streater, for the stone. Gibbons' work was originally shown to the King by John Evelyn: as a reward for the recommendation before which, in Evelyn's words, 'he was scarce known', Gibbons presented Evelyn with a walnut table 'incomparable carved'. Charles was so enthusiastic at what he saw that he rushed out of the room to show it to the Queen – who was less so. Later Charles, supported by Lely and Bab May, had his way. At Windsor, Gibbons, who also ornamented other royal dwellings, was allowed £100 a year. Verrio subsequently came to occupy the post of Chief Painter set up for Sir Peter Lely, at a salary of £200 a year. At the time of the Popish Plot the Catholic Verrio, and some other Catholic stonecarvers, assistants to Gibbons, were protected from the consequences of their religion.[28]

As is the way of the world, not all the payments went directly to artists. The Dutch dealer Gerrit Uylenbergh, a cousin of Rembrandt's wife Saskia, got into trouble when the pictures he was trying to sell the Elector of Brandenburg were denounced as fakes. Reaching England a poor man, he quickly fell on his feet, painted some backgrounds for Lely, and joined the King's service as Purveyor and Keeper of his pictures. Uylenbergh helped to select and arrange the pictures for the private apartments of the King and Queen at Windsor; he was paid £50 for his 'Extraordinary Care and Pains ... and for Several Journeys'. Two young French painters, Nicolas de Largillierre and Philip Dolesam, also set to with their brushes, and, where necessary, fitted the King's pictures into their new frames, carved by Gibbons. The King was particularly delighted with Largillierre's partial repainting of Caracciolo's *Cupid Sleeping*.[29]

At Windsor the only remaining rooms of Edward III were gutted, although many of the old walls remained embedded in the structure. Some of the modernization however brought unexpected problems, as when a series of tanners' skins were found in the water supply. Water was once again used for embellishment at Windsor, on the French model. Charles II was fortunate to be able to enjoy the fruits of the ingenuity of Sir

Samuel Morland, appointed his *magister mechanicorum*. A special feat of Morland's in 1681 caused water to be pumped from the Thames to the top of the castle, and thence in a great jet sixty feet high, which, mingled with red wine, was clearly and splendidly visible.[30]

Today the Windsor revivified by Charles II is best pictured from the Queen's Presence Chamber, with its swirling Verrio ceiling; otherwise, the elegant hand of George IV has once more been at work, sweeping away the older embellishments with the new.[31] In this Presence Chamber the King was wont to dine in public, that strangely intimate glimpse of the monarch traditionally granted to his subjects since mediaeval times. Elsewhere the spirit of Verrio was much in evidence. The new royal apartments were decorated with splendid allegorical paintings in which fantasy brought a comfort denied by reality. Queen Catharine was at last depicted as Britannia – a role for which she had been passed over in favour of Frances Stewart when the new coinage was designed, as being too small. There was more reality in the fact that the Duchess of Portsmouth and her son were granted their own apartments. When four continents were seen bringing Charles II their riches, the King seated on a convenient cloud, then fantasy was certainly rampant.

Yet compared to the extravagance of his father, or for that matter of Louis XIV, Charles II had modest tastes. His own subject the mighty Duke of Beaufort, who with his wife struck terror into the hearts of servants and neighbours alike, kept as much princely state. The Duchess made a daily tour of her domains, instantly sacking any servant not about his or her lawful occasions. The Duke's neighbours planted trees 'to humour his vistas' and 'arranged Hills free of charge'.[32] Queen Catharine made no such tour; the King planted his own trees.

There were also rural pursuits to be enjoyed at Windsor, even if some of them – those of Catharine rather than Charles – smacked a little of the Petit Trianon. The King could fish. The Queen could go on picnics. On one such outing each of the Queen's attendants brought one dish: 'Lady Bath's dish was a chine of beef, Mrs Wyndham's a venison pastry ...', and so on.

Catharine sat under a tree and was 'wonderfully pleased and merry'.[33]

The King's cousin, Prince Rupert, had been made Governor and Constable of the Castle in 1668. The old warrior enjoyed his fortress-residence and made it his permanent home. He was thus able to oversee the King's numerous refurbishments. At the same time he reminded himself of the less pacific past by ornamenting his own rooms with a collection of arms, which made the post-war generation open their eyes wide when they visited him.

Music was another example of Charles II's feeling for culture rather than for formality. He loved music more for its own sake than for the splendour surrounding the performance. In the mid-seventies expenses in the royal accounts for dresses – shepherds, satyrs and the like – for masques recall but do not emulate the great masque world of Inigo Jones in the previous reign. In 1674 Queen Catharine suggested a masque, *Calisto*, to John Crowne. The intention was quite plain: to provide a starring vehicle for the two young Princesses of York, Mary and Anne.* It was only a moderate success. The story of Calisto, in Crowne's own words, posed the problem of writing 'a clean, decent and inoffensive play' on the subject of rape – featuring two girls aged twelve and nine. Neither Crowne nor his leading ladies were equal to the challenge. The masque was dull. The amateurs' voices had to be supplemented by those of two graceful professionals, Moll Davies and Mrs Knight. As both ladies were suspected – with good reason – of unprofessional relationships with the King, this led to considerable tension during rehearsals where the Queen was concerned.[34]

The King's personal preference was for the French instrumental music he had grown to love in exile; Pelham Humfrey was sent to France to learn it, that the English Court might be graced with the innovation. By Humfrey's death in 1674 this

---

* More often known as the Lady Mary and the Lady Anne, according to the convention of the time, which was less lavish with the term 'princess' than our own: Mary and Elizabeth Tudor, for example, were generally termed the Ladies Mary and Elizabeth, despite the fact that they were the daughters of a reigning monarch, Henry VIII.

new type of music was prospering. Violins were introduced into church music at the King's request. As for the royal bills for violinists' costumes – 'Indian' gowns trimmed with tinsel – and garlands for their violins (cost £6),[35] these would have seemed mere trifles, albeit agreeable trifles, to a Louis XIV. One of the beneficiaries of this new style in music was Henry Purcell. Taught by Humfrey, among others, Purcell sprang from a family closely connected with the Chapel Royal. Purcell himself – 'so arch especial a spirit', as Gerard Manley Hopkins described him two hundred yeas later – was a Child of the Chapel Royal. (He features by name in the Wardrobe accounts from time to time for two suits, a bed and so forth.)[36] As such, he was inevitably much in contact with the King. The 1670s saw the metamorphosis of Purcell from a chorister to a composer, but the royal connection was maintained. Two welcome songs to the King and Duke of York respectively brought him into prominence.[37] Many of his early odes hymned such court events as the King's return from Newmarket, his return from Windsor, his reappearance at Whitehall after a summer outing. Later it seems that Charles introduced Purcell to the delights of Italian music as well as French. Purcell's *Sonatas in Three Parts*, dedicated to the King, make some allusion to the introduction.

Queen Catharine enjoyed Italian opera and Italian songs generally (if less so when sung by Mrs Knight). Charles was fond enough of Italian songs – and expert enough in the language – to hold a part himself from time to time at Windsor. He had a great 'thorough-bass' voice. A duet by Carisimi, Charles' favourite composer, exists written out in Purcell's handwriting. Purcell became successively organist at Westminster Abbey in 1679 (John Blow, who probably taught him composition, resigned in his favour) and Composer in Ordinary in 1682.

It was helpful that Charles II had a predilection for experiment, be it scientific or musical: under his influence music was also introduced into the English theatre, on the French model. The French musician Louis Grabu came to England and was appointed 'composer to His Majesty's Musique' in 1665. The appointment of a Frenchman caused some raised eyebrows.[38]

Nevertheless, Grabu was made Master of the English Chamber Musick in ordinary, following the death of Nicholas Lanier. The first public concert in England was also given in the reign of Charles II. It was organized by the violinist John Banister, for a while leader of the King's Band, and held in a large room in Whitefriars in 1672.

Nevertheless, in seventeenth-century England all this kind of expenditure – on music, on art, on building and redecoration – was understood and appreciated; whereas the vast sums visibly deployed on the foreign Popish mistresses were seen as a sign of weakness in the bedroom. Might the King, under such dangerous influences, be equally weak in the council chamber? The question remained. A witticism went the rounds to explain why the Accession Day of Queen Elizabeth I was being celebrated with such warmth: 'Because she being a woman chose men for her counsellors and men when they reign usually choose women.' It was an unfair barb. Women were not the King's counsellors but his concubines – and his companions. But the extravagance which he permitted on their behalf invited it.

In the short term – but only in the short term – the political methods of Danby looked like being as successful as his economic policies. Stoutly Protestant himself, Danby aimed at a political alliance in Parliament which would comprise Anglicans, and other confirmed Royalists, against those whom he conceived of as being the King's enemies. These were the Catholics, the nonconformists, and the opponents of the royal prerogative. It will be appreciated that the latter group included many whom Charles II had sought persistently to conciliate by toleration. Nor did Danby, in his concentration on the alliance of the monarchy and Anglicanism, allow for the special position of the Duke of York in the King's favours.

James was not unnaturally offended and alarmed by Danby's Anglican policies. The shifting nature of political alliances in this period was once more underlined when the Duke of York moved away from Danby's so-called Court party towards the arms of the Protestants Buckingham and Shaftesbury.

All the same, Danby laboured hard at building up his

Parliamentary base: a conglomerate of well disposed MPs has been traced, based on his home ground of the West Riding of Yorkshire.[39] The lop-sided representation of certain areas in Parliament also helped because in general it favoured the Royalist cause. There was another theoretical advantage accruing to the King: the appointment of the Lords Lieutenant, who in turn were responsible for local patronage (although this had to be used with care). Then there was that method of building up a Court party, or any other party for that matter – bribery. Accusations of bribery against Danby were part of the stock-in-trade of his opponents. In fact, some of Danby's payments were disbursements to genuine office-holders. Where did these legitimate payments end and bribery begin? In a situation where office-holding was much complicated by the relics of the pre-war structure on which the post-Restoration structure had been imposed, this is difficult to establish. The important point was that Danby earnestly strove to put together governmental support. It was not easy in an age when party politics as such, to say nothing of the parties themselves, were still in an embryonic state.

The third plank in Danby's platform, after pursuing economic and political solidity, was the strengthening of ties with the Dutch. It was essential to this particular policy that the King should secure sufficient supplies from Parliament to uphold his beloved Navy. Otherwise it was easy to see that the King would have little motive to wrench himself from the lucrative embrace of Louis xiv. When Parliament met again in April 1675 for Danby to secure supplies, the King was all honey to its members. He told them that he wanted to have a better understanding with them and 'to know what you think may yet be wanting to the securing of religion and property'. This was a far cry from his claims of 'supreme power' in ecclesiastical matters. But he did not fail to dwell on the theme of the Navy. 'I must needs recommend to you the condition of the Fleet,' he said, 'which I am not able to put into that state it ought to be, and which will require so much time to repair and build, that I should be sorry to see this summer (and consequently a whole year) lost without providing for it.'[40]

It was all the more important that Danby should succeed in managing Parliament to good financial effect, since his policy of positive Anglicanism went against the King's natural inclinations as well. On 1 May the King signed a declaration expelling Jesuits and other 'Romish priests' from the realm. Already in February, an Order in Council had been made for the strict enforcement of the penal laws against the Catholics, and for the restricting of Catholic chapels to those of the Queen and the ambassadors.

But this session of Parliament proved to be a contest between two equally handicapped opponents. The Commons continued to cry out against the French involvement, demanding that the English troops which had been sent to back up Louis XIV should now be withdrawn under the terms of the Treaty of Westminster. The King promised that further recruitment would be forbidden (in fact, he turned a blind eye to its continuance), but declined to withdraw troops already serving under Louis before the Treaty. The Commons responded by showing intractability over the supplies he wanted for the Navy. They linked them to the Excise – a source of supply he already possessed.

There was even a move to impeach Danby, as the King's minister, for his pro-French attitudes – which would have been a wry turn of events, considering Danby's own attitude to France. Luckily the impulse behind it was feeble and the motion easily defeated. Besides, Danby had his own notion of dealing with possible Parliamentary opposition, by introducing a new type of Test Act promoting 'Non-Resistance'. All office-holders were supposed to take a new oath declaring that resistance to the King was unlawful, and promising to abstain from all efforts to alter the constitution of the Church and State.

The bill had a long and wearisome passage in the House of Lords; at one point the King himself stayed till midnight, following the proceedings. Nevertheless, it might well have become law had not a quite unrelated quarrel broken out at this point between the two Houses of Parliament. The case of Shirley *v.* Fagg rested on the right of the House of Lords to hear appeals from the Court of Chancery, when one of the appellants was a member of the Commons. The Commons considered that by summoning Sir John Fagg, an MP, the Lords had acted in breach of their privileges. The quarrel grew. All parliamentary business was suspended.

The King was aware that at the bottom of 'this most malicious design', as he called the fomented row, was the intention to procure a dissolution of Parliament. Whereas a mere prorogation helped the King, it was the increasing conviction of certain MPs that a dissolution – followed by a fresh election – would produce a House of Commons more favourable to their cause. The King saw through this ploy. And he said so. He appealed to the disputants to patch up their differences and not allow a body of 'ill [that is, wicked] men' to sway them. He also observed, 'But I must let you know, that whilst you are in debate about your privileges, I will not suffer my own to be invaded. . . .'[41]

The disputants were however obdurate. On 9 June the King saw no alternative but wearily to prorogue Parliament. The 'unhappy differences' between the two Houses were, he said, too great. And he spoke bitterly of 'the ill designs of our enemies [that] have been too prevalent against those good ones I proposed to myself in behalf of my people'.[42]

The King and Court went to his delightful new abode at Windsor. When Parliament met again in the autumn, Danby returned with new vigour to the task of carrying through the government's policies. Nor had he wasted his time in the intervening months. Over a hundred MPs had been lobbied by the Secretaries of State, to ensure their attendance. The number of Excise pensioners was increased. Despite these sanguine, if not salutary, precautions, Danby found himself once more desperately bogged down. The *cause célèbre* of Shirley *v.* Fagg still dominated relations between the two Houses; and Danby found himself quite unable to secure the King's financial needs, while the demand for the dissolution of Parliament grew.

The irony of this demand – and irony is never far away from the politics of this period – was that Charles II himself was more or less committed to dissolving Parliament, but in secret, and in his latest negotiations with Louis XIV. It was proposed that Charles should dissolve the English Parliament if its attitude towards France grew too aggressive, or if it failed to vote the King the supplies he needed. In return, Louis XIV would give

Charles II a yearly subsidy of something like £100,000. Did Danby know of the bargain? It seems that he did. Even so, he still pressed on, doggedly trying to secure money for the King via Parliament, for much more than £100,000 was needed to float the Navy.[43]

When Danby failed, it was still open to Charles to dissolve Parliament – as Shaftesbury and his faction so much desired – and call on the French subsidy. Even the Duke of York now supported a dissolution, believing for his part that a new Parliament would not be so rabidly anti-Catholic. But Danby, by pulling out all the stops of his own organization, managed to defeat the motion in the House of Lords. And Charles deftly but determinedly proceeded to prorogue Parliament yet again.

What was more, by taking advantage of France's military embroilment, he managed to secure the French subsidy all the same, while he had not satisfied its condition. The newest secret treaty with Louis XIV, that of February 1676, provided for an annual subsidy, payable in quarters. In vain Danby begged his master to commit himself to the Dutch – the old principle of the Triple Alliance. Charles II once more pursued his own bent, albeit secretly, and signed on with France again for a three-year period. Danby was aware of its existence, but only Lauderdale, 'never more high in His Majesty's favour', and the Duke of York were privy to the actual treaty.

The winter of 1675/6 might be regarded as one of general discontent in England, both in and out of Parliament. The MPs were furious that their fox had eluded them; in addition, the hunt was postponed for an unprecedentedly long period (the prorogation was to last fifteen months). Danby's Protestantism in foreign affairs was not prevailing. Only Charles II himself had managed to survive without any major defeat, 'living from day to day', in the words of the Venetian Ambassador. As for the knot in the comb, he had not forgotten it. But he was not yet ready to try and disentangle it.

CHAPTER TWENTY-ONE

Peace For His Own Time

'For he was not an active, busy or ambitious Prince ...
he seemed to be chiefly desirous of "Peace and Quiet
for his own Time".'

Sir John Reresby, *Memoirs*

B y 1676 it was the opinion of Sir John Reresby that King
Charles II was 'chiefly desirous of "Peace and Quiet
for his own Time"'. But this was not necessarily the
unambitious lethargy outlined by Reresby. 'Peace and Quiet' still
had a wonderful resonance to those who remembered the
troubles of the previous generation. It is notable that when Lord
Halifax in his *Character of a Trimmer* wanted to sum up the
effects of the two political extremes, Absolute Monarchy and
Commonwealth, he conceded the ferment created by the latter:
'[Absolute] Monarchy, a thing that leaveth men no liberty, and
a Commonwealth, such a one as alloweth them no Quiet.'¹ The
views of Charles II on the monarchy remained at this point as
amorphous as those of most of his contemporaries; but he
would have profoundly agreed with Halifax on the subject of
Commonwealths.

'Peace and Quiet for his own Time' had for him no ring of
appeasement. It was a thoroughly laudable aim. Oddly enough,
for a brief period between the prorogation of Parliament in the
autumn of 1675 and its reconvening in 1677, it seemed possible
that he might achieve it without a struggle.

It was true that a 'Country' – as opposed to 'Court' –
opposition was being developed by the coalition of Shaftesbury

and Buckingham. Increasingly this group had to be reckoned with. Although we shall hear more of the Green Ribbon Club towards the end of the decade, its constitution was in existence by 1676, even if its meetings were not yet recorded. The Green Ribbon Club provided an important rallying point for those discontented with the government – particularly when Parliament was not sitting. '*Les mal intentionnés*' was how Charles had described them to the French Ambassador when they persisted in voting against him. The King's Head Tavern, at the junction of Fleet Street and Chancery Lane, proved a convenient rendez-vous. For all the efforts of government spies to permeate the meetings, the Green Ribbon Club succeeded in linking together the various disparate elements – former Puritans, merchants, lawyers and so forth – which would go to make the future 'Whig' party. The first of the long line of English political clubs, it performed a function which even the most capacious private house could not fulfil.[2]

From another angle, the Green Ribbon Club also survived the clampdown on the coffee-houses because it was a private association. It is interesting to consider that beverages like coffee, chocolate and even sherbert, seemingly innocuous to us (because they are non-alcoholic), began life in England as dangerous, expensive and exciting symbols of dissidence. At the new meeting-places, the eternal beer of the English was replaced by a heady combination of coffee – and political sympathy. As a result, the government came to identify the places with the politics. An Order was given in December 1675 to suppress the coffee-houses as once race meetings had been suppressed under the Protectorate.

All the same, the appearance of peace was maintained. And the upswing in the royal and the national finances increased the illusion of a widespread, placid prosperity. As late as June 1677 the King told the French Ambassador that England enjoyed 'a profound tranquillity'. She successfully enriched herself, while other nations were drained or ruined by war. The English would one day thank him, he observed, for having kept them by prudence in 'so happy a state and so advantageous for their commerce'.[3]

In fact, the trade boom broke early in 1676.[4] And as the seventies wore on, the image of a liberal and healing King was being succeeded by something rather different. It is true that towards individuals the King had lost none of his humorous affability. It was a quality which he would retain till his dying hour. He was still the bonhomous monarch who supped with jockeys when at Newmarket. There are several well-known stories which illustrate his particular kind of ironic benevolence. One has the King watching a man who boasted of having invented a new process by which he could stand on the point of a steeple for an unprecedented length of time. At the end of the display Charles announced himself to be duly impressed and said that he would buy the patent of the process – to prevent any of his other subjects using it. Another described him dining with Sir Robert Viner in the City. Viner, overcome with the honour, became hopelessly drunk towards the evening and tried to stop the King from departing. 'Sir, you shall stay and take the other bottle!' cried Viner. Where other European monarchs might have resorted to a ferocious frown, Charles II merely smiled and quoted a popular song: 'He that's drunk is as great as a King.' Then he allowed himself to be led back.

When William Penn, as a Quaker, insisted on remaining covered in the King's presence – an extraordinary piece of *lèse-majesté* for those days – Charles took off his own hat.

'Friend Charles,' Penn is supposed to have asked, 'why dost thou not keep on thy hat?'

'It is the custom of this place that only one man should remain uncovered at a time,' replied the unruffled King.[5]

He remained a most accessible sovereign, in the modern phrase. It was Charles II who set the style by which the royal withdrawing-room, hitherto a select preserve, was open to any 'Person of Quality as well as our servants and others who come to wait on us'. The King would emerge from time to time to discourse with these Persons of Quality: and so the style was set for the official court 'Drawing Rooms' of later centuries. Even his bedchamber, dominated by the great bed, railed in in the French manner, was not particularly intimate. Its door was left open. Here he would receive ministers and favoured individuals; he would also use it to eat in slightly more privacy than the stately public meals allowed. True privacy, in so far as a seventeenth-century prince enjoyed it, was enjoyed in his closet (where he kept the scientific rarities and little treasures described by Evelyn), although even here he would receive certain advisers.[6]

Charles II fell back on another form of privacy. The long legs which had carried him successfully away from Worcester now served increasingly to carry him away from the pleas and complaints of his subjects. As the King grew older, his daily walk in St James's Park was taken at a faster and faster pace, the sovereign considering it enough to scatter random 'God bless yous' about him as he strode, like jesting Pilate, not stopping for an answer. Indoors he took to taking out his watch (wise men made themselves scarce at this signal) and falling asleep after meals, another cunning way of resisting importunities.

Part of this change of image was due to the inevitable erosion of time. The thick black periwig which he now habitually wore recalled in memory, no more, the black love-locks of yesteryear, for the King, having gone grey, was now almost entirely bald. As he was obviously no longer young, he was also no longer debonair. The melancholy which, as we have seen, lay at the core of his being often overlaid the engaging gaiety he had chosen to manifest in the sixties, in public. His face was already lined at the Restoration and adversity was the cause. The later portraits – that of 1675 by Lely onwards – display with relentless truth the deep lines which time had laid on his face; cynicism and an inner weariness at the folly of men – and women – were responsible.

Besides, a new generation was growing up who did not remember the Restoration or those happy years when an invited monarch came from overseas to heal and to forgive. A young man of twenty in 1676 would barely recollect that inauguration of a golden age – as it had seemed to so many – let alone the perils of Commonwealth and Civil War from which the restored monarch had rescued his country.

While the King retained his popular touch with individuals, many of his policies – such as the Stop of the Exchequer –

presented him in a much less attractive light. Then there was the question of his honour. Naturally the full extent of the deceit which he had employed in foreign policy – and was still employing while he received French money – was known to very few. But a feeling that the King's word, like the King's financial bond, was to be regarded with caution, began to pervade Court and political circles, nonetheless. And from there the malaise had the chance of spreading outwards. This is not to suggest that Boy Scout ethics either were or should be expected in a seventeenth-century monarch. But Lord Halifax probably got it about right when he wrote of dissimulation in a ruler, that it was a defect not to practise it at all, and a fault to practise it too much: 'It is necessary and yet it is dangerous too.'[7]

The King's persistent poverty contributed to his practice of deception. Charles II was no exception to the rule that debtors are often liars for the sake of survival, where rich men can afford the luxury of honesty. An anonymous burlesque of 1670 summed up the connection which was felt to exist between the King's lack of money (through extravagance) and the King's lack of truth; Charles was portrayed addressing Parliament as follows: 'You may perhaps think it dangerous to make me too rich, but do not fear it, I promise you faithfully whatever you give me, I will always still want: though in many other things my word may be thought but slender security, yet in this you may rely upon me....'[8]

The sardonic epigram ascribed to Lord Rochester on his master also comes to mind:

> We have a pritty witty King
> Whose word no man relies on,
> Who never said a foolish thing
> Nor ever did a wise one.*

---

* There are many versions of this epigram, which has been transformed into an epitaph in the best known version of all, beginning 'Here lies our Sovereign Lord the King ...'. But since Rochester predeceased Charles II, it could hardly have originated in this form. The epigram does not appear in the early editions of Rochester's works. The version above, with the circumstances which led up to it,

Admittedly Rochester was supposed to have first produced the verse in the following fashion: the King, in his easy way, told his courtiers that 'he would leave everyone to his liberty in talking when Himself was in company, and would not take what was said at all amiss'. At which Rochester saw his opportunity and lunged. Perhaps the King was not totally enchanted by the sally of his friend. For he responded with a thrust of his own blade: his words were his own, he retorted, but his deeds were his ministers'. But, like all slurs with a taste of truth in them, Rochester's wicked little rhyme has survived the test of time, where the King's equally quick riposte is often forgotten.

Even more fatally, Charles II ignored the force of popular prejudice with regard to Catholicism, France, and their hated bedfellow, arbitrary government. That twenty-year-old man alluded to above would contemplate a Catholic Court or, what was almost worse, a French-dominated one, for the links with France were increasingly resented on almost every level. Yet in his youth Charles had shown extraordinary determination in avoiding the Catholic taint while in exile, lest his chances of restoration perish. This degeneration of his sensitivities had come with age. Half of him was aware that the price of 'Peace and Quiet for his own Time' was eternal vigilance where Parliament and the nascent Whigs were concerned, plus a willingness to bow to the strong feelings of the majority of his subjects, however prejudiced and distasteful. The other half relaxed, and hoped that by successful juggling of French money, Parliamentary supplies, and those forces represented by Danby, Shaftesbury and even Buckingham, the same result could be achieved. He would shortly receive a terrible lesson.

Before that happened, Charles II was subjected to an assault of a rather pleasanter nature: from a beautiful woman. The rise – and fall – of Hortense Mancini, Duchesse de Mazarin, demonstrated two things. First, that those closest to the King continued to believe tenderly that he could be influenced by a woman. Second, that the King's sexuality was not yet extinct.

was first given by Thomas Hearne in his *Remarks and Collections* (notes for his historical works) in his entry for 17 November 1706.

The affair with Hortense would be his last very public throw in that direction. But Hortense, unlike Louise, was not of the material of which successful mistresses are made. She was an attractive, self-destructive creature whose wanton disregard for her own best interests (in the worldly sense) seduces from afar, even if it drove her promoters mad.

Once upon a time Hortense could have had the impecunious and throneless King as a husband; as the niece of Cardinal Mazarin, she would have been a useful wife for Charles in the late 1650s. In the intervening years Hortense as well as Charles had seen some revolutionary changes in her state. Her first husband, created Duc de Mazarin in her honour, proved to have a touch of religious mania. The unappreciative Hortense fled to Savoy, a decision which had caused Charles to quip to Madame at the time, 'I see wives do not love devout husbands....'[9] In Savoy an episode with the Duke led to her expulsion from the country after his premature death. But on leaving Savoy, Hortense was noted to be gaily 'bewigged and befeathered' at the head of a train of twenty men, as though nothing particularly humiliating had happened. Accompanied by her black page, Mustapha, she now turned to England to try her fortunes there.[10]

Despite her mature age – she was about thirty – there was something unalterably splendid about Hortense's appearance, in which her Italian inheritance predominated. She was 'one of those lofty Roman beauties', said a French admirer, 'in no way like our Baby-visaged and Puppet-like Faces of France'; Edmund Waller in a poem similarly termed her the 'Roman eagle'. She was blessed with a mass of black waving hair, and eyes said to be of three colours – combining the sweetness of the blue, the Irishness of the grey and the fire of the black. Ruvigny, a Protestant, sniffed that she was not really so beautiful: which, he added as a Frenchman, did not stop her being more beautiful than anyone else in England.[11]

Hortense also had an avidity for life which recalls that of Barbara in her prime. Indeed, in many ways the reign of Hortense represents a short-lived reversion of the King to the type of mistress of his younger days, high-spirited and reckless, as opposed to the domestic docility offered by Louise. In

Hortense's amatory exploits there were hints of sexual ambiguity: as Saint Evremond, commenting on the triumph of this new siren ('Fair beauties of Whitehall give way/Hortensia does her charms display'), saw fit to remark, 'Each sex provides its lovers for Hortense'. Certainly most aspects of pleasure lured her. She was a compulsive gambler, a lover of good food, adored dogs – three favourites were named Boy, Little Rogue and Chop – as well as cats, monkeys and birds which included a white sparrow, a canary, a starling called Jacob, and a parrot called Pretty. She was an excellent shot who could bring down quail. She too, like Charles, loved to swim, if she was not quite so adept at it: we hear of the faithful Mustapha (who luckily swam like a fish) dragging her about in the water on her front and her back. Hortense, wrote a contemporary, thought of nothing but enjoying herself: she triumphed over everything by an excess of folly. These were surely delightful attributes in a lover, if Hortense lacked the fundamental application for such a serious role (as Louise would have had it) as that of royal mistress.

Hortense's ostensible reason for arriving in England in the winter of 1675 was her cousinship to Mary Beatrice, Duchess of York. But her conquest of the King (on whom Louise's domesticated charms were perhaps temporarily palling) was rapid. By the summer of 1676 it was being said that the only time Hortense was *not* at the King's side was when he was bathing. Courtin told Louis XIV in another piece of Gallic chauvinism, 'It is the only decency which they observe in this country. There is a great deal of laxness in the rest of their conduct.'[12] By August Louise was in floods of tears – and Hortense was in Barbara's old apartments.

Naturally the rise of a new mistress caused a flurry of wings in the political dovecots. Arlington, who had attempted unsuccessfully to pursue his early alliance with Louise, now turned to Hortense, hoping to put down Danby. In consequence, Hortense was rumoured to be pro-Dutch. There seems no real proof that Hortense was anything quite so solid-sounding. Besides, Danby quickly adapted to her friendship. But Hortense did create a great deal of trouble by intriguing in a more intimate sphere. For she developed a passionate friendship with Anne

Countess of Sussex, one of the King's two daughters by Barbara. The Earl of Sussex, previously Lord Dacre, had been given the superior title on his marriage to Anne in 1674. The wedding, at Hampton Court, had been a glittering affair, attended by royalties on both sides of the blanket, including Prince Rupert, the Duke of York and the Duke of Monmouth. Anne received a £20,000 dowry from the King, who also played the father's role at the wedding; the bridegroom got a £2,000 a year pension. Despite this *largesse*, the new Lord Sussex intended to be master in his own house.*

He disapproved of the connection with Hortense. Nevertheless, Anne, who had some of her mother's obstinate temperament, persisted in it. The two ladies took fencing lessons together, proceeding to St James's Park for the purpose on one occasion, with drawn swords beneath their nightgowns. The crisis came when Anne announced her intention of sharing a balcony in Cheapside with Hortense at the Lord Mayor's Show in November. Barbara, like many another mother with a purple past, found it in her to write an extremely priggish letter to her daughter from France, advising 'wifely obedience'.[13] Eventually Lord Sussex took his wayward spouse in high dudgeon to the country. But he should have been warned. His troubles with her were not over – nor, for that matter, were Barbara's.

Returning to Hortense and her brief but victorious sway over the King, this was still sufficiently marked in February 1677 for her to be quoted by the French ambassador as being 'in a very prominent position raised above all the other ladies' at the opening of Parliament.[14] By the summer however the eternal Eve in Hortense had reasserted itself. She indulged in a prolonged and public flirtation with the Prince de Monaco. Hortense was dismissed. Louise dried her tears. The King settled back with a shrug into her waiting arms. Since Hortense had not presented the King with a child, alone among his mistresses-in-chief to

---

* The King, as usual, was more generous on paper than in fact. He was a long time paying the various bills, including that of Anne's wedding dress; but this was due to financial necessity. The ceremony, and the King's official acknowledgement of Anne's paternity, certainly made it improbable that she was actually Roger Palmer's child (see page 235).

fail to do so, the main residue of her reign was the unfortunate political impression she created. Marvell expressed the general indignation

> That the King should send for another French whore
> When one already hath made him so poor.

Charles II had not sent for Hortense. But the smear remained.

William of Orange, with the necessary tenacity of the ruler of a small country, had forgotten nothing of his plan for wresting England away from France. Nor after the Treaty of Westminster was he in any position to rest on his laurels. The military campaigns of Louis XIV proceeded apace. The year 1677 would see spectacular advances by the French. Before that date William had already put out feelers concerning marriage with his first cousin Mary, Protestant daughter of the Duke of York.[15] He found a receptive audience in the English Ambassador, the erudite and agreeable Sir William Temple.

Temple had viewed with deprecation England's entanglement with France. He was now in a much stronger position to exert pressure to end it. Having been withdrawn from the Netherlands in 1671 when his pro-Dutch views were clearly incompatible with the pro-French ones of the English government, he was recalled to government service over the negotiation of the Treaty of Westminster. Shortly afterwards, declining both the Embassy at Madrid and a Secretaryship of State (leaving it scornfully to Sir Joseph Williamson), Temple took up residence at The Hague.

The spring of 1677 brought a wave of victories for Louis XIV. 'I have loved war too much,' declared the French King on his death-bed. But his triumphant campaign brought him at the time not only his own heart's desire but also his country's. In the United Provinces William girded himself for another span of heroic defence. Much depended yet again on the attitude of England. Charles II had shown himself able and willing to act as a mediator in the past, once the forced Treaty of Westminster had put an end to his more ambitious plans. Louis XIV, who was paying good money over to his cousin, naturally hoped for

Charles' French sympathies to be exhibited in a more positive manner: neutrality would however be better than nothing. The pro-Dutch party in England, on the other hand, keenly desired England to come to the rescue of that poor beleaguered country.

This projected marriage of the Prince of Orange and the niece of Charles II was one subterranean manoeuvre. Having been backed by Temple in Holland, it was taken up by Danby at home. However, early in 1677 there was a renewed opportunity for Parliamentary interference on the subject of foreign policy. It was time for Parliament to reconvene after its prorogation – high time, in the opinion of such leading members as Buckingham. Indeed, so long had been the gap (fifteen months) that a new and wily argument was developed by Shaftesbury and others for the necessity of a general election. The King had prorogued Parliament beyond the legal limits, so ran the proposition, and thus automatically ensured a dissolution.

It was nonsense, of course. Buckingham addressed the House of Lords on the subject in February. The great Duke had lost his sense of personal magnificence – or did not care. By 1679 not only was he wearing false teeth, but Nell Gwynn, who remained his friend, begged him at least to wear new shoes and a new periwig when he knocked at her door, so as not to stink the place out.[16] Was this the son of the gorgeous George Villiers, whose sheer physical beauty had fascinated two generations? To the King he may have seemed like a curio, preserved for the sake of ancient loyalties from youth and childhood, where a Henry VIII might have employed the purgative axe. Buckingham, no longer the peacock he had once been, was in fact more like a wasp, an angry wasp at that, determined not to recognize the end of his own personal summer; like a wasp, he retained his sting, as the King and Danby would soon discover.

In the House of Lords he certainly made a bold show, attended by a host of followers 'in great bravery in liveries of blue'.[17] The argument was nonetheless rejected by both Houses. The King was furious. He was also deeply worried by the implications of the incident. Was this perhaps that first rumbling of the revolution he had long, consciously or unconsciously, dreaded? Danby pounced forthwith on the four principal peers involved. At the orders of the House of Lords Buckingham was imprisoned in the Tower, as were Shaftesbury, Salisbury and Wharton. It was held at the time to be an over-reaction. Later, when Danby too found himself in the same ominous prison, Bishop Burnet at least thought it a 'just retaliation' for the 'violence' of this incident.[18] But if Danby was the public instrument, there is no doubt that the King approved of the gesture.

Latterly the officials of the law in general were being subjected to his critical scrutiny. There were complaints that the quality of the King's judges was declining. Following the departure of Matthew Hale as Lord Chief Justice in 1676, tenure itself was insecure. In June Sir William Ellis was dismissed from the Court of Common Pleas on the advice of Danby. His substitute, William Scroggs, a sinister if clever fellow described by Roger North as 'a great Voluptuary' whose debaucheries were 'egregious', was, in addition to all this, very much a royal nominee. In 1678 the process continued, Chief Justice Ramsford departing in May and Twisden in December, their respective ages of seventy-three and seventy six being given as an excuse (although even today these ages do not debar incumbents from such positions).[19]

Obviously such a campaign did not pass without remark. Marvell chose to comment on it in his trumpet blast, published in 1677, *Account of the Growth of Popery and Arbitrary Government in England*: 'What French counsel, what standing forces, what parliamentary bribes, what national oaths, and all the other machinations of wicked men have not yet been able to effect,' he cried, 'may be more compendiously acted by twelve judges in scarlet.' He saw it as part of the general decline in English life, set off by the noxious spread of Catholicism; on which topic itself he exploded with eloquent bigotry: 'Were it either open Judaism, or plain Turkery, or honest Paganism, there is yet a certain bona fides in the most extravagant belief ... but this [Popery] is a compound of all the three.'

The meeting of Parliament itself was dominated by the needs of the Navy. The continuation of the quarrel between the two Houses over the issue raised by the Shirley *v.* Fagg case helped

Danby to maintain some kind of control. A stirring speech by Samuel Pepys secured a supply of £600,000 for the ships. So far, so good, even if Danby was probably over-confident in those MPs he listed as supporting the Crown – because such type of prognostication was still in its infancy.

In addition, Danby's strategy was leading him into some strange paths. He may not have fully thought out the significance of what he preached when he urged the King to declare the war in April – against France – on the grounds that *then* Parliament would have to grant him a fully paid-up Army and a Navy, and *then* he would be independent of them....[20] The first implication of this was that the King might well use these forces for a purpose other than that for which they were voted by Parliament. That was not only outside his powers as generally understood at the time, but was also of course the development that many Members of Parliament had been ostentatiously dreading over the years. Had Charles II not constantly denied such suggestions as 'malicious' and 'jealousies'? The second implication, more serious still, was that he might use the Army and Navy to suborn the rule of Parliament.

But the King declined to declare war, either at the instance of Danby or of the House of Commons. The Dutch partisans there continued to agitate for some show of help for Holland, in face of the sweeping French victories. On 23 May the Commons asked in plain terms for an offensive and defensive alliance with Holland. This was quite beyond their rights: public interference with foreign policy undeniably invaded the royal prerogative and the King said so sharply. To mark his displeasure and his determination to preserve his prerogative, he prorogued Parliament until 16 July.

There was an uncomfortable feeling of stalemate by the summer of 1677. Parliament would not vote all the money needed for a war until the King declared that war. The King naturally would not declare war without money. Nor was the opposition quashed. Buckingham emerged from the Tower in July. Marvell believed it to be at the instance of the King's boon companions: 'This was by Nelly, Middlesex, Rochester and the merry gang....'[21] He had already been allowed out for two days in June to oversee the building of his grand new palace at Cliveden – a sign of the King's indulgence or Buckingham's priorities. Shaftesbury attempted in vain to secure his own release by appealing to the King's Bench for a writ of *Habeas Corpus*. He lingered there for the next six months. But his confinement was now much less severe; and, as he was able to receive visits from his colleagues, he was by no means cut off from the opposition's continuing intrigues.

Still without proper funds from Parliament, Charles II signed his third secret agreement with Louis XIV, by which Charles was to hold off his anti-French Parliament until the following May, and in return Louis was as usual to pay up. At the same time Danby was making progress in the negotiations for the Dutch marriage: in this area the King wished to accommodate his minister. It was as though the King were astride a giant see-saw, with William and Danby on one side, Louis XIV on the other, and Parliament determined to upset the whole structure. Rather than let that happen, Charles determined to shift his weight dexterously now to one side, now to the other, rather than lose his balance.

Danby therefore was able to derive comfort from the success of the Dutch marriage project. Temple's mission to tie up the details of the marriage between William and Mary was accomplished. William had characteristically made enquiries about the girl's disposition. Fortunately, Lady Temple was a close friend of the Princess' governess, so that William could satisfy himself on this score: the link with England was evidently not his sole consideration. To Sir William Temple he observed prosaically, if sensibly, on the whole subject 'that if he should meet with one to give him trouble at home, it was what he should not be able to bear, who was like to have enough abroad in the course of his life'.[22] The only unhappy principal in the whole affair was the fifteen-year-old Princess. She wept 'grievously' when she heard the news. She saw herself being exiled for political reasons to an unappealing country, on the arm of an equally unappealing bridegroom: William was several inches shorter than she – to her hysterical eye, virtually a dwarf.

Queen Catharine, ever kind-hearted, tried to make things

better by pointing out: 'Child, when I came to England I had not even seen the King.'

'Madam, you came into England!' exclaimed Mary with the despair and cruelty of youth, 'But I am going out of England.'[23] Shades of earlier Stuart princesses who had made suitable Protestant matches abroad – her great-aunt Elizabeth of Bohemia and her aunt Mary Princess of Orange. The odd thing was that the marriage of this Mary, begun in tears, was to turn out the most successful of them all in a worldly sense. Not for this Mary the years of impecunious exile endured by her great-aunt, the premature widowhood of her aunt. Not only would she occupy the throne of England, but, probably even more to her satisfaction – for she had an essentially shy nature – her marriage of convenience turned into a love affair on her side. She loved her William devotedly and dutifully, becoming a true Dutchwoman in the way her proud aunt had never condescended to do.

It may seem surprising that Charles II should welcome or even tolerate a public event calculated to outrage the susceptibilities of Louis XIV. It is true that Danby pressed the match with great firmness, so that in a sense Charles was able to plead political pressure with perfect accuracy. But Charles, now that he was in his balancing mood, could see another advantage to it. Mary was the heiress presumptive to the throne in the younger generation, or, as it was put at the time of her wedding, 'the Eldest Daughter of the Crown', who was now happily sleeping in 'Protestant Arms'. In his speech to Parliament the following January, Charles referred pointedly to the fact that he had done all he could 'to remove all sorts of jealousies, I have given my niece to the Prince of Orange; by which I hope I have given full assurance that I shall never suffer his interest to be ruined'.[24]

The King trusted that the nuptial arrangements of Mary, deposited in Protestant arms, would distract attention from the fact that her father, who was even closer to the succession, was sleeping in Catholic ones. What was more, Mary Beatrice was pregnant; this always aroused the fear that she might give birth to a son to be brought up a Catholic (she had already borne two daughters). In fact, the baby, born just three days later, was a boy. But the public, who received the news coldly, might have spared their disapproval: by December, this latest Duke of Cambridge had perished like his half-brothers, who had in turn borne the unlucky title.*

But the pregnancy had at least played its part in persuading James to agree to Mary's match, which was otherwise most distasteful to him. Nor, on the occasion of the marriage, could there be any doubts where the popular sympathies lay. According to Pepys, nobody had been pleased at Mary's birth: a disappointing girl and Clarendon's grand-daughter at that. Now, in contrast, such 'bells and bonfires' and general rejoicing had not been seen since the Restoration, wrote Sir Charles Lyttelton.²⁵ Edmund Waller, the Court poet, represented it as a romantic union of a soldier king and a beautiful princess:

> Nor all the force he leads by land
> Could guard him from her conqu'ring eyes...

It was a measure of the general satisfaction at the Protestant combination that it should be rumoured – quite falsely – that Mary had been adopted as the King's own daughter.

All that Charles II actually did at the ceremony in November 1677 was to play the part of a jolly, slightly bawdy uncle. He told the groom to remember 'Love and War do not agree very well together'. When William put down the traditional handful of gold on the prayer book (symbol of all his worldly goods), Charles said briskly to his niece, 'Take it up, take it up. It's all clear gain to you.' And he urged on the prim William on his wedding night, 'Hey nephew, to your work! Hey, St George for England!'

It was left to Louis XIV to exclaim with predictable disgust and horror at the consummation of his worst fears. His reported reactions ranged from the disagreeable ('two beggars were well-

---

* The other children of James and Mary Beatrice – all daughters – died young during the reign of Charles II. It was the birth of a son in June 1688 then called James Edward, known to history as the Old Pretender, which provoked the crisis which led to the departure of James II from the throne.

matched in public') to the histrionic: he behaved as if he had just lost an army when he heard the news, and told the Duke of York, 'You have given your daughter to my mortal enemy.'[26] More to the point, Louis XIV stopped payment of the latest subsidy to Charles II. He also attempted to prick the King's exposed flank by its own Machiavellian means. An obvious weakness of Charles II's position was the dislike of the opposition for Danby – an emotion only sharpened by his imprisonment of Buckingham and Shaftesbury. From the point of view of the French King, Danby's resolute pro-Dutch stance could therefore be circumvented by the time-honoured expedient of pressing money into the palms of his political enemies.

Thus men like Lord Russell and Algernon Sidney – later advertised as champions of liberty – as well as Buckingham were in correspondence with Barrillon, the representative of Versailles (a home of Catholic absolutism, if ever there was one), and, what was more, were receiving funds from that tainted source. At the time, the intrigue was not exactly shocking: it was merely one more manoeuvre in the endlessly complicated wheeling and dealing which went on in Europe at the time, before Louis XIV would and the Dutch could make peace.

Charles II retaliated against Louis XIV's blocking of the subsidy by summoning Parliament for early February – not May, as proposed; he then brought it forward another ten days. By this time he had already allowed Laurence Hyde to sign a defensive alliance with the Dutch on 10 January. Yet the Dutch never ratified the treaty, and the English never went to war as promised; this treaty should be seen as yet another manoeuvre.

Charles' speech at the opening of Parliament on 28 January had a noble ring. He recalled his own efforts at mediation, by which he had hoped to procure 'an honourable and safe peace for Christendom'. It was not his fault, he said, if he now came before them seeking supplies for the Navy and Ordnance, finding that peace was 'no longer to be hoped for by fair means' and that which 'be not obtained by force ... cannot be had otherwise'.[27] But the King's inner hope was not for war. He trusted that Louis would accede to this form of blackmail and negotiate a peace all the same, along lines acceptable to Charles and his nephew William.

The fall of Ghent to Louis XIV on 27 February made the possibility of a compromise peace more remote. At the same time it increased the demands for a positive Dutch alliance in Parliament. In general, the mood there was obstreperous, even ugly, especially on the subject of supplies. William Sacheverell, the rising orator, declared on 4 February that he knew 'what mind the country are of. They will not be pleased if we thrust a sum of money blindly into those hands that have so ill managed affairs.'[28]

Shaftesbury was finally released from the Tower on 26 February. Halifax had presented his first petition a fortnight earlier; but it was not until Shaftesbury had fully and publicly recognized his error, both in demanding a dissolution and in appealing to the King's Bench thereafter, that he was allowed to go free. It all had the air of an abject apology. But wise observers like the French ambassador saw in Shaftesbury's reappearance 'a great mortification' for Danby. Shaftesbury after all understood only too well the art of *reculer pour mieux sauter*. And he was probably aware in advance of Louis XIV's negotiations, since Lord Russell had been a frequent visitor to the Tower. Buckingham, who, like Rochester, had the knack of hitting on the unpleasant truth about his contemporaries (hence his demolition of Dryden in *The Rehearsal*), compared Shaftesbury to a Will-o'-the-Wisp 'that uses to lead men out of the way, then leads them at last in a ditch and darkness and nimbly retreats for self-security'.[29]

All the same, neither side had yet devised a way out of the familiar stalemate – a policy of If No War, Then No Money on Parliament's side; If No Money, Then No War on the King's. Charles II made an equally familiar move on 25 March when he wrote privately to Louis XIV. He suggested that in return for a subsidy of six million livres annually for the next three years, he would secure a proper peace in Europe, along conciliatory lines. But his winning streak had not left King Louis in the mood for territorial compromise: for the time being, he rejected both terms and subsidy.

King Charles was left with the elaborate Parliamentary game of cat and mouse which was being played at home over the question of supplies: with Parliament as the cat and the King for once in the position of the mouse. Later it was claimed in the memoirs of James II that at this point the House of Commons was in reality far more jealous of the King's power than of that of France.[30] Certainly their behaviour lent plausibility to the theory. The opposition bore every sign of being terrified that the King would escape their financial clutches. Although they were armed with their own private subsidies from France, they set up a continual caterwaul that help should be given to the Dutch; yet when money was finally voted which would enable the King to declare war on France (should he so wish), Parliament immediately followed this up by an embargo on French imports. Since the only effective way of raising money quickly was to use the Excise, and since the French imports provided by far the largest share of this, it will be seen that the second action effectively nullified the first.... The result was, as before, a stalemate.

The absolute monarch, Louis XIV, Charles was beginning to find, was easier to cope with than his own elected Parliament. A deft piece of diplomatic blackmail from the English king – the threat of an alliance with Holland, Spain and Austria – did produce the first promised payment of six million livres from the French King in May.

In the meantime, Charles II was not the only one at home who was beginning to think back edgily to the events of 1641 and 1642. So traumatic had been the experience of those days on two generations – the men in their prime and the young who also suffered the consequences – that the survivors tended to see fearful parallels when certain circumstances prevailed. Trouble with the Scots, especially on religious matters, was always held to be a bad omen, so that when an English Parliamentary attack was mounted on the King's regent in Scotland, the Duke of Lauderdale, in May, that too seemed all of a piece. Charles II suspected that the English opposition had been stirring up Lauderdale's new enemies, the Scottish supporters of 'Conventicles', as had previously suspected Shaftesbury of being in touch with the Hamiltonians.

'Conventicles' were a form of independent religious gathering unlawful under the new regime, and a series of moves of increasing severity were made against those taking part in them from 1669 onwards. In fact, the rise of this new type of Covenanter was a manifestation of the Scottish national character which Lauderdale, and by implication Charles II, should have taken more seriously. Originally, they had been animated not so much by political motives as by a sincere desire to practise their religion in their own fashion. It was really impossible to cut out the truly Presbyterian heart of the Scots, as successive rulers had found to their cost.

It was made incumbent upon local magnates to put down Conventicles held upon their land. Yet as the Covenanters were driven towards more violent resistance, it was virtually out of the question for the landowners to carry out this provision without force. And force, military force, should surely be provided by the central government. Furthermore, if it was to be a question of a military crusade against the Covenanters, that raised the second question of who was going to pay for it. In July 1678 the Scottish Parliament voted an extremely large sum – £1,800,000 – for the suppression of the Conventicles. It was quite clear that the raising of this money would be enormously resented by those who did not wish the Conventicles suppressed in the first place. No, the auguries in Scotland were definitely not encouraging.

In England, the address against Lauderdale was carried through the Commons, for all Danby's sedulous efforts to prevent it. Charles, although it was in his nature, as his brother James said, 'to keep measures with everybody', was obviously furious at the impertinence of the Commons. Saying icily that he preferred not to answer the address, he adjourned Parliament for ten days.

In Europe a further impetus towards peace was given by the exhaustion of the Dutch. And Louis XIV, already worried by Charles II's little gambit of proposing a quadruple alliance excluding France, was not averse to being involved in further negotiations. Even so, he retained a very hard-headed notion of the value of his own conquests: the peace negotiations underwent one further check, until Charles II, either in genuine disgust or more probably to bring about the conference he desired, proposed sending some English troops to Flanders to assist the Dutch. The way was finally cleared for the negotiations which led to the Peace of Nymegen on 10 August. By this, France was left with a good deal of the conquered Flemish territory, if not all she had desired; she also secured a workable boundary with the Spanish Netherlands.

The Dutch got the respite that they, rather than William, wanted. William had been reluctant to see his 'mortal enemy' confirmed in so much new ground; nevertheless, he too was able to use the temporary lull of the next few years to build up himself and his country against the final assault. Sir William Temple hailed the role of Charles II in all of this grandiloquently: the King, he declared, was once more 'at the head of the affairs of Christendom'.[31] This was the reassurance the King wanted since the waning of his European prestige after 1673.

The same happy claim could not be made for the King's affairs at home. So ragged had relations between Parliament and King become by the summer of 1678 that it has been suggested that Danby at least was considering the maintenance of the King's authority by use of the Army internally. It has also been proposed that the King himself might have contemplated such action.[32] But there is no proof that Charles II ever contemplated what would have been – by his standards – a disastrous course. Mending and patching, ironing over, smoothing down, these were the natural instincts of Charles II. So deeply were they ingrained that even an outbreak of passion, as over the Lauderdale incident or the Commons' open interference with foreign policy the previous year, was generally followed by a show of regained composure. And there were two good reasons to dissuade him.

First, there was a practical point. He had no money in hand with which to pay the soldiers on any grand scale. It is true that the Commons had voted supplies for the 'disbandment' of the Army on 30 May, the King having told them a week earlier that the issue of peace or war would depend upon their supplies: 'I leave it to you to consider whether to provide for their [the Army's] subsistence so long or for their disbanding sooner.' The Commons opted for the latter course on the grounds that the King was obviously determined not to fight France: peace would leave him in control of just that kind of force the Commons dreaded, unless something was done about it. When the King asked for – and was refused – an extra £300,000 a year on 18 June to ensure peace, the Commons were even more suspicious. The King was, however, left with the 'disbandment' supplies, which he proceeded to use for the Army's maintenance. But this sum alone would not take him very far.

One lesson taught by the Commonwealth was that unpaid soldiers sought new masters. It was true Charles II had emerged from the Restoration with full powers as Commander-in-Chief of the Army. As Sir Joseph Williamson pointed out in 1678, 'I know of nothing that can hinder the King from raising what forces he pleases, if he pays for them himself.'[33] But there was no way that a king hamstrung financially could possibly have financed such an arbitrary force in such a way as to maintain power by it for any effective period.

The second reason, which was psychological, was even more important. Charles II had witnessed at first hand the fatal – because it was unsuccessful – use of the Army by his own father. He had himself been restored by the Commonwealth Army, but in their good time, not his own; his Army in exile had proved useless in recapturing the throne. He loved the new English Army which he had constructed since 1661, devoting much time to details of its welfare. Yet an interest in the special red and black uniforms of his hundred Yeomen of the Guard – 'a livery coat of fine red cloth guarded with black velvet with Rose and Crown, his Majesty's motto and Scroll C R, back and breast, embroidered with silver and gilt spangles. Similar breeches' – should not be equated with a manic wish to take away the Parliamentary bauble by military means, as Oliver Cromwell had once done.[34]

Charles was perfectly prepared to sacrifice a number of things in the good cause of the peace of his kingdom – ranging from the abstract, such as the truth, to the concrete, such as his financial independence; but he was not prepared to sacrifice that peace itself. The use of the Army would have been another 'false Step', like the Stop on the Exchequer; this one might have disrupted the careful structure of the kingdom altogether.

It was easier to prorogue Parliament yet again. Charles II's so-called Long Parliament was adjourned on 15 July. Perhaps peace in Europe would after all be matched by the return of 'tranquillity' at home.

CHAPTER TWENTY-TWO

Against Exclusion

~~~~~~~

'On the other hand, some argued against the exclusion
that it was unlawful in itself, and against the unalterable
law of succession (which came to be the common
phrase).'

Bishop Burnet on Parliament, 1679

The August of 1678 was fiercely hot: a surprise which even
the English summer can sometimes spring. Charles II,
revelling in all the varied enchantments of Windsor, went
fishing and tried to let his cares run softly by the waters of the
sweet Thames.

One of his minor cares was the danger of assassination. It
was a seventeenth- as well as a sixteenth-century weapon (the
first Duke of Buckingham had fallen to an assassin's dagger; the
Royalist conspirators had aimed frequently, if unsuccessfully, at
the death of Cromwell). There had been various plots against
Charles' own life, from the Fifth Monarchists of 1661 onwards.
Given the King's temperament, both courageous and fatalistic,
it is unlikely that it represented more than just that – a minor
care. A man who had the habit of an early morning walk
represented an easy target; a man who regularly promenaded
among his subjects in St James's Park obviously counted on his
popularity rather than his guards to protect him.

Nevertheless, having survived so far, Charles II did not intend
to fall victim either to clamorous opposition in Parliament or
to armed attack elsewhere. As a plotter himself, he believed in
keeping a casual eye on such tendencies in others. He also
appreciated instinctively, better than we can today, just what his

contemporaries might hope to achieve by the death of a king. He had seen the devastation brought upon the monarchy by the execution of his father. The substitution of one monarch for another, be that monarch any one of his assorted relatives, might be plausibly expected to bring about a great alteration in affairs: religious, political, or both.

Shortly before the King left London, a man named Christopher Kirkby warned him about a plot against his life. Kirkby was known to the King because he shared his interest in chemical experiments.¹ With some difficulty Kirkby managed to deliver the first part of his warning just as Charles was entering St James's Park on his morning saunter. Although Kirkby suggested that the assassination might be carried out imminently in the park itself, the King still proceeded on his way. It was only in the evening, still unassassinated, that he hearkened further to Kirkby's dramatic tale. This story was subsequently supported by one Israel Tonge, a slightly dotty Anglican clergyman who had allegedly uncovered the plot.

The plot's substance was however quite incredible: it involved the Catholics in England, notably the Jesuits, and Louis XIV ganging up together to kill the King; then they would all take up arms together to prevent the accession of the Duke of York; the end result would be the conquest of England for France. The assassination complex of the time had taken Charles as far as listening to Kirkby and Tonge – at his leisure – but it could take him no further, given the ludicrous nature of their revelations. It was therefore probably because the accused Catholics included a member of the Queen's household, Sir George Wakeman, that Charles handed the matter over to Danby.² Then he went to Windsor.

In Danby, Tonge found a more susceptible audience. Danby did not love France, to put it mildly, and had a prejudiced Anglican view of the Papists. Besides, it was Danby's duty to ensure the safety of the King. Tonge produced papers which Danby found sufficiently convincing to proceed to a further examination of the subject. It was in this way that another character was summoned onto the stage, one whose sheer roguery should, if there had been any justice, have shown it up at once and for ever for what it was. This was a man named Titus Oates.

Titus Oates had been born in the year of the execution of Charles 1 and was thus nearly thirty at the time of the egregious events for which he was later remembered. Westminster School and Merchant Taylor's, Gonville and Caius College and St John's: all these could claim the honour of his education. Despite these advantages, up till 1678 Oates had had a generally disreputable career. Betrayal was its keynote. He was himself a practising homosexual but had chosen to bring this charge against another man (it was dismissed). From being in Anglican Orders, Oates was converted to Catholicism; instructed as a Jesuit, he abandoned his new faith in 1677. His *curriculum vitae* was certainly not one which should have inspired any confidence in his testimony.

Contemporary descriptions of Titus Oates are almost universally unfavourable. His low forehead, little nose, tiny deep-set eyes, fat cheeks and vast wobbling chins make him sound more like a pig than a man. Once he had achieved fame, or infamy, Oates also showed a taste for playing the dandy which must have made him still more grotesque. But such descriptions also dwell on his voice. It was the 'speech of the gutter' wrote a Jesuit historian: in a tone both 'strident and sing-song' he 'wailed rather than spoke'.[3] One suspects that, like many others whose true impact has perished with them, including Rasputin, Oates was a bit of a mesmerist. Otherwise he could hardly have maintained his remarkable career, even allowing for anti-Popery, over three reigns.

First examined by the Council, at Tonge's suggestion, on 28 September, Oates produced a fusillade of fantastic accusations. Some of his rounds were fired across the water at the Catholic Archbishop of Dublin, Peter Talbot, amongst others. Most of his charges constituted a tarradiddle of lies, easily contradicted. It was only when Oates pointed his weapon wildly but enthusiastically in the direction of the personal servants of the royal family that he met with a piece of undeserved luck. Oates named Sir George Wakeman, Queen Catharine's physician, and Edward Coleman, secretary to the Duchess of York.[4] Using Wakeman's medical expertise, they were supposed to have plotted the death of the King by poison. And very soon the Council did bring to light some highly unwise correspondence between Coleman and the confessor to Louis xiv.

The trouble was that these royal Catholic households presented a sitting target for the charges of the malicious, such as Oates, and had done so since the days of Henrietta Maria. At best, they were tolerated, their existence guaranteed in theory by a marriage treaty, but their numbers were heavily circumscribed and subjected to disgruntled questioning from time to time by the House of Commons. At worst, they were harried and suspected. At all times such Papist enclaves were highly unpopular. As a result, these worlds within a world were Byzantine in character. The men concerned were often cut off from the ordinary life of England for years, even if they had been born there; they were thus quite ignorant of it. And where Catharine of Braganza and Mary Beatrice of Modena were modest, pious, charming women, their servants did not always have the same standards of behaviour. Coleman, the son of an Anglican clergyman, was full of the traditional zeal of the convert. No doubt, on his arrival in the household of the Duke of York in 1675, he did see intriguing with France as part of the work he should do to restore the true Faith to England (although that of course was a far cry from planning the assassination of Charles ii). The King had several times asked his brother to dismiss Coleman (but that again hardly gave Coleman a motive for a daring murder).

Coleman's indiscreet and of course treacherous correspondence had consequences beyond its own intrinsic importance. For, using guilt by association, it enabled a finger to be pointed at the Queen's household. Sir George Wakeman firmly rebutted the charges against him, which were more than usually ridiculous. He was a highly respected physician, a former Royalist and a devoted servant of the Stuarts restored: the death of Charles ii by poison would have broken not only his Hippocratic oath but also his oath of loyalty to his sovereign. As John Evelyn, who was 'well acquainted' with him, commented, he was 'a worthy gentleman' and one who would have totally abhorred such a deed as the assassination.' Yet the discovery of Coleman's correspondence provided the necessary fire to make the smoke go whirling round Wakeman's head. And these clouds of smoke might spread to envelop the Queen.

The relationship of Charles II and Catharine of Braganza had changed since those rather pathetic days when Catharine first came to England. How could it not? Marriage is no exception to the rule that time transforms all alliances. Charles and Catharine had now been married for over sixteen years, almost as long as Charles' parents, before the Civil War separated them. The King, with his ready sense of guilt and tenderness where the fair sex was concerned, now felt quite different emotions towards the woman who had been at his side longer than any of his mistresses – except Barbara, now dismissed.

Besides, the Queen herself had changed. She no longer resembled Princess Katharine of France: there was no more talk of 'bilbo', no oaths sworn by mistake. Like many good women, Queen Catharine had gained support from her virtue over a long period and had emerged as a character of remarkable fortitude. (In this heredity was on her side: both her mother and grandmother had been women of strong character.)

Dryden's play about Antony and Cleopatra, *All for Love*, was first performed in 1677 and dedicated to Danby. Dryden in his own preface purported to 'imitate the divine Shakespeare'. But there is an interesting variation from Shakespeare's construction when Antony's rejected wife Octavia confronts Cleopatra and, from a position of wifely dignity, has the better of the exchange. As Cleopatra angrily exclaims,

> You bear the specious title of a wife,
> To gild your cause, and draw the pitying world
> To favour it...

There is emphasis in general on the respect due to a royal consort – 'Justice and pity both plead for Octavia. For Cleopatra neither,' says Ventidius – and the triumph of goodness – 'My wife has brought me, with her prayers and tears ...,' cries Antony. Both had their echoes in the situation at the English

Court, where Dryden had been Poet Laureate since 1670.

It was not only a case of the King's esteem and that of the Court. Where the English public were concerned, Catharine's dignity and goodness were just the sort of qualities to appeal to them in their Queen over a long period. It was significant that Catharine's servants had been excepted from the ill effects of the Test Act in 1673.

In contrast to the royal mistresses, Catharine displayed no taste for impertinent show. At the same time, she made it clear that she enjoyed the life and pleasures of her adopted country – a feat which may have cost her more pain than she admitted in public, judging from her sad little remark to Princess Mary. The House of Lords in debate positively 'went upon the virtues of the Queen'. When it was all over, the King was able to write with satisfaction to Catharine's brother in Portugal concerning the accusations: 'Such of them as took but time to deliberate how the Queen hath lived found motives to reject the complaint ... instead time was spent magnifying her virtues.'[6] It had taken another foreign Catholic princess, Henrietta Maria, ten years to gain the opprobrium of such as Prynne, who termed her the dancing goblin. Catharine, in a far more anti-Catholic period, spent ten years building up a solid reputation. In public, the Queen also maintained a regal serenity as her husband dallied with a succession of mistresses. She continued to do so until his death: there were to be no more scenes such as had sullied the early months of her marriage – at any rate, in the mind of the King. Like Queen Alexandra, consort of the equally errant Edward VII, she saw that supreme dignity – and love – lay in tolerance.

As yet, the Queen's relationship with her husband had not quite attained that halcyon quality on which observers were to comment in the following eighteen months. A year later Lady Sutherland would cry out that the Queen was 'now a mistress, the passion her spouse has for her is so great'.[7] She was not alone in the view. It had taken the shenanigans of the Popish Plot and the Queen's own behaviour to achieve this 'extraordinary favour'.

In 1678 Charles II, out of neurotic guilt, could not take it for granted that his wife's virtue would protect her. Supposing Wakeman as well as Coleman had been indiscreet, who knew what might be charged against her, however unfairly? In the ensuing proceedings of the Council there is no doubt that the King displayed extreme jumpiness on anything which pertained to the Queen's household, or might prove to do so. Otherwise it is not possible to understand how this sensible and indeed cynical man allowed the fabrications of Oates and his accomplices to have any official credence at all.

Even without the investigations of the Council, the autumn of 1678 bid fair to be a time of unusual tension. A new session of Parliament had been promised by the King, which prospect enchanted no-one but excited not a few. Then in early October an event took place which transformed the whole situation from one of measured enquiry and political anticipation into – strident panic. This was the death of a Protestant magistrate, named Sir Edmund Berry Godfrey, which took place some time between the evening of 12 October, when he left his house to go out to dinner, and 17 October, when his battered corpse was discovered on Primrose Hill. Much later Lord Halifax would sapiently observe, concerning the Popish Plot, that 'the angry buzz of a multitude is one of the bloodiest noises in the world'. The news of the murder (for so it was naturally assumed to be) of Godfrey had a cataclysmic effect on London society. As Serjeant Maynard later declared to the House of Commons, 'The world was awakened.'[8] From now on the angry buzz of the multitude would sound in everybody's ears – King, courtiers, opposition members, Catholic priests, Anglicans, foreign envoys alike – and drown the sweeter strains of reason and common-sense.

The death of Sir Edmund Berry Godfrey has still not been satisfactorily explained three hundred years later. When Godfrey's bruised body was discovered, he had been dead for some days. Murder was the obvious plausible explanation, either by random muggers taking advantage of Godfrey's night walk, or by any one of the enemies a magistrate can acquire in the exercise of his profession. One of these was the drunken Earl of Pembroke, known for his maniacal assaults. But the injuries on Godfrey's body were mysterious; although he seemed at first sight to have been killed by his own sword, the autopsy showed that this wound had actually been inflicted after death.

So another more complicated theory has arisen that Godfrey, who suffered from melancholia, committed suicide; his body was then treated so as to make the cause of death look like murder. There could be two reasons for this: either to avoid the penal laws applied to the estate of a suicide, or, more melodramatically, to throw the responsibility for the crime onto someone else – or onto some persons else, the Papists. But this would have been an elaborate, even over-elaborate, way of going about things. There is no proof that such a concealment ever took place, while random mugging in the seventeenth century was at least a common phenomenon.

As in another classical mystery, the Gowrie House Plot, no one theory of the death of Sir Edmund Berry Godfrey seems able to explain all the known facts. For all the optimism of researchers in the field of historical crime, perhaps the whole truth never will be known.* From the point of view of the biographer of Charles II, the true explanation of Godfrey's death is of secondary importance compared to the furore its discovery caused at the time. It was most unfortunate, with the nerves of London society already on the edge, that Godfrey had recently taken Oates' deposition on oath and was reputed to have given Coleman an informal warning. He was a personal friend of Danby and Bishop Burnet (as well as of Samuel Pepys). Popular imagination suffered from no difficulties in unravelling the cause of Godfrey's death, and at once. It was quite clearly the wicked Jesuits at work. Godfrey had been killed because he knew too much. On 21 October, only a few days after the discovery of Godfrey's corpse, Parliament was recalled. The King still hoped that this assembly could be held to the purpose for which it was intended: to reimburse him for the cost of the army still in Flanders. Anticipating criticism, he explained that although he

---

* J. P. Kenyon, *The Popish Plot*, London, 1972, contains an excellent summary of the various theories in the light of recent research (Appendix A, 'The Murder of Sir Edmund Berry Godfrey').

had not disbanded the army as promised, at least his forces were being employed in ensuring a peaceful situation in Europe. As to the alleged conspirators, he was careful to begin his speech with a firm disassociation from them: he would take as much care as he could 'to prevent all manners of practices by that sort of men, and others too, who have been tampering ... and contriving how to introduce Popery amongst us'.[9]

The King would willingly have kept his eyes fixed on the European horizon, where his own interests lay. But in London the chase was on. Oates' accusations and Godfrey's death represented an opportunity for harrying the 'Catholic' Court which an experienced politician like Shaftesbury was hardly likely to neglect. As Shaftesbury observed, memorably and no doubt truthfully, on the subject of the Popish Plot, 'I will not say who started the Game, but I am sure I had the full hunting of it.'[10] Oates, for example, was in touch with that focus of the opposition, the Green Ribbon Club. Although John Evelyn wrote from the point of view of the Court that the testimony of such a 'profligate wretch' should not be taken 'against the life of a dog', the members of the Green Ribbon Club saw Oates in quite a different light: as a most apposite swallow on the eve of the assembly of Parliament.[11]

London was in ferment. So profound was the atmosphere of fear and agitation that fashionable ladies took to going about with precautionary pistols in their muffs. Indeed, the rumours which now abounded concerning the presence of priests everywhere can best be compared to the fear of German parachutists landing disguised in Britain during World War II. But the search for weapons, supposedly concealed by the rabid Catholics in preparation for their insurrection, produced a singularly unheroic armoury – 'from the Widow Platt, one old gun', and so on. Nevertheless, so fierce was the fervour that another Catholic widow was advised by a JP to marry a Protestant to cover herself; while Christopher Wren, as royal Surveyor, duly searched the cellar of the House of Commons for a latter-day Guy Fawkes, and was ordered to put padlocks on the communicating doors of the Spanish Ambassador's house, to fence in this notorious Papist.[12]

Shortly after the recall of Parliament, Oates had some further resounding revelations to make. He charged five Catholic peers – Lords Arundell of Wardour, Powis, Petre, Stafford and Belasye – with plotting to kill the King. These were honourable men who had on the whole led slightly obscurer lives than their position in society warranted – for the sake of practising their proscribed religion in peace. They had a great deal to lose by involving themselves in any plot, nor was there a shred of evidence against them. The King burst into laughter at the idea of the aged Lord Arundell as commander of the insurgent forces. Lord Powis was a man of over sixty, liberal-minded enough to have helped the Quakers in their own religious troubles on occasion. William Howard, Lord Stafford was a Fellow of the Royal Society. A devout Catholic, he was also, like many of his co-religionists, a loyal adherent of the established order. Nevertheless the five Catholic peers were arrested on the orders of the House of Commons. Their vast combined ages made them a touching group of dignity at bay, reminiscent of those long-bearded Roman senators who decided to await the barbarian hordes in silence, motionless within the Capitol.

On 2 November Shaftesbury judged the time ripe to demand the exclusion of the Duke of York from the Privy Council, in a speech quite as dramatic in its effect as his famous cry over Holland: *'Delenda est Carthago!'* A Bill was introduced into both Houses to debar Catholics from sitting – a far stronger measure than the Test Act of 1673, which had only been concerned with the actual office-holders. The royal households were also attacked, but the servants of the Queen were once more excepted – an even greater tribute to her prudence than that of 1673. The King appeared to bow. He persuaded the Duke of York that it would be unwise to attend the Privy Council, and, as to the Catholics, he told both Houses that 'he was ready to join with them in all the ways and means that might establish a firm security for the Protestant religion'.[13]

Although the measure was passed, Danby fought a brilliant rearguard action which was to prove the last triumph of the parliamentary organization he had sought so hard to establish. James was excluded from the Act. The measure had thus netted the mice but lost the lion, since one Catholic heir presumptive, still legally at liberty to sit, was worth a clutch of Catholic MPs and peers excluded. Nor was the King himself quite so meek as he pretended. As the dirty tide of prejudice swilled through Whitehall, leaving behind its debris of false accusation, the King did not lose his own balance. William of Orange had on occasion complained of the English Court, how it blew hot and cold, and how his uncle should pay heed to the words of a pilot he had heard at the helm of a ship during a storm: Steady, steady, steady. Charles II's conduct at this juncture showed steadiness. He refused to allow his old friend Father Huddleston to be included in the general proclamations against the Catholic priests. But he tried and failed to protect his armed forces, and disbandment was once more pressed to the clamour of MPs determined to prove a Catholic connection with the Army.[14]

November was ever a notorious season for anti-Popish demonstration. There was a new venom in the celebration of Guy Fawkes Day in 1678. Pope-burnings had been on the increase recently: one such conflagration had been provoked by the arrival of Mary of Modena as a bride in November 1673; in 1677 a figure of the Pope was burnt in the streets of London and the presence of some yowling cats imprisoned inside the effigy was generally held to add to the artistic effect. In 1678 there were several effigies to be seen.[15]

Further west in the city, at the beleaguered Palace of Whitehall, the Court attempted to put on an equally bold, if less outrageous, show. This was for the birthday of Queen Catharine, which by an unlucky coincidence fell about the same time. She was forty. 'I never saw the Court more brave,' wrote John Evelyn on 15 November. But the flickering of the anti-Popish bonfires and the cries of the rabble made a coarse accompaniment to celebrations in aid of a gentle Queen. Besides, the King was more occupied in fighting off the attacks on his wife than in dancing attendance on her birthday. On 24 November, at the second of his two meetings with Oates during that month, the King listened to accusations coupling Queen Catharine with Wakeman in trying to poison him.

Oates had now been joined by a worthy accomplice, 'Captain'

William Bedloe (he had no right to the military title but had found it useful in his early career as a confidence trickster). Like Oates, Bedloe knew the Jesuit organization from the inside, having been employed by them on sundry missions, and was able to profit from his knowledge to make some lethal accusations against the priests in the royal household. Bedloe was now a member of the criminal underworld.[16] Attaching himself to Oates' soaring coat-tails, he offered evidence on the Godfrey murder which was, despite his scandalous past, received with joyous credulity. The importance of Bedloe was that, having joined in the anti-Popish hue and cry, he was prepared to perjure himself without hesitation. He could thus provide the essential 'first-hand' witness to these rumoured misdeeds which would be required by a judge at a proper trial. He could 'corroborate' Oates. Or he could himself be 'corroborated' by much vaguer witnesses.

Not for one instant could the King credit that his wife had conspired to poison him. Throughout the examination of Oates, the King had represented the voice of common-sense, pointing out for example that Oates had called the Spanish Prince Don Juan, an alleged conspirator, tall and dark, whereas he was actually short with red hair. When Oates in his new testimony mentioned the Queen's apartments where the plotting was supposed to have taken place (he could not even describe them), the King reacted swiftly. He confined Oates to his rooms in Whitehall under guard; there the perjurer remained briefly until the Council had him released.

At the end of November, Coleman, a less innocent figure, was tried for high treason. The presiding judge, William Scroggs, spoke of him being condemned by 'his own papers', which had been seized; they were in fact ruled treasonable by the judges before the trial. (The testimony of Oates and Bedloe proved dangerously lame on examination and was quickly glossed over at the end of the trial.) It was thus for the treason of his papers that Coleman was condemned to death and executed on 3 December.

How different were the fates of Oates and Bedloe: despite this demonstration of the perjured nature of their evidence, both received State apartments in Whitehall; Bedloe was granted a modest allowance at the request of the House of Commons. Oates' state was more splendid: with his allowance of £1,200 a year, he might have been a national hero – Admiral Nelson himself.

In view of the King's instantaneous strong defence of the Queen, and in view of their success in other areas, it can be argued that Oates and Bedloe made a psychological error in trying to implicate Catharine in the first place. Charles blamed Shaftesbury, the fair-haired villain, at the time.[17] But Shaftesbury, with his superior intelligence (and superior knowledge of the King's mind), had not attempted to attack the Queen. Of course the element of calculation in Oates' behaviour, once he had tasted the heady wine of popular approval, should not be exaggerated; it would have been an elementary precaution to have ascertained the nature of the Queen's apartments, for example. Yet Oates, in concentrating on the Queen, had touched on one of the King's few genuinely sensitive spots: he might let Clarendon go without too much regret, and sacrifice Danby perforce; but, as he had already shown over the prospect of a divorce, Catharine was another matter.

He told Burnet, *à propos* the Queen, that 'considering his faultiness to her in other matters, it would be a terrible thing to abandon her now'. He went on to say that he knew that he had led a bad life ('of which he spoke with some sense'), but he was breaking himself of all his faults and he would never again do a base and wicked thing. And more strongly than that: 'They think I have a mind to a new wife; but for all that I will not see an innocent woman abused.' Queen Catharine wrote a most moving letter to her brother the King of Portugal on 'the care which he [Charles II] takes to defend my innocence and truth. Every day he shows more clearly his purpose and goodwill towards me, and thus baffles the hate of my enemies.... I cannot cease telling you what I owe to his benevolence, of which each day he gives better proofs, either from generosity or compassion.'[18] The result naturally was to draw the royal couple still closer together. By acting as knight errant to his Queen in distress, Charles had at last found a way of atoning to Catharine for all the pain he had caused her.

None of this however enabled him to dismiss Oates' allegations. He was obliged rather to rebut them and to strike back. In another sense therefore Oates' attack on the Queen was a brilliant (if unintentional) coup. By involving the King so personally, Oates ensured that the whole matter of the Popish Plot was given a gravity it lacked in essence. Meanwhile Shaftesbury whipped up his pack, ready for the full hunting of the game so conveniently started for the opposition.

At the end of November the House of Commons presented the King with a Bill for placing the Militia under the control of Parliament. This, the very measure which had precipitated the Civil War, was a sign of hostility to the prerogatives of the Crown which Charles II was hardly likely to miss. For the first time in his reign the King employed his veto to put an end to the Bill.

So far he was holding his own. But the King had an Achilles heel in politics as well as in private life. This was the position of Danby. September had seemed to mark splendid new advancement in Danby's success, when he married his daughter Bridget Osborne to the King's illegitimate son by Catharine Pegge, 'Don Carlo', the Earl of Plymouth. Then there was his coup in carrying the amendment concerning the Duke of York's position through Parliament. But Danby was a marked man where the opposition was concerned. When an opportunity came to hunt him down in his turn, it was likely to be taken with gusto. Less important to the King emotionally than the attack on his wife, the crisis over Danby represented a far more critical assault on the position of the monarchy.

The occasion of the attack was provided by yet another unsavoury character, if not in the same class as Titus Oates either by birth or behaviour: Ralph Montagu, the English Ambassador to the Court of France. Women brought luck to Montagu. He married an heiress. Before he was appointed to the Court of France as Ambassador Extraordinary at the time of the Secret Treaty of Dover, he had worked his way up the Stuart household ladder; he was successively Master of the

Horse to Anne Duchess of York and Queen Catharine. It was he who attended and reported the piteous death-bed of Madame in France. As a ladies' man, Grammont described him as one to be feared more on account of his assiduity than his appearance – the most dangerous sort of gallant.[19]

Returned to the Court of France as full Ambassador, Montagu became the lover of that full-blown expatriate beauty, Barbara Duchess of Cleveland; but he also allowed himself the luxury of trifling with the affections of her daughter, Anne Countess of Sussex. This promising *Liaisons Dangereuses* situation was spoilt by Barbara's unpredictable temper; she incarcerated her wayward daughter in a convent. But Anne, lured by Montagu, bounced out again. Barbara peppered Charles II with letters of outraged complaint. Montagu was now 'the most abominable man'; Anne had been 'up with Montagu till 5 a.m.', sending her servants away. Like many another ageing courtesan, Barbara clearly found herself gravely shocked by the morals of the younger generation. 'I am so afflicted that I can hardly write this for crying,' she exclaimed.[20] In revenge, Barbara revealed some of Montagu's intrigues with Danby (he was a great intriguer, as well as a ladies' man). Montagu returned to England to defend himself and was sacked for making the journey without permission.

The motto of all this might appear to be that Hell hath no fury like a mother scorned in favour of her daughter. But as a matter of fact Montagu, an Ambassador scorned, now ran Barbara close. And, in sheer damage done around him, he far outstripped her. In view of the prolonged secret relationship of Charles II and Louis XIV and his own position as intermediary, Montagu obviously had some powerful weapons at his command. He also had an ally in the French Ambassador in London, Barrillon, no friend to Danby and the pro-Dutch policy he represented.

Buoyed up with French money and French promises, Montagu now stood for Parliament himself – nor could Danby's much-vaunted organization prevent him from being elected, an eloquent commentary on its growing failure in these late days of 1678. Montagu's intention was to gain immunity for his attack on Danby.

In vain Danby tried to seize Montagu's papers. Two crucial letters eluded the snatch. Supported by Barrillon, Montagu revealed their contents to the House of Commons. They were lethal. Here was Danby undeniably proposing to Louis XIV that England would settle the war in return for a substantial whack of cash. It would have taken much less than that to bring the gleeful cry of 'Impeachment!' to the eager lips of the members of the House of Commons.

For all his charms and intrigues, Montagu was not an adept politician. He was not, for example, in the same class as Charles II, whom he had dismissed airily but inaccurately as 'a governable fool'. Montagu's declared intention was to secure the acknowledgement of Monmouth as Prince of Wales, and he took strength from the fact that Louis XIV seemed not averse to such a prospect. But the French King's real interest was in the promising confusion which a disputed succession would bring about in English affairs. Barrillon, echoing his master in wiliness, never paid Montagu all the money he had been assured. And Charles II, recognizing danger when he saw it, employed that potent weapon which remained quite unblunted in his hand – the termination of Parliament at the sovereign's will.

In a sense, the attack on Danby was a familiar crisis: Charles II had grown up against a background of impeachment, or threatened impeachment, of a minister, ever since that day when, as a child prince, he had pleaded with Parliament for Strafford's life. But in another sense the move against Danby was part of the grave new threat to the position of the monarchy. The fact was that Montagu's former position – he may even have known the full truth of the Secret Treaty of Dover – made him peculiarly dangerous. The King acted with swiftness and decision. At Danby's suggestion, he wrote, 'I approve of this letter C.R.' on the drafts of Danby's letters produced in Parliament to protect him.[21] And to protect himself he then got rid of Parliament on 30 December by dissolving it.

Shaftesbury and the Whigs had nevertheless scented blood. The smell encouraged them wonderfully. Their noses were firmly pointed towards the man at the King's side, the man described by Montagu as a 'wilful fool', as opposed to his 'governable fool' of a brother: James Duke of York. For it was a fact that James' position as heir presumptive remained as yet officially untouched, despite all the attacks upon it – just as the Crown's ability to control the timing of Parliament was also untouched. It was time, felt Shaftesbury and his associates, to remedy that disagreeable state of affairs.

The General Election of February 1679 was the first to be held for eighteen years. Not only was the experience therefore novel to the country as a whole, but that country was also in a continuing bubbling state of ferment, attendant on the 'Popish' revelations of the previous autumn. In the quick-heating capital, there were many unpleasant manifestations of the unpopularity of the Court. Louise Duchess of Portsmouth continued to embody that kind of alien immorality which even the greatest English sinners saw it as their duty to resent. Lady Gerard, who was taken for 'the French whore', found her chair surrounded by a hostile mob (as a respectable woman, she did not have the wit or the opportunity to deal with the situation as Nelly did). At the Duke's Theatre the real-life duchess was booed and the theatre closed in consequence.[22]

Louise's loss was Nell's gain. For Nell was now the recipient of new praise. Aphra Behn, for example, that ornament to Nell's sex and the playwright's profession, dedicated a play, *The Feign'd Curtezans*, to her in 1679 (in this war of the dedication, Louise would score three years later with *Venice Preserv'd*, from Thomas Otway). There was a swings-and-roundabouts element about it all. *Janna Divorum*, a study of gods and goddesses by Robert Whitcomb, referred to Nell as possessing the primitive wisdom of Apollo, the pristine wit of Mercury, the greatness of mind of Juno, the delicate beauty of Venus, and the God-like courage and brave spirit of Hercules. With such high-flown praise sounding in her ears, Nell could afford to ignore those critics who described her somewhat less pleasingly as 'puddle Nell', the 'hare-brained Whore', and the 'darling Strumpet of the Crowd'.[23]

The Court wits continued to snarl out their smutty jokes. They exhibited nothing but derision for Charles II at this juncture. Rochester, for instance, took pleasure in hammering home the message that the King cared for nothing but sex. In 'The Royal Angler' he alluded crudely to the 'fatal bait' which Rowley would always greedily swallow:

> And howe'er so weak and slender be the string,
> Bait it with Whore, and it will hold a King.

Buckingham with equal rudeness referred to the monarch as one who could sail a yacht, trim a barge and loved ducks, tarts and 'buttered buns'.[24]

But the King's comrades did not necessarily see behind the mask of indifference he wore. And perhaps he chose them for that very reason. No doubt Charles II would far rather not have dealt with a major political crisis in the nineteenth year of his restored reign. As we have seen, he had originally tried to coast through his political difficulties, 'living from day to day'. But given the challenge of the Popish Plot and Montagu's machinations, leading to the Whig attack headed by Shaftesbury, the King responded to it.

In the spring of 1679 he took a solemn decision concerning the future of his brother. His contemporaries, fooled by the mask, did not immediately appreciate that it had been made. There were also interested parties, like Shaftesbury and Monmouth, who either believed or wished to believe themselves that the King favoured Exclusion – and certainly wanted to convince those around them that he did. As Henry Sidney wrote in his diary later in the summer, they did great harm in that respect, bringing MPs to quite the wrong conclusion concerning the King and Exclusion – 'Which everybody knows he is utterly against'.[25] Indeed, for the next six years, Charles II was steadfast, even obstinate, in support of James' claims to succeed, as he had been over very few things in his essentially flexible life.

On the surface, the King appeared to be pliant in the face of necessity, as so often before. In February he told the Duke of York that he must leave England for the time being. The King's letter to his brother was couched in gracious terms: 'You may easily believe that it is not without a great deal of pain I write you this, being more touched with the constant friendship you have had for me than with anything else in the world...."[26] Nevertheless, this was no more than a characteristic allusion to shared family loyalties in the days of yore.

The crucial observation was that made by the King to Parliament at the end of April. As the new session was ending, he volunteered to accept any law whatsoever that the House of Commons could devise 'that may preserve your Religion' – provided that there was no interference with 'the Descent of the Crown in the right Line' – that is, the legitimate succession. There is no clearer statement of the conviction Charles II had reached with regard to the future of the monarchy. The Lord Chancellor's long explanatory statement reiterated the point at the end: 'If anything else can occur to the Wisdom of the Parliament, which may further secure Religion and Liberty against a Popish Successor, without defeating the Right of Succession itself, his Majesty will most readily consent to it.'[27]

Why had he reached this conviction? First of all, he was not fighting for an absolutist role for his brother; he would subsequently show himself willing to accept various kinds of compromise concerning James' actual position, including the humiliating concept of a guardianship of James by his own children. When it was all over and Exclusion defeated, the King even told Barrillon that he might have agreed to it if Parliament had offered more money and they had not attacked his prerogative at the same time – particularly as it would not have stopped James succeeding all the same!

Nor did Charles II reach this conviction out of an increased opinion of his brother as a potential ruler. James was no Hamlet, 'like to prove most royal'. While Charles continued to respect James' bull-necked strength of character, he also continued to deplore the lack of tact which went with it. To the last years of the reign of Charles II belong his various unflattering references to James, featuring *'la sottise de mon frère'*. When James remonstrated with Charles for his famous habit of walking in St James's Park, frequently unattended, Charles is supposed to have replied lightly, 'I am sure no man in England will take away my life to make you King."[28]

Most famous of all is that remark made to William of Orange, when Charles observed that Exclusion would make little difference in the end, since if James succeeded to the throne, with his 'turbulent and excessive temperament' he would not stay on it four years.[29] This judgement has gained prominence for the wrong reason. Because it proved uncannily correct as a prophecy, it is generally held to be illuminating about the character of James II. But its real importance lies in the light it casts on Charles II. Here was a king who had decided, *faute de mieux*, that he must uphold the principle of the legitimate monarchy; in his usual clear-sighted, if cynical, way, Charles recognized the material he had to deal with in implementing his decision.

The conviction of Charles II concerning the need for 'the descent in the right line' was based on the present danger to his own monarchy rather than on any future dangers to the monarchy as a whole. He identified attacks on the legitimate succession as part of a campaign which would turn on the royal prerogative, decimate the other wide powers of the Crown, and in general transform the face of English politics. From there, the slippery slope led downwards all the way, via political strife in Parliament to the dreaded abyss of civil war and revolution. Thus 'descent in the right line' became closely, almost mystically, linked in the King's mind with that beneficent order he sought to preserve in his kingdom.

The temperament of Charles II as he approached fifty was turning to pessimism. The steel of his youth, that essential quality of public hope which had carried him from Worcester to exile and back to England again, was no longer necessary. Charles II's famous remark about his brother and the future sprang from his own deep-seated conviction of the essential melancholy of human affairs.

The Duke of York, accompanied by Mary Beatrice, sailed for the Netherlands on 3 March. The ostensible reason for his journey was to visit his son-in-law and daughter, William and Mary of Orange.

He left behind him a political scene unpleasantly transformed by the recent General Election. This, which has been described as the first English General Election fought along 'distinctively party lines',[30] resulted in a happy triumph for that Country group increasingly identified as the Whigs over those of the Court nicknamed Tories.* It was also incidentally marked by such heavy drinking on all sides that 'Sober Societies' were later formed in towns – an interesting example of locking the stable door after the horse had fully refreshed itself. Far from gaining new adherents, the government did not gain more than thirty seats, against 150 to their opponents. The Crown had miscalculated.

The men who now mustered at Westminster were later described in James' memoirs as being like 'so many young Spaniels that run and bark at every lark that springs'. But they were not wholly without a sense of purpose. Quite apart from the subject of Exclusion, there remained the unsettling matter of Danby. The King probably hoped that Danby might be allowed to settle his affairs – and the King's – and then depart with something like dignity. Danby probably hoped, with Charles' support, to be able to ride the storm and survive afloat.[31] But the 'young Spaniels', organized by Shaftesbury, were not content with such a tame solution. The Commons requested Danby's arrest and the Lords agreed. This of course posed a threat to Danby's actual safety as well as his ministerial position.

Danby, reluctantly, offered his resignation. On 25 March the King, after assuring the House of Lords that he had authorized the Montagu letters, accepted it. Afterwards Danby blamed the King's decision on a new man in his counsels: Robert Spencer, Earl of Sunderland. Originally designated as Montagu's successor in Paris, Sunderland belonged to the rising generation (he was in his thirties) which would increasingly dominate political events in the last years of the King's reign. But Sunderland was merely echoing the general feeling of the Court party that Danby had to go.[32] Besides, Charles himself could propose no better solution to save Danby than to pardon him for all the offences he had committed up till 27 February.

---

* As the Tories took – or rather received – their name from Irish brigands, the Whigs were dubbed after the Whiggamores, Scottish Presbyterian rebels. (The word was originally spelt 'Whigg'.)

Even this caused fearful trouble with the House of Commons. As William Sacheverell, the fiery Whig MP, put it, 'If they confirmed this pardon to Lord Danby, they made the King absolute.... What difference was there between that and arbitrary power?'[33] The King insisted. The House of Commons did not budge. In the end, Danby was imprisoned in the Tower. It was now that his treatment of Buckingham the previous year came home to roost. Danby was not even allowed to visit his wife, who was believed to be on her death-bed. Buckingham and his friends had vindictive memories.

The introduction of the First Exclusion Bill was in the King's opinion a further manifestation of the general attack on his position. When one considers Sacheverell's sentiments yet again, it is difficult to think the King was wrong. Sacheverell did not take his stand on the need for a Protestant king. 'Let the King and the Council be as Popish as they will,' he cried. He took his stand on the far more dangerous point that it did not matter if the King was Popish – so long as 'we can wind the King to a good will and liking of what we shall do'. In short, 'The foundation of Government is in the People's hearts, and upon the same foundation the King came in at his Return....'[34] This cut at the very root of the royal position. More to the point, it cut at the root of the practices of a Charles II. If the foundation of government was in the people's hearts, then clearly the monarchy was not the strongest force in the country, for it lay below that of the people, as expressed by Parliament. The appearance of such radical arguments goes far to explain the personal horror Charles II felt for Exclusion, over and beyond its consequences in banning his brother from the succession.

For the time being however the Exclusionists were weakened by their own internal disagreements. Exclusion was a comparatively new concept. Essentially it was personal to James: the First Exclusion Bill sought to exclude the Duke of York in particular from 'the imperial crown of England' – not any unnamed Catholic successor. But no-one had quite decided how the hand should be played. If James were debarred from succeeding, the main contenders for the throne were his two daughters: Mary, married to William of Orange, and Anne, as yet unmarried (she was only just thirteen). Then there was 'the Protestant Duke' – James Duke of Monmouth, still the crowd's darling, still unlegitimized. All sorts of combinations of these figures would be suggested in months to come; but immediately there was no obvious winning card. Anne's youth obviously ruled her out, but at this point Mary's marriage made her equally suspect. For it is important to realize that the Whig attitude to William of Orange in 1679 was quite different from what it subsequently became. By no means did he represent a kind of dream candidate. William was at this point regarded preeminently as a Stuart, and as such an authoritarian figure.

Monmouth too was an uncertain quantity. 'Young Jemmy was a fine lad' – so ran a popular song. But was he? Sir John Reresby described him as having a fine exterior but not being all of a piece inside, which was probably an accurate assessment. In appearances he had markedly Stuart looks, with that slight heaviness of chin and sensuality of mouth with which many of the members of his family were endowed. But he was undeniably handsome. In character he lacked weight. He could not, for example, conceive of a course of action or an opinion without wishing to give it immediate expression. He had none of the secrecy and substance of his father, the constancy of his uncle the Duke of York. One remembers Evelyn's charge against his mother, Lucy Walter, that although beautiful she was 'insipid': perhaps it was from her that Monmouth derived his own fatal lightness. Or perhaps, more simply, Monmouth was spoiled. 'So pretty a child', he had been indulged but not properly educated by his grandmother, Henrietta Maria; that was a dangerous combination.[35]

Like many exhibitionists, Monmouth was also quite ignorant of other people's feelings. As Buckingham wrote, he lived 'as if the world were made only for him'. It was typical of Monmouth that he described his mistress, Henrietta Wentworth, as his wife on the grounds that he had been too young to know what he was doing when he married Anne, the heiress of Buccleuch. As a contemporary wrote, it is 'a pretence, very airy and absurd'.[36]

Nell Gwynn, in her witty way, hit off Monmouth's mixture of royalty and impudence when she christened him Prince Perkin, a nickname which somehow fits him better than the languishing lines of Dryden on the subject of Charles' children:

> Of all this numerous progeny was none
> So beautiful, so brave as Absalom.

The King of course loved him – and also spoiled him. But where Charles was concerned, that did not necessarily mean blind, uncritical appreciation. Charles was on the contrary well aware of Monmouth's instability. As a father, he may have loved him all the more for frailty; as a monarch, he could not help seeing in Monmouth's flawed character, in particular his lack of judgement and his choice of 'knaves and flatterers' as counsellors, another of his own problems.

Monmouth's sponsors were not put off by his flawed character – nor, for that matter, by what was described as his 'flawed title'. There was even an argument in favour of choosing a prince thus handicapped: he would take care to govern well, as Lord Howard put it, because he could not dispense with popular support. It was basically Monmouth's Protestantism which made him attractive to backers in the succession stakes. In the November of 1678, as anti-Catholic prejudice mounted, toasts were drunk to Monmouth, the first real indication of his candidature.[37] Even so, in the spring of 1679, his genuine backers were not really very numerous. Shaftesbury, for example, still harped on the idea of the King divorcing the Queen (which, with its implied consequence of a new wife and a new family, was the very reverse of supporting Monmouth).

This was where Monmouth's lack of acumen hampered him. As he swaggered on the political stage, he could not perceive the obvious fact that his cousins, Mary and Anne, and least of all William of Orange, were hardly likely to support his pretensions. Their reasons were straightforward ones of self-interest. William told Monmouth quite frankly that 'if he aimed at the crown he could not be his friend, but in all things else he would'.[38] The King never supported Monmouth's pretensions publicly for a moment.* Of course, daydreams could and would be spun concerning Charles' secret intentions. Yet to secure the succession, with so many disadvantages and opponents, Monmouth needed to work like a mole underground. He was however one of nature's roosters and could not emulate a mole to save his life (as events in the reign of James II would show).

Returning to the supporters of Exclusion, it will be seen that their campaign, like Monmouth's title, was flawed: it had no positive objective as yet, only the negative one of keeping out the Duke of York. Against Exclusion, not only the King but many within Parliament were prepared to argue, as Burnet put it, that 'it was unlawful in itself, and against the unalterable law of succession (which came to be the common phrase)'.[40] Yet even without unity on the part of the Exclusionists, the situation was quite ugly enough for the King. In Parliament he was being pressed on all sides, not simply for or against his brother's cause. In particular, his faithful servant Lauderdale was being attacked: like the assault on the Duke of York, the campaign smacked of insult to the monarchy.

Lauderdale's situation, both in England and in Scotland, was acute. In Scotland there had been the predictable outburst after the imposition of taxes for a 'Highland Host' to suppress supporters of the Conventicles. Three thousand Lowlanders and six thousand Highlanders neither managed to suppress these spirited Covenanters nor to ensure peace in the troubled land. In England Shaftesbury chose the spring of 1679 to mount a violent attack on Lauderdale's Scottish regime in the House of Lords. He took it to symbolize the way things were going generally – downhill towards absolutism. On 25 March he described Scotland as 'the little sister' of England. The only difference was that in Scotland slavery was to come first, then Popery; in England it was to be the other way round.[41]

Charles II stuck by Lauderdale. He reckoned to be able to protect him, where the discovery of his 'treasonable' correspondence had made it impossible to save Danby. In any case,

---

* According to Evelyn, Monmouth admitted on the scaffold that Charles II had 'indeed told him he was but his base [illegitimate] son'.[39]

of the two men, the King felt infinitely more bound to Lauderdale, for reasons of long association and political sympathy.

In Ireland the Test Act had been strictly enforced: Catholics who had crept into the corporations had been hastily eliminated from them and priests proscribed. In Ireland too there was rising tension. Inevitably, Ireland felt the effects of the Popish Plot: where Catholicism was concerned, it was a case of England sneezing and Ireland catching cold.

In 1677 the Duke of Ormonde, Ireland's best friend where stability and mercy were concerned, was once more put in charge of the country. Despite his disgrace at the hands of the intriguing Buckingham, Ormonde had been kept in touch with Irish affairs by the former Lord Lieutenant, Essex – another example of the latter's good sense. Ormonde had not achieved the post without a struggle. The nature of it reveals once again the selfish indifference of the English Court – including its King – towards any interests in Ireland other than its own aggrandizement. For there was an opposition manoeuvre to make Monmouth Lord Lieutenant, a post he would however continue to occupy in the salubrious atmosphere of London, while Lord Conway, as Deputy, did the dirty work on the spot. Although this scheme had the support of both Danby and the Duchess of Portsmouth, for internal reasons to do with their own English-based intrigues, Ormonde emerged triumphant.[42]

He now tried to sort out what was undoubtedly the curse of Ireland at the time: the incredibly complicated situation with regard to land titles. This was the product of forty years of settlement and counter-settlement, larded over with unfortunate grants made by the English Crown, often quite ignorantly. Clare and Connaught were in a particular state of chaos. After all, if Charles II placated his suitors with grants of land which actually had lawful occupants already, he was not likely to feel the consequences personally. It was not incidentally that Charles acted more selfishly towards Ireland than the rest of his contemporaries. Like Cromwell in the previous generation, with his ferocious genocidal victories, Charles merely personified the English attitude of his time. But the result was 'a mere scramble'.[43]

A second problem facing Ormonde was that of law and order. The brigands – the original Tories – continued to multiply. Characteristically, Ormonde tackled both the land question and the rising anarchy with measures designed to cast a mantle of forgiveness over the past. The legislation he proposed included a Bill of Oblivion. There was considerable opposition to Ormonde's plans, some of it comprehensible, since obviously some interlopers might find themselves confirmed in their titles.

It was in this sense that the Popish Plot, naming the Catholic Archbishop of Dublin, Peter Talbot, and potentially smearing all Catholics, came at an awkward time. Shaftesbury was only too easily able to play on folk memories of the 'massacre' of 1641 by suggesting that there would be another Irish insurrection. It is hardly likely that the Irish off-shoot plot for a French invasion ever existed, any more than the alleged conspiracies of the English Catholic Lords; it was correctly described later by Oliver Plunkett, Archbishop of Armagh, as being 'all plain Romance'. Nevertheless, as in England there were casualties. Archbishop Talbot died in prison in Dublin late in 1678, and about the same time Plunkett was arrested. Plunkett was a man of the greatest probity, of whom nothing worse could be said than that he had not left Ireland when the Catholic hierarchy was officially banished: yet a charge of high treason was later fabricated against him. Since it proved impossible to find an Irish jury to convict him, two years later this particular witch-hunt was destined to move to England – the land of more amenable jurymen, where a Catholic prelate was concerned – with scandalous results.

Meanwhile, in England the summer of 1679 seemed unlikely to provide a happy resolution from the King's point of view. Danby was gone, leaving no obvious successor. The trial of Sir George Wakeman, with possible injury to the Queen, was pending. Parliament was sitting and about to debate the Exclusion Bill. The King as usual lacked money. Popular prejudice had, if anything, heightened since the previous autumn. It is true that Catholics were not actually being torn to pieces by the mob – a negative achievement – but the atmosphere of hysteria was such that no-one, whatever their allegiance, could be

97

confident such a thing would not happen. A satire on 'Affairs of State' demanded:

> Would you send Kate to Portugall
> Great James to be a Cardinall ...?
>   This is your Time.
> Would you send confessors to tell
> Powis, Stafford and Arundell,
> they must prepare their souls for hell?
>   This is your Time.[44]

It was certainly the time of Titus Oates. In April he was able to postulate publicly such extraordinary fantasies as the fact that James 1 had been murdered, that the Great Rebellion and the death of Charles 1 were due to the Jesuits, and that the Duke of York had started the Great Fire! Useless to suggest that no sane person could believe such mad perversions of reason and common-sense – when popular prejudice is aflame, the very madness of such tales brings with it an orgiastic release to hearers: the greater the madness, the greater the satisfaction.

A famous pamphlet of the time – a best-seller – is a classic illustration of this. Protestant citizens were adjured to go to the top of the Monument in the City and imagine the consequences of Popish rule:

> the whole town in flames, and amongst the distracted crowd, troops of Papists ravishing their [the Protestants'] wives and daughters, dashing out the brains of their little children against the walls, plundering their houses and cutting their throats in the name of [being] heretic dogs. And, tied to a stake in the midst of the flames, they were to picture themselves their fathers or their mothers screaming out to God with hands and eyes uplifted to heaven.[45]

What chance did the real Catholics – obscure, oppressed people – stand against this dramatic image?

In its deliberate excitation of the most basic fears in every human breast, this is the language of the rabble-rouser down the ages. Sir John Reresby wrote afterwards of 'the Torrent of the Times' that no one who had not actually witnessed them could conceive 'what a Ferment that raised among all Ranks and Degrees'.[46] But those who have lived through similar periods of irrational persecution, that of the 'Reds' in Macarthyite America, for example, can imagine them quite well.

Related afterwards, the actual events which took place might not amount to much in terms of massacre or the kind of mayhem which chills the blood centuries later. If the innocent died, they died after due – if not fair – trial. But it was an atmosphere in which rational decision and steady action were, if not impossible, exceptionally difficult. No-one knew what the next day would bring, whether they were a Catholic fearing slaughter, or a righteous Englishman fearing the assassination of the ruler, followed by armed insurrection. The predatory Shaftesbury, blowing his hunting-horn to encourage the Whigs, added both to the excitement and to the confusion.

Charles II maintained his balance by firm adherence to twin principles – for the Queen and against Exclusion.

CHAPTER TWENTY-THREE

A King at Chess

~

So I have seen a King at Chess
(His Queens and Bishops in distress)
Shifting about, growing less and less
With here and there a pawn.
                    Charles Sackville, Earl of Dorset, 1680

An unacknowledged deadlock existed between Charles II and his Parliament after the fall of Danby in March 1679. There was no obvious candidate to replace Danby as chief minister, one who would both be acceptable to the King and succeed in managing Parliament. The King listened to the advice of Sir William Temple. It might be that the time had come for a political experiment. He now instituted a new type of Council, consisting of thirty members, half of whom were to be ministers and half without office (Temple himself was a member).

It was an intelligent move. Such a choice had the desirable effect – from the King's point of view – of promoting discord between those who were selected and those who were not.[1] At the same time, it was the intention of this Council to transform poachers, such as Shaftesbury and Lord Halifax, into game-keepers. The distinction between these two professions was not necessarily so rigid: unlike most poachers, Shaftesbury and Halifax had been gamekeepers once upon a time. Halifax, member of a great Yorkshire family and endowed with even greater brilliance of intellect, had been made a Privy Councillor in 1672; he had supported the Test Act. Although Halifax accepted the authenticity of the Popish Plot, where James was concerned he did not take a hard line. Halifax stood more for the limitation of James' powers than for his total Exclusion.

The other members of this Council, trainee gamekeepers, included Sunderland and Laurence Hyde – 'Lory'. Like Sunderland, he was in his thirty-ninth year, eleven years younger than his master. He had been a diplomat (accredited to The Hague) as well as an MP; he was made one of the new Lords of the Treasury in March 1679, when Danby fell. Hyde had inherited from his father, the once mighty Clarendon, a certain arrogance. But he had also inherited Clarendon's great loyalty towards the monarchy. Hyde was considered personally close to the Duke of York and, although he regretted James' Catholicism, was against Exclusion.

Then there was Sidney Godolphin, in his early thirties, another Lord of the Treasury appointed in March. Since 1668 he had been an MP, first for Helston and later for St Mawes, and he had included a variety of royal appointments in his career: page of honour (when Charles described him as never *in* the way and never *out* of it), groom of the bedchamber and finally in 1678, Master of the Robes.[2] But he also had close Dutch contacts and disliked the Duke of York. The junior member of the group was the Earl of Mulgrave, barely thirty. One of the Wits and Dryden's noble patron, Mulgrave had also been a naval commander; he was now colonel of the 'Old Holland' regiment of foot. Mulgrave preferred the Duke of York to Monmouth, for whom he had felt a military jealousy.

From their youth, these men were to be known as 'the Chits'. A mark of this generation in 1679 was a capacity to remain on friendly terms with Shaftesbury and his associates, as well as with the Court, where their natural interests lay, unless there was some specific and dangerous issue. Indeed, there is a fluidity about the stance of men like Sunderland and Godolphin which echoes the generally confused political alliances of this period.

The new Treasury commission after Danby's fall was however headed by a figure of greater maturity: the Earl of Essex, recently returned from his spell as Lord Lieutenant of Ireland. At the new Treasury it was felt that Essex's 'clear, though slow sense' would make him 'very acceptable to the King'.[3] Indeed, Essex's instinctive moderation was illustrated only a few months later, when he advised the King to disband his newly raised Guards, as being unnecessarily provocative.

Later Essex favoured Exclusion. And even the wise Essex would lose his head, believing in such a far-fetched notion as the guilt of the aged Lord Stafford, and involving himself in the Rye House Plot. But at the time when the King's experimental Council was formed, the employment of a man like Essex, coupled with Shaftesbury, Halifax and the younger men, represented a positive decision to try and break the deadlock which existed between King and Parliament: a deadlock which had virtually brought government to a halt. The plan was that this Council should transact all business, and for reasons of convenience it was therefore divided into committees for Intelligence, Ireland, Tangier and Trade and Plantations.

It is true that as this perturbed spring turned into a still more hectic summer, the King tended to lean more and more on those members of this Council who were sound on the subject of the royal prerogative. But this was inevitable, given that the prerogative was under renewed attack, and given the King's anxieties on the subject. The rise of the influence of Essex, Hyde and Godolphin was not implicit in the constitution of the Council when it was first formed; nor is it necessary to suppose that Charles II formed the Council in a derisive mood, as a kind of blind to his real activities. The formation of the Council was an intelligent move in its own right, because it stood to bring strident members of the opposition within the nullifying orbit of the government. As a pragmatic operator, the King would have been perfectly content had the Council succeeded. In any case, the burning issue of Exclusion, filling Parliament with both smoke and fire, was occupying all his positive energies.

On 29 April, as an effort against Exclusion, the King agreed to considerable limitations on the powers of any 'Popish' successor. These included lack of control over judicial or ecclesiastical appointments (a limitation which would put this Popish sovereign in a very weak position indeed, compared with his predecessors). Parliament was also to assemble immediately on the death of the sovereign, as of right – another important sacrifice of the royal prerogative. It was not enough. Shaftesbury and his clique continued to demand the sacrifice of James. Thus the Exclusion Bill was given its first reading and carried.

On 21 May it was also carried on the second of its three necessary readings, before going to the Lords. The majority was large, without being overwhelming (207 to 128, and there were over 170 people who did not vote). The Commons was not however likely to be in great haste to accord the Bill its third reading, since relations with the House of Lords were still in that state of nagging discord which is an important political feature of this period. Once they had passed the Bill finally, the Lords would probably reject it. The King therefore, as an experienced general, fell back on the tried weapon of prorogation. On 27 May he prorogued Parliament until 14 August.

Parliament was not the only front where the royal authority was directly threatened. In Scotland, the murder of Archbishop Sharp on 13 May meant that the precarious peace there could no longer be maintained. Archbishop Sharp had gratuitously attacked the Covenanters for what were undoubtedly sincere religious beliefs, but, as with all acts of terrorism, the shocking nature of the deed shifted the balance: the Archbishop was dragged from his coach and hacked to pieces in front of his daughter's eyes. In June the government's forces, under John Graham of Claverhouse, were defeated by the Covenanters, and had the rebels now not indulged in the eternal sport of Scottish dissidents, internal bickering, their cause might well have flourished outwardly, as it did in the hearts of the Scottish people. As it was, the main outcome of the Scottish insurrection, from the English point of view, was a change in the position of Monmouth.

The dashing young 'Protestant Duke' was presented with a nice opportunity to shine when he was despatched north to command the loyal militia. He was appointed Captain General. It was Monmouth's finest hour. Not only was he officially responsible for the government's triumph at Bothwell Brig on 22 June, but he also issued instructions for mercy thereafter, understanding the essentially harmless nature of most Conventiclers. As the 'clement victor' in Scotland, Monmouth acquired a *kudos* which his actions at the English Court had not brought him.

Meanwhile, the English Parliament had passed one Act which should have been enough to immortalize it – had anyone at the time realized the consequences of what they were doing.[4] This was the Act since known as Habeas Corpus, and widely regarded as one of the cornerstones of English civil liberty. At the time it was loosely known as 'Shaftesbury's Act', but that did not mean that Shaftesbury alone understood what was involved: the Act caused little stir with anyone at the time when it was passed, slipping on to the Statute Book, rather than marching on to it in glory.

Previously, a writ of Habeas Corpus, as the Latin indicates, had required the body of a person to be brought by his jailer before a judge or into court; its advantage lay in the fact that, once the aforesaid person was produced, the nature of his custody – lawful or otherwise – could be investigated. So far, so good. But recently there had been extraordinary difficulties made over the granting of writs. Once granted, the difficulties were not over: as many as three writs had on occasion been needed for the prisoner to be produced. Nor was bail necessarily granted thereafter. Political detainees were not the only ones to suffer: those on criminal charges were subject to the same ordeal.

One of the questions asked was whether any court other than the Court of the King's Bench had the right to issue such a writ. Then there was the whole issue of imprisonment at the King's command – that is, by royal warrant. To suggest the abolition of this was a clear attack on one aspect of the royal prerogative. But by the end of the debate MPs were merely demanding the abolition of various abuses to do with this type of imprisonment. Equally, the Act of 1679 simply specified that there were to be no delays in granting the writ, without touching on the question of the courts involved. In effect, all parties had shied away from the issue of the royal warrant, which was really at the centre of the abuse.

It showed how little the significance of the Act was understood that the King himself was mildly favourable towards it. He saw it as a useful means of protecting Danby and the imprisoned

Catholic lords – the latter, at least, the victims of a tyrannical incarceration quite as arbitrary as anything a Stuart monarch could provide. There is also a persistent story that the Act only passed through the House of Lords as a result of a piece of impudence on the part of the teller, who boldly counted one exceptionally stout peer as ten. Be that as it may, *31 Chas II* was duly entered on the Statute Book.

Then Parliament was duly prorogued. The King was under no illusions on the subject of Exclusion. He was aware that the reassembly of Parliament would be rapidly followed by a return – probably successful – to the painful subject of the Bill. Having granted himself a breathing-space, he cast his thoughts, as before, towards means of ruling without this tiresome assembly.

Renewed negotiations – or intrigues, as the opposition would have termed them – with France was one answer. Charles II had never yet turned to Louis XIV totally in vain. The reopening of discussions on the subject of a French subsidy was planned in the summer. Throughout the autumn these deliberations with the French Ambassador, Barrillon, would continue.

There was another possibility – that expedient contemplated, if only for a moment, by Danby twelve months previously: the use of the King's standing army to solder together the worn surface of his personal power. There were of course plenty of commentators who discerned this intention in the King's slightest move. In particular, the raising of new royal guards in July (that measure condemned by the sensible Essex as being provocative) aroused the familiar suspicion that 'governing by an army' was on its way. The King however scoffed at the criticisms and raised his guards all the same. As far as he was concerned, all the reasons which had militated against a military solution in 1678 still obtained.

In June five Jesuit priests had been put to death. The King had no means of knowing that the impending Wakeman trial would represent the turning of the tide where reason and justice were concerned in London. The Scottish situation was hardly encouraging, and Monmouth's success brought its own problems where Exclusion was concerned. The so-called Triumvirate of chief ministers in the King's Council – Essex, Halifax and

Sunderland – were now convinced that a proper dissolution of Parliament was essential. They feared that otherwise, when Parliament returned, Shaftesbury would introduce a newly triumphant Monmouth as his Exclusion candidate. It has been established that the Triumvirate were mistaken, and that Shaftesbury had no intention of supporting Monmouth at this juncture: but this is hindsight.[5] On 3 July the King raised the question of dissolution in his Council, and after discussion it appeared that the majority were against it.

A week passed. Then, on 10 July, the King dissolved Parliament all the same. The thoughts of Charles II at this critical period can only be divined. He was careful to avoid committing them to paper. The written word had proved a dangerous medium where Danby was concerned and he had never much favoured it in the first place, either out of laziness or some profound need for self-concealment. The move to dissolution was the effective termination of his experiment with a new type of Council: he had ignored its decision. But then the Council's decision would have interfered with his royal prerogative to prorogue or dissolve Parliament at will. Charles had not anticipated this particular confrontation when he set up the new Council. But where the prerogative was concerned, he knew where the royal interests lay.

A further week later, on 18 July, Wakeman, the Queen's physician, was acquitted by a jury presided over by the Lord Chief Justice William Scroggs. At the time it was widely believed that Scroggs had been got at – bribed, for example, by the Portuguese Ambassador. Certainly he met a fair reward at the Court for presiding over such a welcome verdict: at Windsor thereafter it was noted that 'the favourites of both sexes rejoiced', and the soft white hands of the Duchess of Portsmouth were supposed to have patted the unwieldy form of the Lord Chief Justice in gratitude.[6] But this was after the event. It has been pointed out by legal historians that Scroggs' conduct of the case cannot be faulted by the conventions of his own age. He cast well-founded doubts on the testimony of Oates and Bedloe. Scroggs' own language to the jury was also more impressive than the contemporary reaction might indicate. He told them,

'Never care what the world says, follow your consciences.' And of his own participation, Scroggs observed, 'I would be loath to keep out popery by that way they would bring it in, that is, by blood and violence. I would fain have all things very fair.'[7]

There is in fact no evidence that Scroggs was influenced. Given that Wakeman was innocent, and given that his defence (unlike that of the Jesuits) was efficiently organized by some person of authority whose identity is unknown, Scroggs simply allowed justice to take its course.[8] Afterwards a dead dog was thrown at his coach. The Popish issue was not yet equally dead – the trial of the Catholic lords was to come – but at least some progress had been made in killing it off.

The acquittal of Wakeman on the one hand, and the possibility of renewed Anglo-French manoeuvres on the other, meant that by August 1679 the King could at last hope for the ease which had been denied to him during the last horrendous twelve months. Virtually everything he held dear, both of a private and a public nature, had been under attack. But the essential sea wall had not yet been breached. It was at this point, by one of those strange flukes of personal misadventure from which the course of history is never wholly free, that the King fell violently ill.

This dramatic twist to events – occurring at a moment of maximum uncertainty concerning the succession – was all the more startling because it was so unexpected. The King was famous for his superb health. Like many men who consider physical exercise the best panacea, he had a cheerful disregard for the medical profession, 'ever laughing at physicians', and 'would not come under their hands'.[9] No one at Court was foolish enough to suppose that their King, who had survived so much, would actually elude the ordinary laws of mortality as well. Charles II was now in his fiftieth year. The constant fuss over the succession, the care taken to guard the King's person against assassination: all this illustrates a general preoccupation with the future. But his *imminent* death had never been contemplated.

It is relevant to Shaftesbury's tortuous policies over Exclusion, for example, that he was working towards a future he never expected to see. Nearly ten years older than the King, with a sickly and twisted body, Shaftesbury could not legitimately hope to outlive the vigorous, athletic monarch. The Duke of York himself was only three years younger than his brother and Charles was always reckoned to be the healthier of the two. James thought it worth recording in his memoirs that he too had not expected to outlive Charles II.[10]

Now, from one moment to the next, all that was changed.

On 22 August at Windsor the King was struck down. He was seized with an acute fever, probably of the malarial origin which was so common in seventeenth-century Europe, since he was cured by 'the Jesuit's powder', actually an early form of quinine imported from the South American bark *cinchona*. Appropriately enough, the King owed his cure to his own zest for scientific knowledge.[11] Although the bark had been known in England since the time of Cromwell, the dosage was not yet fully understood and the established doctors regarded the new cure with baffled suspicion. But Charles, being 'the most inquisitive King in the whole world who is also the greatest patron of empirics', had looked favourably upon one Robert Talbor, an early expert on the subject. He had joined with him in experiments using the new powder, and chided the physicians for their lack of interest. Even so, they might have denied the King his own cure in 1679 had they been able to think up anything else to administer. Evelyn tells the story of Dr Lower's continued childish reluctance to admit its efficacy; eventually, faced with the King's undoubted recovery, he fell back on the formula that it was 'a Remedy fit only for Kings'! The King, more gratefully, knighted Talbor and granted him a pension.

Returning to the royal sick-room at Windsor, here no such happy outcome was predicted at the time of the King's collapse. According to the prevalent insanitary custom (when infection was not understood), the poor King had his chamber crowded with his councillors – anxious as much for themselves and their future as for his. The councillors, standing on their own right to be present, warded off still greater crowds, but the spectacle of their grim and enquiring visages looming over him can only have added to the King's fevered dreams. One unresolved question faced them. What was to be done about the Duke of York, lurking in unofficial exile at Brussels?

James' legal position as heir presumptive was quite unaltered. Councillors could foresee an ugly situation arising if the King died, the Duke of York took over the throne which was his by right – and they had somehow neglected to acknowledge this fact. On the other hand, it was equally possible that the Duke of York, being absent, would fail to secure the throne: Monmouth, dominated by Shaftesbury and bolstered by his position as Captain General, might grab it; that spelt catastrophe for his former opponents. Presence often constituted right in a doubtful succession, as the weak Richard Cromwell gained over his stronger brother Henry, at the time of Oliver's death, simply because Henry was absent in Ireland.

On 24 August Sunderland, faced with this dilemma, sent word to James that the King was ill. A day passed and it was suggested he should return. On 2 September James arrived back in England.

It was a decisive moment. Admittedly, by this date the King himself was recovering; he exchanged water-gruels and potions for the more robust fare of mutton and partridges. Soon he was demanding to go to Newmarket – no doubt to escape the claustrophobia of his closely watched sickroom. The doctors forbade it on the grounds that the season was too advanced and, as a result, 'the Air too serene' (meaning not so much calm as liable to a noxious twilight dew, from the Latin *serus*, 'evening'). All the same, it was a decisive moment because James made it so. Such an ambiguous situation brought out the best in the military-trained Duke, accustomed to a lifetime of decision and command in the field and at sea. Suddenly his stalwart figure appeared as a bastion against contention and the worse evil of civil strife.

The Duke of York went back to the Continent three weeks later, but not before he had been assured that, had the King died, the Lord Mayor of London would have proclaimed James as his successor. The point was taken by courtiers and politicians alike that, were a similar crisis to arise, the Duke of York would be the gainer. The King's health could never again be taken for granted: it was about this time that a 'sleeping chair' was ordered for the King's progresses, symbolic of a general easing up in his restlessness.[12] In the following May he was ill again (with twice-daily bulletins on his progress). Thus the whole episode secured an ascendancy for the established candidate, in which the pretender Monmouth was the inevitable loser. Monmouth still had much to prove, and he did not help matters by his own behaviour.

It was in vain that Monmouth had attempted to prevent the return of the Duke of York. His own welcome from Scotland as the 'clement victor' was now eclipsed. Charles II preferred the interests of his brother – representing the 'descent in the right line' – over those of his son (although Monmouth and his backers seemed unable to take in the point). It was Monmouth who was deprived of his general's commission and, like the Duke of York, was asked by the King to absent himself from the felicity of the royal circle for a while.

The people had rejoiced to see Monmouth. Bonfires in abundance were lit in the streets on his behalf. But mob appeal, which Monmouth clearly possessed, was no substitute for his father's *imprimatur*. There were those at Court who wondered whether the King's attitude was 'but a feint'; wiser heads decided that he was 'in good earnest'.[13] Monmouth, unconvinced, lingered for a while disconsolately. Then he headed for The Hague. There he managed to cause the King even more annoyance by striking up an unholy alliance with William of Orange: something which Charles, in a sharp autumnal mood, believed was directed against his own French interests.

The ascendancy of the Duke of York was not achieved without sacrifice. Charles was prepared to protect his brother's right to the succession, but no more than that. In return for the dismissal of Monmouth as Captain General, James was obliged to agree to leave the centre of things himself. He was appointed as yet to no official position in Scotland; it was a year later that Lauderdale resigned 'for your own solid and wise reasons', as the King put it. Nevertheless on 27 October 1679 James and his family, whom he had collected from Brussels, set off north.

It was significant of what had passed that it was something in the nature of a royal progress. Gentlemen took care to greet the heir presumptive to the throne on his way. It was an expression of that law described by Halifax: 'Men's thoughts are naturally apt to ramble beyond what is present; they love to work at a distance ...',[14] and put even more poetically by the great Queen Elizabeth: 'Men ever seek to worship the rising sun....'

At the centre of things, Charles II was left to cope with what was present. There was a trail of damage left by his illness and the behaviour of his brother and son. Meanwhile, the General Election of the summer had given him another House of Commons. The bitterness of the anti-Popish mood of the capital persisted. The popular celebrations in November reached a new pitch not only of hysterical malevolence, but also of organization. What was more, the date was shifted from 5 November – Guy Fawkes Day – to 17 November – the Accession Day of Queen Elizabeth. The shift was deliberate. The famous Queen's image was menacingly paraded, with its implied reproach to a lesser sovereign. As Marvell's satiric 'Dialogue between the Two Horses' had it:

> A Tudor! A Tudor! We've had Stuarts enough,
> None ever reigned like old Bess in a ruff....

In the organization, the Green Ribbon Club took a hand. Buckingham also put his knowledge of the theatre to brilliant, if Luciferian, use. The result was a show at once spectacular and inflammatory. So dazzling was it to the eye that even the poor Catholics it was directed against could not resist watching it, as the Jews might have watched the great military rallies pass in Nazi Germany. So rousing was the show to the spirits of the rabble that many felt compelled to express the anti-Popish fire within by lighting real bonfires in the streets.

One of the newspapers supporting Oates, *Domestick Intelligence*, gave a gleeful report of it all. The centre-piece of the show was still the Pope himself. His figure cost £40 in wax alone: indeed, the total cost of the whole show, including claret for spectators, was nearly £2,500, a colossal sum for the times. Figures of devils attended the Pope – 'Hail Holy Father' – but more ominous to the Court were his other attendants: nuns – 'the Pope's Whores' – labelled 'Courtesans in Ordinary'. Another typical placard showed a Jesuit with a bloody sword and pistol and the legend: 'Our Religion is Murder, Rapine and Rebellion.' The spectre of Sir Edmund Berry Godfrey demanded vengeance.[15] Finally, as Dryden put it, 'the mitred poppet [doll] from his chair they drew', and the Pope was duly consigned to the fierce bonfire which, it was hoped, symbolized his ultimate destination.

In such an atmosphere, it was hardly surprising that when a new Plot was put forward for popular inspection by one Thomas Dangerfield, it was not found wanting. Dangerfield, a scurrilous rascal, belonged to the tradition of Oates and Bedloe as a witness; his novel invention consisted of uncovering a plot involving the Whig leaders, including Shaftesbury. When that failed, he turned the plot on its head and vowed that a Popish conspiracy, centring on the death of the King, lay at the heart of it after all. This new farrago was nicknamed the Meal Tub Plot, after the hiding-place where a Catholic midwife was supposed to have concealed incriminating papers. The King, commenting that 'he loved to discover Plots, but not to create any', made it clear that he regarded it all. Whig coup d'état and Popish assassination, midwife and meal tub, as dangerous nonsense.[16] But there was no doubt that the absence of a clamorous House of Commons assisted him in maintaining this firm view. The whole parading mob, with their lighted torches, were not half as threatening to him as a few vocal Members of Parliament.

Under the circumstances, animated also by the renewal of the French negotiations, the King decided not to meet his new Parliament. At this point, Shaftesbury went too far for the second time. Just as he had infuriated the King in the autumn of 1673 by his open attack on the Duke of York, which then seemed *lèse-majesté*, he now called a meeting of the Privy Council to discuss James' projected departure for Scotland. He suggested the matter should have been discussed in the Council first (he pretended to believe the journey was being made without the royal assent).

The King dismissed Shaftesbury instantly, and the next day drove the message home by telling the Council that he did not propose to allow Parliament to meet until the following January. The 'Chits' were appointed with Laurence Hyde replacing Essex as First Lord of the Treasury. On 10 December the King let it be known that he had thought better of that date too, and, still further buoyed up by the progress of matters with France, indicated that Parliament would not actually meet again until November 1680. By December 1679 the irrepressible Monmouth had still further blotted his copybook by returning from the Netherlands against the King's specific orders. Monmouth's – and his backers' – reasoning was that the absence of the Duke of York in Scotland provided a heaven-sent opportunity. Monmouth could build up just that kind of solid support which he needed to press his own claims and, thinking ahead, secure the King's acknowledgement of them. There were many fingers in this Protestant pie, some of them the pretty, meddling fingers of the royal mistresses. Nell Gwynn, for example, justified her popular reputation as a staunch protagonist of that religion by supporting Monmouth; later even Louise Duchess of Portsmouth, her Catholic counterpart, took part in an intrigue to get the King to name his own successor.

But it was unwise to count on the susceptibility of Charles II to petticoat government. The King was plainly furious with Monmouth; Nelly's poignant descriptions of the wan looks of Charles' once-beloved son, his Absalom, did nothing to allay his fury. They might cry 'God bless Monmouth' in the playhouses, but at Court the young Duke was ostentatiously stripped of his various civil and military positions. In February the Duke of York was permitted to return from Scotland. In the absence of a Parliamentary session, an angry war of pamphleteering concerning the claims of the rival dukes (and not ignoring those of the two Protestant princesses) broke out in the late summer.

In particular, the legend of the King's marriage to Monmouth's mother, watered by the hopes of the opposition, grew apace. The campaign of rumour had begun in the late summer. All sorts of stories were given credence, generally on the sanguine principle that two improbabilities added together make a possibility, and four improbabilities a certainty. It was pointed out gleefully that James had once tried to deny his marriage to Anne Hyde; another comparison was made to Edward IV's refutation of Lady Eleanor Talbot in order to marry Elizabeth Woodville. The fact that James had been contracted to Anne Hyde, and the supposition that Edward IV had been contracted to Eleanor Talbot, were given as proofs that Charles' refutation of Lucy Walter was also false: it was smear by analogy.[17] Even details of the supposed marriage were now given: solemnized by the late Bishop of Lincoln (who was of course dead) in the house of an innkeeper at Liège, and witnessed by certain lords. The marriage certificate was said to be preserved in an exciting 'Black Box', one of those objects of which it could be said that everyone knew of someone else who had definitely seen it.[18]

The trouble was that a putative marriage was by far the most convenient way of establishing Monmouth's claim: it hurt no one (except the Papist Duke of York, and who cared about that?) and provided a neat solution to the problem of the succession – so at least ran the argument of Monmouth's sponsors. Thus the rumours nagged and badgered the King and would not go away.

The total lack of substance in these rumours need not be reiterated. By the spring of 1680 Charles was beginning to feel rather the same way. For a long time his instinct had been to ignore the matter as being too ridiculous to dignify with official discussion. Early in 1679 however he had made, with some reluctance, a declaration to four of his councillors, including the Archbishop of Canterbury. Two months later he repeated this declaration to the Council as a whole, and also committed it to paper, 'it being all written and signed in his Majestie's own hand'. This he judged to be the best way to kill this particular snake.

The document, dated partially according to the old style by which the year began on 25 March, is worth quoting in full:

> For the voiding of any dispute which may happen in time to come concerning the succession to the Crown, I do here declare in the presence of Almighty God, that I never gave

nor made any contract of marriage, nor was married to any woman whatsoever, but to my present wife Queen Catharine ['Queene Catarine' in the original] now living. Whitehall the 3rd day of March 1678/9. Charles R.

The impatience can be seen in the handwriting, the words 'Almighty God' being the only ones written with any care at all. This document was ordered to be kept in the Council Chest.*[19]

But the snake was scotched, not killed.

In the summer of 1680, driven beyond endurance on the subject, the King decided to put an end to these rumours once and for all. The *London Gazette* of 8 June, the official government organ, gave a prolonged recitation of the steps leading up to this decision, with the preamble: 'We cannot but take notice of the great Industry and Malice wherewith some men of a Seditious and Restless Spirit, do spread abroad a most false and scandalous Report of a Marriage or Contract of Marriage....'

In particular, care was taken to nail the story that there was 'a Writing yet Extant' – that is, a marriage certificate; it was pointed out that the very lords said to have been present at the marriage had been examined and had denied the allegation. Then the *London Gazette* printed the King's own declaration to his Council in full.

'Though I am confident that this Idle Story cannot have any effect in this Age ...', wrote the King. But the idle story persisted simply because it suited men's purposes at the time. It would haunt the first year of James II's reign for the same reason, and bring the wretched Monmouth to his death.

In general, the spring of 1680 was a period redolent of anger and disgust on all sides. Halifax wrote frankly in January that it would be pleasanter in a wasps' nest than in London at the present time.[20] In January also seven Catholic priests were tried merely on grounds of their ministry (although it was stated that they were not on trial for their lives, unlike those priests already

* It is now in the Pierpont Morgan Collection, New York, having been purchased from an unknown source in the present century.

executed in the provinces). Lack of cash meant that even members of the royal household were clamouring for their salaries. The King, encouraged by Sunderland, took refuge in the hope that foreign policy would once more rescue him from his bonds.

Sunderland's strategy was based on the notion of a series of treaties bringing in Spain, the Austrian Empire and even the United Provinces.[21] It was of course the reloading of the see-saw. France was not likely to view this new weighting with approval. Charles II acknowledged the change by making no official gesture at the time of the wedding of Louis XIV's son. The secret talks with Barrillon were however not excluded, as they had not been excluded during the sway of the pro-Dutch Danby. Sunderland, like Danby, simply occupied one end of the see-saw. The Austrian Emperor, however, a vital character in the proposed new alliance, declined to commit himself. In common with the rest of Europe's happily absolute monarchs, he was anxious to see how the King of England would deal with this obstreperous Parliament of his. Thus the foreign policy of Charles II, which he trusted to free him from Parliament by the manipulation of foreign powers, remained uncomfortably dependent upon it.

Many in England at the time believed that the Crown itself was threatened. James Duke of York had written to William of Orange the previous year that 'the monarchy itself is in great danger as well as his Majesty's person ...'. To a certain extent the King himself shared this view. There had been a rumour at the time of his illness in August that a Commonwealth would be set up if he died. At all events, he was quite prepared to take a series of steps to ensure that the country did not become further inflamed. Essentially he saw himself as forced to take these steps. They were produced out of a situation which was not of his own making, a situation which might otherwise lead to revolution. That was the King's angle. Seen from another angle these steps represented quite simply the beginnings of tighter, even absolutist, control. In May, for example, the judges (now far more the King's men than before, thanks to the new policy towards judicial appointments) gave a unanimous opinion to the Council that the King might prohibit all unlicensed news-books and pamphlets in the interests of good order. The King had another asset in the crucial royal warrant by which municipal corporations were granted their charters. It was in essence a question of control over the composition of the House of Commons. Four-fifths of the MPs at that time were city or borough members, and, by packing the governing body of a corporation in charge of their election – or in fact selection – attractive results could in theory be gained. The technique was to recall the charter of a given corporation on the excuse of a misdemeanour, using a *Quo Warranto*, if it was not surrendered voluntarily. This was not a new issue, nor were the steps which the King now began to take new:[22] it was the confidence he showed in his attack which was new.

Back in the 1630s his father had struggled with the City of London over its charter; Cromwell, following the Stuart trend in power, had fought with the City of Colchester. It has been pointed out that there is evidence of Crown efforts in the 1660s to impose some kind of control by using the uncertain position, after the Restoration, of many corporations whose charters had been granted by Cromwell. These early manoeuvres, in which the Duke of York seems to have played a part, came to an end not so much out of fear of the corporations, as out of fear of the House of Commons defending their own privileges in this respect.

By 1680 there was no question of the King avoiding a clash with the House of Commons: as he saw it, the Whigs were snapping at his privileges. Moreover, his dissolutions of Parliament had been disastrous: he found himself with a more Whiggish body each time. By calling in the charters, he might provide a more satisfactory selection of Parliamentary candidates. Once again he saw himself combating a trend; others might view the situation differently.

It was true that the summer of 1680 also saw the beginnings of the inevitable blacklash which violent happenings – and the possibility of violent change – bring. This backlash worked naturally to the advantage of the monarchy. Francis North, in his judicial progresses at the time, witnessed 'some dawnings of loyalty to the Crown'. The reprinting of the works of Sir Robert Filmer (begun in 1679) was another notable manifestation of Tory resurgence: he was the only theoretician in the 1630s who had actually supported Divine Right. The lapsing of the government order against unlicensed printings meant that the summer was loud with a cacophony of propaganda, Tory as well as Whig. Roger L'Estrange, an able and vituperative Tory journalist, conducted a pamphlet war against the Whigs in general and Titus Oates in particular.[23]

In Scotland the latest anti-government revolt, in June, brought to prominence the Cameronians – named for one of their leaders, Richard Cameron. These rebels styled themselves as standing for the 'anti-popish, anti-prelatic, anti-erastian, anti-sectarian, true Presbyterian church of Scotland' and, not surprisingly with such a sweeping ideal, forswore allegiance to the King of England. They also believed in preventive murder – in other words, terrorism. The Cameronians were however easily defeated and their leaders killed. Scotland under the Duke of York (who returned there in October) was to enjoy at least a stability of administration which was to his credit. Although his reputation was blackened later, the suppression of terrorism was at the time seen as essential, and James' methods no more severe than those generally sanctioned at the time in Scotland. To many of the nobility and gentry, the presence of the King's brother was welcome, while he himself became 'highly esteemed'.[24]

Meanwhile, back in England, there was a meeting of ministers in June, known as the Althorp conference, which included Halifax, as well as Sunderland, Hyde and Godolphin. It was agreed that these ministers should labour to produce a more amenable Parliament. The King promised in return not to ask Parliament for money unless his foreign alliances necessitated it; and he gave securities against Popery (but not against the succession of James). Halifax pronounced himself satisfied with such a position. The Althorp conference was an earnest of the kind of reasonable accommodation the King might be able to achieve in the future.

As a portent however it was far outclassed by certain outrageous public events which promised a very different outcome of the King's struggles. Most notable of these was the attempt by Shaftesbury to indict the Duke of York as a Catholic recusant and Louise Duchess of Portsmouth as a common prostitute before a Whig Jury in Middlesex. The penalty for the latter crime was unthinkable for the royal mistress (Louise stood to be incarcerated in the stocks, amongst other painful humiliations). The penalty for the former was purely financial. Nevertheless the joint attack was a calculated piece of provocation on the part of the Exclusionists. In the event, Lord Chief Justice Scroggs had the jury discharged. And so the matter ended; although it had the effect of sending the terrified duchess scurrying over to the Exclusionists, hoping to save herself by abandoning the cause of James. The King's mood became ever blacker and more withdrawn.

'Our most solitary sovereign,' Thomas Bruce called him. A rhyme by Lord Dorset, circulated that autumn, compared him to a King at chess, who has already lost his rooks and knights:

> (His Queens and Bishops in distress)
> Shifting about, growing less and less
> With here and there a pawn.

One effect of this withdrawal was to make him increasingly inscrutable. As Barrillon wrote back to France, 'His conduct is so secret and impenetrable, that even the most skilful observers are misled. The King has secret dealings and contacts with all the factions and those who are most opposed to his interests flatter themselves that they will win him over to their side.'[25] It had never been particularly easy to gauge the secret emotions of Charles II, since his youth had trained him to hold his feelings, like playing-cards, close to his chest. Charles had, on the other hand, prided himself on being able to gauge the emotions of others – which gave him a double advantage. Now, in the momentous autumn of 1680, this inscrutability was to be a prime factor in the ultimate fate of the Second Exclusion Bill.

For there is no doubt that a large proportion of those who voted in favour of it genuinely believed that the King was prepared to ditch his brother. As Halifax reported, by October 1680 half the world was absolutely confident that the King would quit the Duke of York and the other half absolutely confident that he would not.[26] Yet, as has been expressed, the King had in fact no intention of doing so: so that one-half of the world was (as often happens) confident but absolutely wrong. Baffled by the King's prudent secretiveness, the Exclusionists allowed optimism about his intentions to sway their judgement. They expected support from him and none came.

Admittedly, the opponents of the Bill gained no great royal support either. The King had called Parliament for quite another purpose. Tangier, the Queen's dowry, was in danger as an outpost, being beset by the Moors. Only vast injections of cash to raise more troops could be expected to save it from falling into their hands. The French discussions were still covertly proceeding, but, as Louis XIV appreciated, 'He [Charles II] only treats with me to derive an advantage in his future negotiations with his subjects.'[27] Under these circumstances, King Louis was in no hurry to conclude yet another secret agreement which might bolster up King Charles, but leave England officially no better disposed towards France than she had been before.

Charles II therefore opened Parliament in October strongly on the theme of Tangier and its desperate plight. In the summer its defender, the Earl of Ossory, Ormonde's son, had been killed. Charles had written a personal letter to his parents concerning the great loss, in which 'I take myself to be an equal sharer with you both'.[28] Without new fortifications – which had to be paid for – Tangier was lost: 'Therefore I lay the matter plainly before you, and desire your advice and assistance.' Throwing in assurances about the maintenance of Protestantism at home the while, the King pleaded for money which would provide 'greater strength and reputation both at home and abroad'. He would also bring King and Parliament together. For above all he desired 'a perfect union among ourselves'.[29]

The answer of the House of Commons to this powerful pleading was to introduce the Second Exclusion Bill. The so-called Tangier Parliament did not share the King's concern at the fate of this outpost – quite ignoring its strategic position on the Mediterranean; later one member of Parliament would refer to the King's preoccupation with Tangier as being like Nero's decision 'when Rome was on fire, to fiddle'. The first reading of that Bill which the Commons considered so much more important took place on 2 November; the Bill was carried.[30]

On 6 November the House of Commons moved that Exclusion did not apply to the children of the Duke of York; their title would be unimpaired. But the next day the King sent a message to the Commons, offering once again to agree to any securities with regard to the maintenance of Protestantism, provided the 'descent in the right line' was not touched. The day after that the House of Commons, ignoring the King's suggestion, moved that Mary, James' elder daughter, should inherit the throne (as would have happened if her father had been dead).

At this point Sunderland moved over to the Exclusionist cause, to the indignation of the King. Sunderland's point was that Exclusion represented the only viable alternative to a French involvement. He also dreaded dissolution and the prospect of yet another unsatisfactory Parliament. And he threw in for good measure that it safeguarded the King's own life. But Charles, intent on his own steady course, referred to Sunderland's behaviour, in an audible aside, as 'the kiss of Judas'.[31]

The meetings of the Commons also took place against a dramatic background of movement on the part of the rival claimants. The Duke of York, who had returned from Scotland in February, was despatched thither again by the King in October. Monmouth, who had still not learnt his lesson about the limits of the King's indulgence, set off on a series of progresses around the country which aroused a satisfying loyal chorus of support from those who witnessed them. It is possible that Monmouth was encouraged in this unlicensed display of strength by Shaftesbury. If so, Shaftesbury also had not yet understood the King's capacity for sharp action when tried too far; the lesson would shortly be rammed home for him.

The Commons, having passed the Bill on the third reading, with the question of James' descendants left open, passed it on to the Lords. And at this point the Lords, seeing an opportunity to avenge themselves for the various insults and insolences dealt them by the Commons during this period of warfare between the two chambers, joined battle.

In 1678, for example, the House of Lords' right of originating Bills of Supply (that is, money bills) had been attacked by the Commons. The latter claimed that 'all aids and supplies ... are the sole gift of the Commons'. Later the Lords counter-attacked on this particular subject; but in the autumn of 1680 the defeat of the Exclusion Bill offered the possibility of revenge in a different area.

The King himself paid the debate in the House of Lords the closest attention; a practice he had begun in the days of the Roos Divorce Bill, another measure which had seemed likely to affect the fortunes of his family. On occasion he threw in a word himself, and was formally thanked by the House. The King's posture in the House of Lords was characteristic: he began by sitting on the throne, then moved to the fire, where he felt more comfortable, and finally went round like 'a common solicitor', as Burnet vividly expressed it, lobbying on behalf of his own interests.[32]

Many of the speeches – so far as can be judged from the existing texts since the debate has only come down to us in fragmentary note form – expressed a reassuring conservatism. The contribution of old Lord Ailesbury was one such example.[33] Ailesbury was certainly over-optimistic when he suggested that James might turn Protestant, as Henri IV had turned Catholic (how that celebrated conversion continued to haunt the descendants of Henri Quatre!). But when he spoke along these lines, 'If the right heir should be thrown out may we not be subject to invasions abroad or Wars at Home. More insecurity from Wars than to suffer him to Reign', he was striking exactly the note of alarm which had long sounded in the King's ears. Lauderdale prayed that 'We must not do Evil that good may come of it' and reminded the House – another significant touch – that the Duke of York was 'Son to Charles the First of Blessed Memory' as well as 'only brother to King Charles 2d'.

But the key speech came from Halifax. Only details of Halifax's superb and successful effort remain:[34] but from these it is clear that he dwelt firmly on the possibilities of revolution – or at least an armed rising under James – which the passing of the Bill might offer. These references to the power of the Duke of York in Scotland, Ireland and elsewhere 'with the Fleet', caused fury when they were reported to the Lower House. One MP exclaimed angrily that Halifax should be told, 'If the Duke had such power, it was time to take it out of his hands.' But Halifax remained steady. The Catholic succession, if it occurred, could be dealt with by other means, such as limitations. To throw out the Duke of York's claim by means of a Bill was to provoke exactly the kind of trouble they all wished to avoid.

It is clear from the reports of contemporaries that Halifax's decision to oppose Exclusion proved crucial. Only Halifax had the trenchant style necessary to cut down Shaftesbury, capable of demonic leadership in such a cause. There was one particularly telling exchange. Shaftesbury suggested sarcastically that Halifax could not really believe the Duke to be a Catholic, since he 'combated with such warmth' their own reasonable precautions against the Duke's Catholicism. To this Halifax riposted that of course he knew the Duke to be a Catholic. Since he feared the consequences of the Duke's Catholicism, he had opposed the Declaration of Indulgence (which Shaftesbury had supported) and worked for the Triple Alliance (which Shaftesbury had worked against). At this Shaftesbury was 'much disconcerted'.

Dryden afterwards paid tribute to Halifax's influence: his

> piercing wit and pregnant thought
> Endued by nature and by learning taught
> To move assemblies ...
> So much the weight of one brave man can do.

During the ten-hour debate Shaftesbury never got up to speak without Halifax answering him. The final verdict was that Halifax's rapier was 'too hard' for Shaftesbury.

At the end of the day the Second Exclusion Bill was defeated by sixty-three votes to thirty. And so the issue of the succession was, unexpectedly to many, disastrously to not a few, settled for the time being in favour of the Catholic Duke, who represented the old order as well as descent in the right line. As for Exclusion, another satiric couplet summed up its dismissal in lines not quite up to the level of Dryden, but pithy nonetheless:

> Our Renowned Peerage will not have it so,
> The Demi-Gods and Heroes thunder, No.[35]

PART FIVE

His Autumnal Fortune

'In his autumnal fortune ... yet there remaineth still a
stock of warmth in men's hearts for him.'
LORD HALIFAX, *Character of King Charles II*

CHAPTER TWENTY-FOUR

Bolder and Older

〜

'Men ordinarily become more timid as they grow old;
as for me, I shall be, on the contrary, bolder and firmer
and I will not stain my life and reputation in the little
time that perhaps remains for me to live.'

Charles II, March 1681

With the defeat of the Second Exclusion Bill, it might
appear that Charles II, that expert on the subject of
survival, had survived yet again. To Sir John Reresby,
on the eve of Christmas 1680, the King had never seemed more
at his ease, his sang-froid never more marked. At his *couchée*,
that semi-official gathering of an evening, Charles weighed in a
humorous vein against the fallacy and emptiness of those who
pretended to a greater degree of sanctity than their neighbours:
they were most of them 'Abominable Hypocrites'. Above all, as
the King had told Reresby the previous month, he was aware
of the need of sticking by his old friends, otherwise 'I shall have
no Body to stick by me.'[1]

Much of this must be regarded as whistling to keep the royal
spirits up – as well as the spirits of those surrounding the royal
person. The King's real mood was better expressed a few
months later at that classic confrontation, the Oxford Parliament,
when he observed something along these lines: 'Men ordinarily
become more timid as they grow old; as for me, I shall be, on
the contrary, bolder and firmer and I will not stain my life and
reputation in the little time that perhaps remains for me to
live.'[2] The deaths resulting from the Popish Plot, the persistent
chicaneries (as he saw them) of the Whig opposition, the attacks

on his wife, mistress and ministers, had produced a new 'Severity in his Disposition'.

James Welwood attributed this directly to the Catholic executions: and Welwood, although writing some time after the event, at the request of Mary of Orange (he was her physician), knew the Court gossip.[3] It is also possible that such severity had always been latent beneath the courageous forgiveness which Charles II displayed at the Restoration. But a more plausible case can be made for the fact that all the Stuarts became more conservative as they became older – those that survived to do so. James I, who died in his late fifties, certainly developed a kind of obstinacy very different from the dexterity he displayed as monarch of Scotland. It scarcely needs stressing that Charles I, who was executed at the age of forty-seven, had shown these tendencies; James Duke of York had been marked for his rigidity since his thirties. Charles II, a far more flexible character in every way, who had learnt in a hard school the value of pliancy, was nevertheless not quite immune from the same tendency.

The next few months constituted the greatest challenge yet to the King's nerve. He discovered in the course of them that this new boldness, the boldness brought by age, led to triumph, not disaster. This result did not encourage the King to revert to his previous easy-going stance. The concept of 'peace for his own time' was abandoned since, like so many other attitudes of appeasement, it had manifestly failed.

The day after the defeat of the Exclusion Bill, Shaftesbury struck again. He still did not reckon himself to be totally overborne on the subject of the King's successor. 'Sick in health', he was 'yet in action nimble and busy as a body louse'.[4] If Monmouth's chances had temporarily vanished beneath a hail of mockery from Halifax, then the other expedient (of divorce) could be resurrected. In the House of Lords the next day, Shaftesbury outlined another project 'as the sole remaining chance of liberty, security and religion'. This was designed to separate the King from his existing Queen, and provide him with an opportunity for 'a Protestant consort', and thus leave the Crown to his legitimate issue.

This gained little support in the Lords. It also offered the King an opportunity to demonstrate his loyalty to his wife publicly. That night he ostentatiously supped with the Queen, when he had been in the habit of supping with the Duchess of Portsmouth. And, even more ostentatiously, he took his post-prandial nap in the Queen's chamber. It was a signal rebuke to Shaftesbury's plans. Queen Catharine had been ill that autumn, her fragility producing the usual unattractive speculation about her possible successors, including some cold 'northern princesses' and the daughter of the Earl of Manchester. Now the King had made it clearer than ever that she could not be attacked with impunity.

His speech to Parliament on 15 December was one of bitterness and disappointment. He had not succeeded in obtaining those funds which would enable Tangier to be made secure; as he saw it, Parliament had preferred to concentrate on this perpetual bickering over his successor, while forgetting the wider issue. He had hoped for a united front; they had responded with dissension. He had given them assurances concerning religion and they had not responded with any kind of financial backing. 'I should be glad to know from you,' exclaimed the King, 'as soon as may be, how far I shall be assisted by you, and what it is you desire from me.'

One further piece of Parliamentary presumption he ignored. During the autumn session the House of Commons had reacted to the King's new treatment of the judiciary by asking for a change in the tenure of the judges – or else for some limitation to their powers. The King made no reference to this request. All the same, the mantle of royal protection could not be flung out much further than the King's own circle. In January the House of Commons made a move towards the impeachment of Lord Chief Justice Scroggs (in the event, the House of Lords refused to take him into custody and then Parliament was prorogued). More serious was the move of the House of Commons against Lord Stafford.

The five Catholic lords were still languishing in the Tower of London, to which they had been committed two years before. Although various Catholic priests, mainly Jesuits, had been put to death, and others condemned, no trial had yet taken place of these far more prominent victims. Scaffolding had been erected in May with a view to preparing Westminster Hall for such a magnificent public event. The mob, with its taste for gloating rhyme, had sung of the preparations beneath the windows of the imprisoned peers.

The death of one of the chief movers of the plot, Bedloe, in the summer of 1680, was a blow to the prosecution: it was not until the autumn of 1680 that it was decided by the House of Commons to move against Lord Stafford.

This particular peer was chosen because the witnesses against him had the greatest air of plausibility.[6] Thus the verdict of guilty which was given against him was in a sense justified by the evidence produced – except that it happened to be perjured evidence. Witnesses happily swore that Lord Stafford had bribed them to kill the King, that Oates had delivered to him a commission to act as Paymaster-General for the Pope's Army, and so on and so forth.

The condemnation of this decent and harmless old man was a blot on the age in which he lived. Already the ridiculous 'Pumpkin Plot', as it would be described satirically two years later in Otway's masterpiece *Venice Preserv'd*, was beginning to be revealed for what it was: 'It is indeed a Pumpkin-plot, which, just as it was mellow, we have gathered, and now we have gathered it, prepared it and dressed it, shall we throw it like a pickled cucumber out of the window?' But in his prologue Otway spoke more soberly of the period of suspicion through which he had lived:

> In these distracted times, when each man dreads
> The bloody stratagems of busy heads;
> When we have feared three years we know not what,
> Till witnesses begin to die o' the rot.

It was thanks to the 'bloody stratagems of busy heads' that, while the pampered Protestant ladies shivered in their coaches, Lord Stafford was executed on 29 December.*

---

* The attainder on the Stafford title remained in force until 1824. The original Bill of May 1685, to reverse the attainder, was dropped at the outbreak of Monmouth's rebellion.

His fellow lords remained in prison for the next five years, with the exception of Lord Petre, who was released earlier by death. But there were no cheers from the crowd when Lord Stafford's head was held up by his executioner. The publication of his affecting last speech, the 'Brief and Impartial Account' (which was, unusually, not forbidden), brought further waves of uneasy sympathy. 'My good Child,' so Lord Stafford addressed his daughter Delphina, 'this is the last time I shall write unto you, I pray God bless you. Your poor old Father hath this Comfort, that he is totally innocent of what he is accused of, and confident of God's mercy....'[7]

Charles II told Thomas Bruce that Lord Stafford's blood was on the heads of those who had brought about his murder – 'I sign with tears in my eyes'; and he made clear his anger and disgust at those peers who had voted guilty, especially those whom he considered to be supporters of the Court.[8] But he did not reprieve Stafford, as he would later fail to reprieve Oliver Plunkett. He could only remit the more extreme penalties for treason, including the traditional and disgusting mutilation – and even this merciful remission was criticized by the House of Commons, who wondered whether the sovereign had the right to grant it.

Then, on 18 January, the King dissolved Parliament and announced that the next Parliament would meet in March – and in Oxford.

It was an audacious move. It indicated that the King was at last prepared to take the initiative. Even before this, the Crown was at last mounting some kind of propaganda campaign, equivalent to the agile manoeuvres of Shaftesbury and his associates.* The anti-Tory Green Ribbon Club had after all proved itself to be a more dangerous enemy than the anti-Popish mob. Noise merely

---

* For example, one of Nahum Tate's pedestrian reworkings of Shakespeare, *The History of King Richard the Second*, which opened at the Theatre Royal, Drury Lane, on 11 December 1680, was taken off after three days: the government hastily assumed that the plot must elevate the nobility (that is, the Whigs) at the expense of the King. In fact, the play had no such message, as Tate himself indignantly protested in his Preface to the printed text.[9]

battered the ears; propaganda wooed them. The point was there to be taken. There were the efforts of Roger L'Estrange in particular. Certainly the new Parliament turned out to be no *more* Whig in complexion than the previous one, and possibly slightly less – a notable improvement on the record of the previous two years, when each successive Parliament had marked a further setback for the King's party. Against this background, the choice of Oxford, whose University was a secure Royalist nursery, was inspired. Here was no London mob, hostile to so many of the King's entourage. Perhaps the setting was the suggestion of Danby, for although still immured in the Tower, he was now able to receive visits and thus proffer advice. Eighteen months before he had proposed: 'Parliament to be called to some other place; the King to reside out of London', in a memorandum.[10]

The removal of Parliament from the seething capital did not merely recognize the dangers threatening the monarchy; it also took advantage of the very wide powers remaining with the King. It is true that he had not felt himself able to save Lord Stafford, but a man who could choose the *venue* of Parliament without contradiction was still in a very strong position. There was much aggressive talk in the capital in February. One of the City MPs, Sir Thomas Player, a notorious anti-Papist, answered boldly when questioned at dinner as to why Parliament would not raise money to preserve Tangier and pay His Majesty's debts.

'Hang Tangier!' he replied. 'We resolve to raise no money to pay the whores at Whitehall and arbitrary government. And, as the King has called us to Oxford, we know the next will be to York, but for all that we will give him no money.' Sir Thomas went on to say that the disposing of the Crown was in the Commons and as alterable as the exchanging of pipes between men, 'and taking up pipes in his hand [he ex-]changed them'.[11] For all this kind of public boasting, the Commons had not the ability to deny the King his choice. To Oxford, then, reluctantly but without the ability to resist, came the Whig leaders.

The King and Court did not come there directly, but took in the spring race meeting at Burford, twenty miles away in the stony, beautiful Cotswolds. It was a meeting at which the King's twelve-stone heats for the royal Plate were due to be run. However, on this occasion Burford was transformed into something of a political Ascot; the Duke of Monmouth was amongst those who contested and there was a quality of nervous display about the whole occasion. Only the King himself kept up that appearance of relaxation which subsequently trapped his enemies and destroyed them. He hawked across the nearby fields and dined with Sir John Lenthall, son of the celebrated, if acquisitive, speaker of the Commonwealth House of Commons.

Once the Court reached Oxford, the scene was a curious mixture of the significant and the profane. Of course the Court was not unknown to the university city. Nor for that matter was Parliament. The King had been careful to reassure himself on that front, in an age when precedents, however dubious, were held to cover a multitude of sins. There were one or two (including Charles himself) who could remember Oxford as the seat of his father's government nearly forty years ago; but it was only fifteen years since not only the whole Court but also Parliament had merrily romped off to Oxford to be out of danger at the time of the Plague. It was then that Barbara had given the King her Christmas present of a son, born at Merton College. Now both the Duchess of Portsmouth and Nell Gwynn were in attendance, as was the Queen; but the atmosphere was more political than lascivious, and there were to be no presents of such an exciting nature. Once again Merton was a Royalist stronghold, as were Christ Church and Corpus Christi. The Whigs concentrated on Balliol: Shaftesbury directed that 'the younger sort of students' should retire to make room for the elderly politicians.

There remained that concomitant of courtly pleasure, the theatre; while that concomitant of the theatre, a good row, was also to be found. The King's Players petitioned furiously to be admitted, despite the claims of the Irish Company, which were supported by the Duke of Ormonde as Chancellor of Oxford University. The Irish were 'a barbarous Mass', said the King's Players, and in the end this xenophobic view prevailed. More satisfactory than this squabble was the actual performance attended by the King on 19 March: *Tamerlane the Great*, by Charles Saunders, with an Epilogue by Dryden to make the message even more acceptable.[12]

Troops of soldiers as well as actors were present. Even more than the players they set the scene. It seems that their total did not exceed five hundred.[13] Yet since they lined the roads on the way to Oxford, and lounged in the streets of the city itself, the impression of a trial of strength was there. The Whigs arrived at Oxford marked out by the bows of satin in their hats, blue and with the words 'No Popery! No Slavery!' woven into the material at a cost of two shillings a yard (these impudent bows were afterwards used to arraign Shaftesbury).* But the Whigs, like the King, were armed with something more serious than satin bows. They brought their own troops with them, if they did not have the possibility of a full standing army to back them. At St Mary's, that same church where the young Charles had shocked his governor by laughing and eyeing the ladies in the congregation, the rival parties now carefully took their places according to political allegiance and eyed each other across the church.

And of course the Press was there. A flurry of news-writers gave the scene at Oxford something of the air of a modern party conference – except that on this occasion both parties were present. Cartoons played their part. So did lampoons. The Whigs made as much use as possible of the weapon of satire, some of it gross, in order to portray the King's choice of Oxford as an act of absolutism. 'The Raree Show' depicted him as a man with a travelling peep-show, a pack of Parliamentary motions on his back, and the 'Saints' pulling him into the mire. The Duke of York was shown, more venomously, as a figure half-Jesuit and half-devil, setting fire to London.

> Halloo! The Hunt's begun,
> Like Father, Like Son . . .

---

* Blue, now the colour of the (Tory) Right in contrast to the red of the (Socialist) Left, was then adopted in opposition to the traditional scarlet of royalty; the Covenanters also wore blue, based on a Biblical text which adjured the children of Israel to put on 'a ribband of blue', and Presbyterian preachers threw blue aprons over their preaching-tubs.

so ran the verse (before proceeding with considerable indecency). It was a gloomy and, as it turned out, inaccurate prediction. A loyal poem of the time, occasioned by seeing the ageing King walking near the river, was nearer the mark when it adjured him:

Go on, blest Prince! the power of years defy...[14]

The King's opening speech to his new Parliament on 21 March was however placatory rather than defiant. It is true that there was a warning contained in the phrase, 'I, who will never use arbitrary government myself, am resolved not to suffer it in others' (the classic anti-Whig position). But at the time it seemed more important that the King stressed his continued affection for his dissident Lords and Commons: 'No irregularities in parliaments shall make me out of love with them.' It was a gruesome echo of those words uttered by the King shortly after his Restoration: 'I need not tell you how much I love Parliaments. ... Never King was so much beholden to Parliaments as I have been.' Then the King had felt quite a measure of love for the body which had shown the good taste to restore him; how, seventeen years later, love had well and truly grown cold, but the question remained how the King was to deal with his inconvenient old flame.

On the subject of religion and the succession, the King went out of his way to emphasize that he wanted 'to remove all reasonable fears that may arise from the possibility of a Popish successor's coming to the Crown' and was therefore ready 'to hearken to any such expedient, by which the religion might be preserved, and the monarchy not destroyed'. Was the King contemplating imposing some form of regency upon James, to be undertaken by William and Mary jointly, under the influence of Halifax? The words were at least capable of that construction and gave hope to the 'moderate' Exclusionists in the Commons, who believed that the King was to be counted amongst their number. But the rest rated this a 'subtle and crafty' speech, 'so unexpected that they should be put upon taking new measures'.[15]

Shaftesbury, in the makeshift House of Lords sited in the

Oxford Geometry School, wasted no time in returning to the attack. He demanded the consideration of a Bill, already passed by both Houses, which would give relief to nonconformists but not to Catholics. The House of Commons, in cramped quarters which gave rise to complaint, reverted to their favourite subject of Exclusion. Fatally – from their own point of view – the Commons felt no particular urgency. The debate was postponed until the following Saturday, 26 March, so that there might be an opportunity for compromise, possibly along the lines touched on in the King's speech.

During the next few days the King, brilliantly, paid out the rope for the Whigs. Shaftesbury, for example, was encouraged to come right out with his own solution. This was the legitimization of Monmouth by a Parliamentary Bill. But of course this had the effect of dividing the opposition. Many Whigs quite sensibly preferred Mary of Orange (who was generally understood to represent rule by William) to Monmouth. Here was descent in the right line of a sort, since Mary, as James' heiress, would receive the Crown one day in any case; while to know the wayward Monmouth was not necessarily to trust him in a position of authority. Time was rectifying the Whig distrust of William's 'Stuart' authoritarianism; whatever the nature of the animal was, William clearly did not resemble his uncle the Duke of York, nor for that matter his grandfather, Charles I.

The House of Commons in the meantime concentrated on the fortunes of yet another Pumpkin Plotter, one Edward Fitzharris. In an age when plots were endemic, as poison to the age of the Borgias, Fitzharris does not shine out as a particularly fascinating figure. It remains obscure where his allegiances lay and as a plotter he lacked the baroque, if horrifying, imagination of Titus Oates. Nevertheless, Fitzharris was to have a significance beyond the revelations he proffered. In themselves, these were contradictory; on the one hand, Fitzharris knew of a plot whereby the Duke of York would kill the King; on the other hand, he possessed the draft of a pamphlet in which the King was accused of being a Papist like his brother. The Commons at Oxford decided that these matters were best dealt with by impeachment for high treason in the House of Lords, instead of by a straightforward trial.

The Lords declined to impeach Fitzharris. All the old antagonism between the two Houses – from which the King had already profited – was aroused all over again, and at the very moment when the latest Exclusion Bill was to be read in the Commons: Charles himself, advised by Halifax, even went so far as to suggest a regency of the Princess Mary. It was probably a gambit, for it was however about this time that Charles II made those remarks, quoted at the beginning of the chapter, on the subject of boldness and age, which concluded, 'I do not fear the dangers and calamities which people try to frighten me with. I have the law and reason on my side.' Under the circumstances, it seems more likely that the King was still paying out the rope for the Whigs to hang themselves than that he was actively contemplating such a regency. James, as he well knew, would never agree to such a humiliating proposition. To agree to it was tantamount to condemning the country to civil strife on his death – the one course he was determined to avoid.

This debate in the Commons took place on the Saturday, 26 March. Taking advantage of the Commons' complaints of their uncomfortable accommodation, the King pleasantly suggested that they should meet the following Monday in the Sheldonian Theatre.

The Sunday was passed by the King in secret conference at Merton College.

On Monday the King took his place in the House of Lords, now set in the Hall of Christ Church. There was nothing out of the ordinary about his costume. But Thomas Lord Bruce, who knew him well, received 'a most gracious smile' and noted his exceptional bonhomie.[16] As for the peers, they too were in ordinary dress, having been given no notice to put on their robes. Very few present were aware that the King's own robes and crown, those trappings essential to a dismissal of Parliament, had been secretly smuggled into the building.

The King proceeded to send for the House of Commons, who were engaged in discussing the various precedents over Exclusions from the throne. Indeed, one of the members was in the very act of complaining at the isolation of Oxford in that respect: 'Amongst our misfortunes in being called to this place, we are far remote from Records and Books.' He went on, 'I have heard of Record 4.E.3 where when the Earl of March—' At that moment the official, Black Rod, arrived, to command the Commons' attendance at the House of Lords.[17] So off the Commons trooped, and the member's clinching comparison with the past was never completed. The Commons however trooped off not so much disconsolately as eagerly, expecting some new offer or concession.

The entrance to the Hall was narrow, down a little flight of steps. There was a crush as the Commons pressed through it. The sight which met their eyes – the monarch attired in full robes and crown – was both unexpected and for one moment inexplicable. The Lords themselves had barely taken in the sudden transformation. There was a babble of voices, and in the confusion the Serjeant at Arms had to call for silence three times before the noise died away. Then the King in a single sentence ordered the Lord Chancellor to dissolve Parliament: 'All the world may see to what a point we are come, that we are not like to have a good end when the divisions at the beginning are such.'[18]

Finch carried out the King's command. Charles promptly left the Hall. He had wasted neither time nor breath. These, the last words he would ever speak in Parliament, were brusque to the point of incivility. They came from a man otherwise famed for the graciousness of his manner. They represented the end of a downhill road and a long-declining relationship.

Afterwards, however, the King displayed 'a most pleasing and cheerful countenance' as he took off those smuggled robes. It was the MPs who greeted the news with 'dreadful faces' and 'loud sighs'. The King, good humour fully restored, observed to Bruce, 'I am now a better man than you were a quarter of an hour since; you had better have one King than five hundred.'[19]

Charles then dined in public, as was his custom; but he did so with exceptional rapidity. Then it was down the backstairs and into Sir Edward Seymour's coach, standing ready. The King joined his own coach at the next stage, to which he had prudently sent it in advance. And so he went on to Windsor, along a route discreetly guarded – another precaution. The King's Oxford troops clattered away unused. The Whigs, baffled and outpointed, had no choice but to leave as well, taking their own unused troops with them. Many of them had furnished their Oxford lodgings for a long stay – the measure of their astonishment.

Gradually Oxford became quiet again. Parliament never met again during the lifetime of King Charles II.

It is logical to suppose that the King arrived in Oxford with a rough plan of action already in his head. It was time to take on the Whigs. Given that he was prepared to act with decision, it was in fact an uneven match – not so much because the King was inordinately strong as because the Whigs were extremely weak. Nothing so far had gone right for them. In the House of Commons they had not succeeded in acquiring control of the Militia, for example, but had both alarmed and alerted the King by demanding it. Their battles with the House of Lords, also not yet conclusively won, occupied much of their attention, and had distracted them at several crucial moments. In terms of Whig policy, they concentrated their minds wonderfully on the question of the King's Papist successor; yet the King was not a Papist himself and no one (*pace* Fitzharris) seriously supposed that he was.

All this loaded the dice in favour of a sovereign with very wide theoretical powers at his command, who was also able to demonstrate the sheer intransigence of the Whigs by appearing to offer compromise. Above all, the Whigs had not made up their minds about the practical possibilities of resistance to the Crown, if any. It was scarcely likely that they would succeed against the sovereign until they did.

Nevertheless, the nerve demanded from the King by the dissolution was considerable. There were troops present – on both sides. Armed clashes in the streets of Oxford, and the further nightmare of civil strife, were to be dreaded, whatever their outcome. Oxford University was Royalist, but the city itself was known to be Whig. The feeling that revolution – some new violent turnabout – was pending was not confined to the King. Men could read the signs, or thought they could. A correspondent wrote to Pepys in January, 'I cannot but pray God to preserve us from the tumults, confusions and rebellions of 1641 and 1642, which seem to threaten us on one hand as much as Popery on the other.'[20] No-one wanted a return to unsettled times; the man who risked plunging his country once more into such 'tumults, confusions and rebellions' bore a heavy responsibility if his plan went awry. It was therefore relevant that on 8 April, the day on which a long Declaration from the King on the subject of the recent Parliament was ordered to be read throughout the country, he also received the first payment of a new subsidy from Louis XIV. The two events were closely connected.

This fresh agreement had been negotiated by word of mouth between Barrillon and Laurence Hyde. About the same time Hyde also spoke comfortingly to Barrillon on the subject of England's tiresome involvement with Spain, that treaty negotiated by Sunderland a year back: Charles II would gradually divest himself of this obligation, which of course cut quite across French interests. Hyde, shortly to become Viscount Hyde and then Earl of Rochester after the death of Charles II's sardonic friend, certainly deserved Dryden's sobriquet of Hushai: 'the friend of David in distress'. For without this agreement, it is doubtful that the English King – in the character of David – could have grappled so successfully with his 'Goliath' of a Parliament.

The confidence that Charles II needed to organize his abrupt dissolution came from France. Even though the Whigs had not made up their minds to anything except to press raucously and childishly for the Exclusion of the Duke of York, this mental disarray might not prevail for ever. It was not even a question of the money which Charles II would now receive from Louis XIV – about 4,300,000 *livres* or over £300,000 spread over the next four years; although it was true that that would enable the King to jog along comfortably without Parliament for the time being.* Once more, as in the 1660s, Charles II drew strength

---

* The actual agreement with Louis XIV was for more; five million *livres* for a three-year suspension of Parliament.

from the notion that Louis xiv was on his side and would help him, if need be, to uphold his 'legitimate authority'.[21]

Armed with this knowledge, the English King was able to display those qualities of attack and surprise which constituted one side of his nature; the other side, which craved ease and knew that delay often brings its own solution to difficulties, had enjoyed a long run. Fortune, which traditionally favours the bold, smiled upon the new determination of Charles ii.

The Declaration on the subject of the recent Parliament, ordered to be read aloud in all churches on 8 April, was as long as the message of dissolution had been short.[22] It was also hypocritical. No-one should be persuaded that he was not going to use Parliament in the future, declared the King: this was merely 'the restless malice of ill men who are labouring to poison our people, some out of fondness for their old beloved Commonwealth principles, and some out of anger at being disappointed in their own ambitions'. He repeated his familiar theme: no 'irregularities' would make him out of love with Parliaments. The King showed more of himself in disdaining responsibility for what had happened: 'Having done our part ... it cannot be justly imputed to us that the success hath not answered our expectations.'

Charles ii had done with dealing with five hundred Kings. In future he would deal with one French King and rest master of his own fate.

The summer of 1681 bore a very different air from that of the previous year. Then there had been some dawnings of loyalty to the Crown visible to a discerning eye. Now the reactionary sun's rays could be felt in a variety of ways. 13 April 1681 saw the first issue of Roger L'Estrange's newspaper *The Observator*. Nahum Tate wrote of L'Estrange's energies in attacking the Whigs, playing on his paper's name: 'He with watchfull eye/Observes and shoots their treasons as they fly....' When the King and Queen went to dine at the Guildhall, the people's rejoicing as they entered and left the City was considered to be in marked contrast to the coolness of previous years. As Henry Sidney wrote in his *Diary* at the end of June, 'But which is most extraordinary is the favour the Queen is in.'²³ She had emerged unscathed from the crucible of the bad years. It would take further time for the Duke of York (still in Scotland) to recover his lost popular prestige: nevertheless, the rehabilitation of the Catholics was part of the overall popular shift away from Whig influences.

It was true that the summer of 1681 witnessed the dissection of yet another Pumpkin Plot at the trial of Edward Fitzharris. But Charles II's cool and vigorous attitude towards this episode demonstrated as much as anything else how far he had moved from the worried stance of 1678. Optimists among plot-watchers expected, as usual, great things from Fitzharris' revelations, and a connection with the household of the Duchess of Portsmouth was deemed encouraging.²⁴ In the event, the King made it quite clear that he expected to see this petty informer condemned and executed. And executed he duly was, on 1 July. Justice was certainly done, since Fitzharris had sought to bring about the execution of a great many more. All the same, it was a public blow to the repute of the Whigs, notably Shaftesbury; it demonstrated how far their vicious control of these events had slipped. The condemnation and execution of another informer, an anti-Papist joiner named Stephen College (amongst whose alleged crimes was the singing of the gross ballad 'The Raree Show' at Oxford),²⁵ continued the trend.

About the same time quite a different trial, that of Oliver Plunkett, Archbishop of Armagh, showed up both English justice and the royal character in a less attractive light. Plunkett's trial on a charge of high treason was a travesty. Dragged to England and kept in prolonged imprisonment there, he was unable to secure satisfactory Irish witnesses because of the expense and difficulty of travel. Those that did manage to arrive presented an alien spectacle, with their thick, often incomprehensible Irish accents, and were correspondingly badly treated in court. The witnesses produced on the other side, for this conspiracy that never was, puffed up with their own perjury, received a gentler welcome.

Thus Oliver Plunkett was found guilty and on 1 July went

presumably to his heavenly reward.* As Sir Charles Lyttleton wrote, he was 'generally pitied and believed to die very innocent of what he was condemned'.[26] Yet no one cared to save him, not the Earl of Essex, who, as former Lord Lieutenant, knowing the Irish scene, might have protested effectively against his condemnation – nor, for that matter, the King. Charles II could see the significance of condemning Fitzharris, but, in common with most Englishmen, no matter how liberal, could not see that there was much to be gained from saving this Irish archbishop.

The royal eye was fixed elsewhere. The newly piercing glance of the King was focused on Shaftesbury. On 2 July, the day after the executions, Shaftesbury was arrested. The King's move was not unexpected. Shaftesbury had wagered his strength against the King's in a series of provocative actions, including the attacks on Louise and James as prostitute and recusant, as well as the sallies at Oxford. Shaftesbury was also on excellent terms with those the King considered his enemies, such as the arch-informer Titus Oates, still at large, if not quite the popular hero of yester-year.

The charge against Shaftesbury was frankly weak, as weak as some of the charges against the Catholic priests who had died (the fact has to be faced that Charles II did not regard the course of justice as imperturbable, any more than the Whigs had done). Shaftesbury was accused of treason because he had conspired to levy war against the King at Oxford; but the most cogent piece of evidence against him was a Bill of Association, a list of people who were to be invited to protect the King and prevent the Catholic succession.

The truth was that Shaftesbury's arrest was an aggressive action which Charles II now felt himself strong enough to make. He was also animated by his strong personal dislike of the fair-haired villain. This dislike, like his rare outbursts of jealousy, stood out in contrast to his generally mild attitude to politicians. On the whole, Charles was content to be guided by their

---

* Later his heavenly status was confirmed. He was beatified in 1920 and canonized in 1975.

usefulness. In this way he amiably agreed to a reconciliation with the 'Judas' Sunderland in the following summer after some pleading from Louise, Sunderland's long-term ally.[27] But Shaftesbury was different. He was the burr under the saddle of the King, as Charles' obstinate pursuit of his trial and conviction this autumn proceeded to demonstrate.

It would have been wiser to have let Shaftesbury depart for the Carolinas, as he himself wished.[28] Shaftesbury had business interests there. An absent Shaftesbury was all the King really required in terms of safety. Instead, carried away one must believe by an animosity founded on fear, the King demanded a trial. He was punished for deserting his own former policies of forgiveness and flexibility. The new Lord Chief Justice, Pemberton, made strenuous efforts to secure Shaftesbury's condemnation. He quoted the Act of 1661 by which it was treasonable to try and interfere with the King's liberty. This, it was claimed, Shaftesbury had done at Oxford, supported by the presence of armed men. The famous blue silk bows in their hats were quoted in evidence against him. But on 24 November a Grand Jury composed of resolute Whigs returned a verdict of *Ignoramus* and Shaftesbury went free.

In short, the King had struck too far too soon. He should have been more wary of the deeply Whig sympathies of the City: at the Lord Mayor's Banquet a few weeks earlier 'every little fellow' was said to have censured both the King and 'his proceedings at that time'.[29] The acquittal of Shaftesbury was a personal blow. The Lord Mayor himself, on the King's instructions, refused to allow the bonfires or rejoicing which the Whigs wished to mount. But neither King nor Lord Mayor could prevent the striking of a celebratory medal in honour of the event, adorned with the humiliating motto *Laetamur* – 'Let us rejoice'. The obverse showed the sun emerging radiant from clouds over the Tower of London. *Laetamur*! No, the King did not rejoice.

There were however other causes of rejoicing. There is an interesting juxtaposition between public and private happiness in the lives of famous men. The presence of private happiness can always atone for the lack of public fulfilment, if the man himself will suffer it to be so. The personal life of Charles II during the last years of his life was extremely happy, even serene. Queen Catharine, comforted by his championship, had settled into a role which suited her and did not conflict with the King's other pleasures. She had, for example, protected Catholic Louise from the consequences of the Test Act of 1678 by including her name in the list of her own ladies who were not to be expelled. In explanation Catharine said that Louise had always behaved 'decently' towards her, unlike Barbara, who had been 'cruel'.[30] By now, the King's mistresses resembled the great ships he also loved, floating grandly on the tide of the royal favour, their hulls weighed down with jewels and other riches. They flew their ducal titles like pennants, their ennobled offspring following in their wake like flotillas of lesser boats. Emotionally however the King had reverted to the 'monogamy' of the first decade of his reign, on which Pepys had commented.

While Nell Gwynn retained what Aphra Behn called her 'eternal sweetness', the solace of the King's later years, Madame de Maintenon to his Louis XIV, was Louise. Relaxation, not religion, was however what Louise offered. Just as the King's accord with his wife and her own popularity were the subject of comment, the domestic ascendancy of Louise was also remarked. She had grown plumper, more 'fubbsy' than ever, as her later portraits show; it only increased her air of luxurious cosiness.

Absence was one test of the King's affections. With her son, Louise paid a visit to France in the autumn of 1684; she secured the settlement of the Aubigny estates and dukedom upon the boy as a result of Charles' intercession with Louis XIV. The King's delight at her return was unqualified. He also passed that other test of love, the appearance of a rival. When stories were circulated of Louise's dalliance with Philippe de Vendôme, nephew of Hortense de Mazarin, Charles had the presumptuous swain thrown out of the country. To celebrate her ascendancy, Louise had her own medal struck, embellished with a Cupid and bearing the legend: *Omnia Vincit* – it was a more flirtatious form of insolence than Shaftesbury's.

It is impossible to be certain when – if ever – the sexual bond between King and Duchess ceased. In January 1682 there were rumours that the King had not slept with the Duchess for four months. Bruce's testimony that the King supped with Louise 'without intent' is to be taken more seriously because of Bruce's intimate position in the King's household.[31] Yet no outsider can pronounce with complete confidence on such matters. Given the continued healthy vigour of the King, absolute cease seems unlikely. What is much more certain is that the domestic bond increased. In principle, King Charles, Queen Catharine and Duchess Louise created a master triangle in which all parties, for the first time in their lives, were roughly content with the status quo.

The King does not appear to have practised any form of birth control – there are no references to the topic by any of the interested parties. He also derived a great deal of happiness from his children. As far as one can keep track of them, the total of those that survived long enough to feature in the royal records was a round dozen. As Buckingham brightly observed, a King is supposed to be the Father of his People, and Charles II was certainly the father of a good many of them. These twelve known bastards were born from seven women: Lucy Walter, Elizabeth Killigrew, Catharine Pegge, Barbara Villiers (mother of five), Nell Gwynn (mother of two), Moll Davis and Louise de Kéroüalle. The King certainly did not suffer from that complex characteristic of some Casanovas who must claim the paternity of every child conceived within their orbit: to be cynical, he could scarcely afford to do so, since paternity for a sovereign was a serious (financial) business. At the same time he honoured his genuine paternal obligations with a mixture of love and liberality.

The royal accounts include payments which have a distinctly nursery flavour – rattles, cradles and so forth. As the children grew older, more substantial sums were disbursed. In April 1684 Lady Mary Tudor, daughter of Moll Davis, received a suite of tapestry hangings, a looking-glass, a little crimson damask bed for country use, a bed of druggett for her gentlewoman, and for her chambermaid, laundry-maid, page and footman 150 ells of Holland to make six pairs of sheets. There were wedding expenses, which any father might expect to pay (the King's heart was in the right place: as we have seen over the wedding of Anne Fitzroy, he accepted the responsibility, even if payment came at a characteristically slow pace). There were dowries and allowances. As late as 1693 Charles Duke of Southampton was still being allotted an allowance of £6,000 a year.[32]

Where the emotions were concerned, so affectionate were the relations of Charles II with his illegitimate children that it was all the more regrettable that he should lack legitimate heirs. The next century would see disputes between royal father and son become the norm, not the exception. Since children tend to reproduce the family pattern they have experienced, a terrible chain reaction was set up. King and Prince of Wales were in constant conflict. The boy dreamt of by Queen Catharine in her delirium would have had a happier fate, since Charles II had always enjoyed delightful relations with Charles I. For that matter, Charles I had been greatly loved by his own father. The Stuarts, for all their weaknesses in other respects, made good parents; unlike the Hanoverians, they were characterized by warm family relationships. Charles II would have been an excellent father – within the marriage bond.

As it was, he did make an excellent father – but outside it. His blood courses down through the veins of the English aristocracy into the body of English life. His descendants, if not quite as numerous as the sands of the sea, are at any rate numerous enough for the line to be unlikely to die out. 'Six bastard Dukes survive his luscious Reign': so Defoe summed up the King's achievement; and it is a point often made today in attacks on the hereditary House of Lords that so many dukedoms derive from the *amours* of King Charles II.* Such critics would undoubtedly approve the contemporary satire of Marvell on the subject:

---

* But since the dukedoms were originally introduced into England and Scotland only for the King's sons, not for ordinary peers, Charles II was, in fact, behaving in an enlightened manner by not penalizing his sons for their illegitimate birth.

The misses take place, each advanced to be duchess
With pomp great as queens in their coach and six horses,
Their bastards make dukes, earls, viscounts and lords,
With all the title that honour affords...

In fact, six of the King's sons received nine dukedoms: Monmouth and Buccleuch for Lucy Walter's son; Southampton, Northumberland and Grafton and Cleveland, on her death, for Barbara's three boys; St Albans for Nelly's surviving son; Richmond and Lennox (joined together) for Louise's only child.* Monmouth's marriage to Anne Duchess of Buccleuch in her own right, led to the pair being created Duke and Duchess of Buccleuch in England jointly. After his death, Duchess Anne was allowed to retain her own Scottish Buccleuch title, although that of Monmouth was swallowed up in her husband's disgrace.

But Charles' daughters were not forgotten. Some were married off to lordlings, who were then further ennobled. Mary Tudor was granted the rank and precedence of a Duke's daughter at the same time as her step-brothers gained their coveted dukedoms. Two of the King's sons made political alliances – Henry Duke of Grafton married Arlington's daughter, and Charles Earl of Plymouth married the daughter of Danby.

Taken all in all, they were an agreeable bunch, with no real black sheep amongst them – unless one counts Monmouth. Out of a dozen children, that was not a bad record. It is true that none of them showed the exceptional calibre of their father, and what one must suppose to have been the exceptional talents of their mother in one direction at least. But then exceptional parents rarely breed exceptional children. Charles II's extraordinary qualities had been largely forged by adversity: these children enjoyed quite a different upbringing.

Nor can it be argued that the children of Charles II were noted for their waywardness. Charles Duke of Southampton and later Duke of Cleveland on his mother, Barbara's, death,

---

* Today four of these dukedoms still represent the quasi-royal line: Buccleuch (although Monmouth's own dukedom of Buccleuch is still under attainder), Grafton, St Albans, and Richmond and Lennox.

was described by her in one of her accesses of maternal disgust as a 'kockish idle boy' while at Oxford; and she sent for the Dean of Christ Church to tell him so.[33] But such undergraduate behaviour must be regarded as the rule, not the exception. Some of the girls were flighty: not only Anne Countess of Sussex but Mary Tudor, who married the Earl of Derwentwater, caused her husband distress. Yet such infidelities were hardly above the average for well-born ladies during this period. As for the King's favourite, the solace of his later years, Charlotte Countess of Lichfield, her sweetness and impeccable virtue bore out a pleasanter axiom: that an amoral mother will often produce a paragon of a daughter – for she was the offspring of the hot-tempered Barbara Duchess of Cleveland.

Charlotte Countess of Lichfield is one of those characters whose goodness survives differences of style and period to charm us still. Her appearance was appealing rather than beautiful: her mouth (like her father's) was too large and so were her eyes; her face and chin were too small. It was her personality rather than her looks which won hearts. Whether bearing and rearing her enormous family (at the age of nineteen she had four children and gave birth to a total of twenty), playing basset, crimp or billiards, going riding, adorning her houses, her attitude to life recalls that of Queen Charlotte a hundred years later: she wanted each day to bring its own pleasure.

She was married off in 1677 at the age of twelve, her husband being rewarded with the Lichfield title. The new Earl also received the more spiritual reward of great happiness. Together the Lichfields enjoyed a married life of forty-two years. Their shared monument in Spelsbury Church commemorates the fact that 'at their marriage they were the most grateful bridegroom and the most beautiful bride and that till death they remained the most constant husband and wife'.

To King Charles II, in a series of fond if scribbled notes often enclosing money, she was his 'dear Charlotte', as once Madame had been his 'dear sister'.[34] He was her 'loving' and at other times her 'kind' father. There is a vignette of Charlotte tickling the King's bald pate as he took his post-prandial nap. Other glimpses of family intimacy include fatherly advice on

Charlotte's building plans for a new house, which should not disturb those of her sister Anne, but 'I think it a very reasonable thing that other houses should not look into your house without your permission.' When Charlotte is pregnant, the King is delighted and hopes to see the child ere long; when they are apart, he is sorry he will be so long deprived of seeing his 'dear Charlotte'.

As for the boys, the King was proud of his fine brood of dukelings: Evelyn's wry pen gives a portrait of him receiving communion at Easter 1684 with Richmond, Northumberland and St Albans, 'sons of Portsmouth, Cleveland and Nelly', three boys on his right hand – and three bishops on his left. Barbara's second son, Henry – 'Harry' – Duke of Grafton, was rated the handsomest; he also pursued a career as a sailor. These two attributes were sometimes in conflict. 'Your brother Harry is now here and will go in a few days to Holland,' wrote the King to Charlotte. 'By the time he returns, he will have worn out in some measure the redness of his face, so as not to fright the most part of our ladies here.' Charles Earl of Plymouth – 'Don Carlo' – much resembled his father. Said to be 'a fine youth', he was authorized to raise Plymouth's Foot for Tangier; he died there in October 1680 before his promise could be fulfilled (he also left a mass of debts including tailors' bills, so his promise was not entirely military). But the Duke of Northumberland, Barbara's third son, he who had been born so festively at Merton College, Oxford, was generally considered to be the most like Charles – at eighteen he was 'a tall black man like his father the King'. Because he was also 'well-bred, civil and modest', Evelyn rated Northumberland the 'most accomplished and worth the owning' of Charles' children.[35]

Nelly's sons, one of whom died at the age of nine, and Louise's boy, belonged to a later period. They were duly ennobled after the frantic efforts of their mothers – Louise's son was only three when he was raised to the peerage – but were still only in their early teens at the time of their father's death.

In general, all the bastards were easily and unselfconsciously treated by their legitimate relatives, whether they pursued the Whig connection of William and Mary or the Jacobite one of

James. Their Stuart Christian names emphasized rather than diminished the connection: no fewer than four of the King's sons were named Charles, two of them James, and Barbara's third son, like the third son of King Charles I, was christened Henry and nicknamed Harry. The girls were Charlotte, a name otherwise hardly known in England at that date,* or Anne or Mary, the names of Stuart princesses. The King's daughter by Elizabeth Killigrew was named Charlotte Jemima (for James) Henrietta Maria, a Stuart mouthful. Surnames employed were unashamedly royal: Fitzcharles, Fitzroy, Tudor. The name of Crofts, taken from his guardian, was only used for Monmouth in the desperate days of exile, when a royal connection was not necessarily blazoned. (On his marriage to an heiress, Monmouth took his wife's surname of Scott.)

The Duke of York was particularly devoted to his niece, Charlotte Lichfield, and corresponded with her while he was in Scotland;[37] he also favoured Harry Duke of Grafton. Charlotte Jemima Henrietta Maria Fitzroy had a daughter by her first marriage, Stuarta Howard, who became a lady-in-waiting to Mary of Modena. Mary Tudor was the mother of the two Jacobite Earls of Derwentwater, who died respectively in 1715 and 1745 in the cause of their Stuart relations; they had been brought up as companions to James Edward, the so-called Old Pretender. Harry Duke of Grafton, on the other hand, supported William of Orange and was rewarded by being integrated into the Whig establishment; he died as a soldier under Marlborough's command in 1690.

The King was also extremely fond of Charles, Earl of Burford and then Duke of St Albans, surviving son of Nelly. He too was 'very pretty' in youth. There is evidence that Charles worried over Burford's education more than that of his other children: as though Louise, the *bien née*, could be trusted with that of her son (in fact she gave him the playwright Wycherley, Barbara's former lover, as a tutor), but Nelly, the girl of the people, could

---

* When the King was godfather to Sir George Carteret's daughter in Jersey the diarist Chevalier was at some pains to explain the derivation of the name Charlotte as being somewhat eccentric.[36]

not. In 1682 George Legge, the King's intimate, commented on the King's fondness for the boy: now he was of an age 'to be bred into the world', he was to be trusted to Lord Preston in France. Here the King wished him to study mathematics and the art of fortification (two of his own preoccupations), as well as observing the progress of Louis XIV (another of them). Nelly herself was torn between coveting this glorious future for her boy, and not wanting him to leave England before 'some settlement' had been made upon him.[38] Later Burford justified his father's faith by fighting the Turks in Hungary – his colonelcy was not to be regarded as a sinecure – and his mother's by marrying an heiress.

If the whole effect of the Popish Plot and its aftermath on Charles II was to bring about 'a severity in his disposition', this was the public monarch. Halifax later commented on this new sharpness, which we may suppose to be the outward sign of the inward decision to be yet bolder and firmer. He developed, says Halifax, 'a very peevish memory': in his anger, scarcely a blot escaped him.[39] In private the King's life was marked by new contentment as he grew older, and, in terms of good relations with his growing children, he led a life of richness which many men of his age might have envied.

CHAPTER TWENTY-FIVE

Another Way of Ruling

'I learnt from a Great Man, that we were in no Way
of having a Parliament, there being some near the
King, who advised him to another way of ruling the
Kingdom.'

Sir John Reresby, *Memoirs*

Charles II spoke directly on the subject of government to
Lord Bruce some time after the Oxford Parliament. He
confided to him, 'I will have no more Parliaments unless
it be for some necessary acts to be passed that are temporary
only as to make new ones for the good of the nation, for,' he
added, 'God be praised, my affairs are in so good a posture that
I have no occasion to ask for supplies.'[1] In the winter of 1684
Sir John Reresby was informed by a certain 'Great Man' that
there was no question of a Parliament, since those near the
King had 'advised him to another way of ruling the Kingdom'.

Certainly in the last years of the life of Charles II another
way of ruling was tried out. It was found highly satisfactory –
from the King's point of view. The nation as a whole also
enjoyed that happiness ordinary people are often content to
desire, knowing too well the hideous possibilities of disruption
which change brings in the lives of the lowly. The connection
between prosperity and happiness being ever strong, it was
relevant that England enjoyed a trade boom in the early 1680s.
This boom, which has been traced in the customs figures,
happily transformed the receipts from this source.[2]

Unaware of these blessings about to flow, Charles II took a
firm line about his own finances. The French subsidies could

be counted on to settle outstanding military needs. Where Court and personal expenditure was concerned, the value of economy – an unpleasant prospect, but anything to avoid having to call a Parliament – was recognized. Retrenchment in general was noted at the Court in the spring of 1682: the King was cutting down at his own table and that of everyone else, 'except that of the Maids of Honour to the Queen'. More painful to him must have been retrenchment in the number of his horses. The Queen herself played her part and remitted to him her marriage settlement for one year, 'so that his Majesty seems to have taken serious thoughts of endeavouring to live without subsidies from his Parliament', as an observer (correctly) commented.[3] It is true that the essential needs of a sovereign could not be transformed overnight; bills for beds, one of crimson and orange velvet and silver tissue, costing nearly a thousand pounds, continued to disfigure the accounts. There were new lodgings in Whitehall and a twelve-oared barge for the Queen in 1683.[4] This period also included a major building programme for a new royal palace. But that, as we shall see, was envisaged by the King more as a political move than as an architectural foray. The point remained that the King was by now taking the business of ruling without Parliament more seriously than ever before, even if it meant cutting down on the courses at his own table, the horses in his stable.

These were negative gestures. More positive and more practical were those measures taken to consolidate the political base of the monarchy. That these measures were deliberate is generally agreed. A rhyme of April 1684 summed up the angry astonishment in certain quarters at the turn-round in the royal fortunes:

> Who could have thought in '78 that we
> So much enslaved by '84 should be.[5]

The extent to which the King himself took an active interest in extending his own powers is more difficult to assess. This royal leopard did not choose to change his protective spots of apparent laziness and even indifference. Under the circumstances, it is certainly possible to make a case for the Duke of York as the master-mind of this absolutist trend.[6] James returned from Scotland for good in June 1682. He had made a brief return in March, but headed north again to fetch his Duchess. It was a disastrous expedition. On the way back James and his entire party was shipwrecked off Yarmouth with much loss of life, although as James himself rather callously remarked, no one 'of quality' was drowned. The opportunity was given to his enemies to spread the canard by which James had thought only of saving his strongbox, his priests and his dogs. James himself was in fact more guilty of an obstinate and characteristic refusal to abandon ship in face of danger. It was his entourage who beat off the desperate 'lesser' passengers with their swords.[7]

In Scotland James had conducted affairs justly enough by the standards of a troubled time. His administration brought about calm in the Highlands – no mean achievement – and he also coped competently with the Scottish militia and all the problems of Scottish finance. A new Oath of Allegiance imposed upon all officials the necessity of upholding the Protestant religion (from London the King approved it). That hit the extreme Covenanters. But the Catholic minority – who were not officials in the first place – were able to live in unofficial peace. James also approved of much in the Scottish spirit and law, including the fact that the death penalty was imposed for perjury. As he told his niece Charlotte Lichfield grimly: 'If it had been so in England so many innocent people had not suffered.'[8] The only exception to the orderly quality of his rule was his clumsy attempt to eliminate the Earl of Argyll. This ended with the Earl's escape and the Duke's red face.

In England James was not without natural sympathizers. He had for example employed the powers of patronage he possessed in the Army both widely and wisely. Many of the bright sparks of the day owed their advancement to the Duke of York, including John Churchill, George Legge, Sir Charles Lyttleton and Henry Jermyn. His native honesty and courage won respect, as they had done throughout his career (although his father's 'peremptoriness', so different from the affability of Charles II, was detected in his manner).

James' climb back to favour and power is one of the features of the reign's end. By the beginning of 1684 Sir John Reresby commented that the Duke 'did now chiefly manage affairs', adding another dig at his 'haughtiness'. By the end of that year, James' 'indefatigability' at the King's side was generally remarked. James had certainly always possessed more obvious indefatigability that his brother, who took care to show as little as possible of this worrisome quality. From there it was a short step to assuming that James was actually deciding on the direction government should take.

But the case for James as master-mind is not proved. The fact was that James' ideas and policies were now convenient to the King. James, for example, approved in his memoirs that campaign for calling in corporations' charters begun in 1680 and shortly to be stepped up: 'His Majesty had at last taken those vigorous counsels, and resolute methods the Duke had so long pressed him to.'[9] James had been keen on such measures in the sixties – without success. That still did not mean he was responsible for the new initiative. It was Charles who decided when the time was ripe. The indefatigable James was allowed his hand on the tiller just because he was guaranteed to steer the ship in the direction his brother now approved. It was in this way that the royal brothers drew closer and closer together, just as they had grown apart when James had shown himself a liability to Charles. Charles respected his brother but he did not fear him. He had been the senior partner all their lives; he did not desert that position now.

If James' 'absolutism' is rejected, there is an alternative explanation of the events of the King's later years: that Charles sank into happy cynicism, now that things were going well in the short term, leaving all to his younger ministers. It is an attitude summed up not so much by the prophecy of Louis xv – '*Après moi le déluge*' – as a more devil-may-care '*Après moi je m'en fou . . .*'. Neither attitude – reliance on James or indifference – seems however to accord psychologically with the decisive, vigorous and above all cheerful King who dismissed the Oxford Parliament; nor with the wily sovereign who would play a subtle hand at foreign policy during the next few years.

Implicitly Charles II agreed with the doctrine of Sir Robert Filmer, posthumously published in the 1680s, that a king was a father of his people.[10] Even Charles I had not adhered to Filmer's extreme doctrines concerning Divine Right; and, where Divine Right was concerned, Charles II certainly did not. But when Filmer wrote that 'anarchy is nothing else than a broken monarchy, where every man is his own monarch or governor', his words found an echo in the breast of Charles II. They also of course found an echo in the hearts of the people. The King instinctively appealed to those sentiments aptly phrased by Oliver Goldsmith eighty years later. Goldsmith denigrated the great Whig leaders who

> blockade the throne,
> Contracting regal power to stretch their own...
> When I behold a factious band agree
> To call it freedom when themselves are free...
> I fly from petty tyrants to the throne.

As a father, Charles II had not yet abdicated his responsibilities.

In May 1682 the King endured another bout of illness, but, as in previous years, he gave the appearance of a complete recovery. Once restored to health, the pattern of exercise was unabated, including such famous killers of the middle-aged as tennis games with much younger men. He rode and hawked as before. Buck-hunting remained a passion: in the course of his sport he was able to introduce his Italian sister-in-law, Mary of Modena, to the English countryside, including Dorset and one of its jewels, the hunting retreat at Cranborne.[11] Physically, this was not a monarch in decline: whatever sharp warnings of the future were being administered in the shape of these attacks, they were intermittent signals delivered to a still active man. There is no reason to suppose that, mentally, the King was in decline either.

People saw what they wanted to see. Where Reresby witnessed the Duke's indefatigability at the expense of his brother's indolence, Roger North, writing the life of his brother Lord Keeper Guilford, described quite a different phenomenon: how the King, after his various illnesses at Windsor, 'appeared to be more considerative, and grew more sensible of the niceties of State Government, than he had been before, especially relating to the Treasury'. Charles' words to Burnet – spoken with regard to his championship of Catharine – will be recalled; in the autumn of 1678 he described himself as having led a bad life which he now wished to amend. He was 'breaking himself of all his faults'.[12] Among those faults it is plausible to suppose that he listed a lack of interest in the *minutiae* of government. 'Another way of ruling' represented his own attempt to redirect his energies. And in so far as the Duke of York and ministers gave to outsiders the air of being in control, it was because their thoughts and policies coincided with those of the King.

The attempt to secure a friendly judiciary was an essential part of 'another way of ruling'. For all the indignation of the Whigs, the calibre of the new men was not low.[13] Thomas Raymond, Edmund Saunders, Robert Atkins and Francis Pemberton, Evelyn's 'very learnedest of the judges', were all estimable appointments. What they did share however, and share with the Crown, was the view that their tenure sprang from that Crown and depended upon it. Once again the King was taking advantage of tradition, the judiciary merely failing to flout it. (It is however that kind of flouting which leads to progress.)

Most significant of all was the appointment of the Chief Justice, Francis North, as Lord Keeper in succession to Lord Nottingham in December 1682 (North was created Lord Guilford the following year). North was a good man and a distinguished judge: the manner in which he swayed the trial of Stephen College to secure the desired guilty verdict in August 1681 was probably the only blot on his career. But he was famous for his loyalty to the royal prerogative. It was his declared opinion that 'a Man could not be a good lawyer and honest, but he must be a Prerogative Man. So Plain were the Law Books in these cases.'[14]

In 1683 Jeffreys, not such an agreeable man, succeeded as Chief Justice on the death of Sir Edmund Saunders. Under his presidency, the King's Bench began to produce the pro-governmental verdicts for which the King and his *coterie* hoped.[15] By the end of 1683 eleven judges had been removed – at the King's wish – and a new model judiciary had come into being. It is true that the difficulty the King experienced in getting Danby released would show that this new model was not totally subservient. But as Guilford's words on the prerogative amply demonstrated, their hearts – and their judgements – were in the right place.

The other angle to any verdict was provided by the jury. It was here that the great weakness of the King's flank had been demonstrated in his attack on Shaftesbury: the City of London continued to throw up Whig juries, because juries were 'pricked' or chosen by the sheriffs and the London sheriffs were Whigs. At midsummer 1682 Tory sheriffs were duly elected, although the skulduggery of the manoeuvres involved did not bear inspection.

More charters of corporations were called in, along the lines referred to earlier in chapter 23, whenever some light excuse of misdemeanour could be found to justify it. The excuse given for calling in the charter of York had at least a nice period touch to it. The Lord Mayor was said to have refused a mountebank permission to erect a stage, although the fellow had been recommended by the King himself.[16]

In the last year of the King's life, towns in the four corners of England were included in those who lost their original charters. Colchester, Swansea, Lyme Regis and Wigan … east and west and south and north the King's messengers, like those of Lars Porsena, went forth. On occasion the arrival of the new charter was greeted with loyal demonstrations which underlined the popularity of the settled regime, or at least of a skilful Royalist mayor; at seaside Lyme there were all-night bonfires and great shouts of 'God save the King and the Royal family.' Elsewhere, at Berwick and at Malmesbury, for example, there was a disturbing air of resentment.[17]

The varied popular reaction was less important than the fact that the warrants on the new charters all contained the vital clause which gave the King a veto over the election of the officers. Suitable Tory figures locally would see to it that equally suitable Tory figures were returned to Westminster – if the occasion ever arose.

The apex of this campaign was the great struggle to secure the charter of the City of London. It was said that the Common Council there had imposed an illegal tax at the time of the rebuilding of London after the Great Fire; and, furthermore, the Council had sent in a disrespectful petition in 1680. In June 1683 the Court of the King's Bench voted that, consequent upon these heinous acts, the charter should be put in the King's hands. At last, as Jeffreys put it, 'the King of England is likewise King of London'. By 1684 the charters of the Livery Companies in the City of London, including the Plumbers, Goldsmiths, Grocers and Apothecaries, were being surrendered with petitions for their renewal.[18]

About the same time as the collapse of the City's independence, the Convocation of Oxford University passed a decree condemning 'certain pernicious books and damnable doctrines, destructive to the sacred person of princes, their state and government, and of all human society'. The decree only survived until 1688.[19] Since it explicitly denied that there was any compact between a prince and the people, that a prince forfeited his right to rule through misgovernment, and that civil authority itself was in any way derived from the people, it represented a highwater mark of Royalist theory.

In the country the Crown's approaches, if more subtly deployed, were twofold. Authority over the country magistrates was built up, and so long as care was exercised not to infuriate the local magnates, the King was able to re-emphasize his right to appoint and dismiss Lords Lieutenant.

A Commission for Ecclesiastical Preferments was set up in 1681 to review appointments. These were monitored carefully, both by William Sancroft, Archbishop of Canterbury, and by the King's minister Rochester. Their conservative (as opposed to Catholic) tenor was illustrated by the fact that many of them had connections with the Duke of York. Francis Turner, Bishop of Ely, had been his personal chaplain, as had William Thomas at Worcester; Thomas White, Bishop of Peterborough, had been chaplain to Anne Duchess of York. For the Duke of York, as a political figure, continued to represent a kind of solid con-servatism at variance with his actual religious beliefs.

In the last year of his life the King even revoked this commission. He resumed a free hand in the election of bishops, and as there were a notable amount of sees falling vacant, received an ideal opportunity to strengthen the number of his personal nominees (such as Thomas Ken, his chaplain, and Thomas Sprat, Dean of Westminster) in bishoprics.

The printed word continued to be regarded as the dragon's teeth. Francis Smith was put in the pillory in June 1684 for disseminating that famous and gross libel, 'The Raree Show'. Savage penalties were extended to James Holloway in April of the same year for that astonished rhyme on the change-round in the royal fortunes already quoted. On 17 December 1684 Sunderland, on behalf of the King, granted to Roger L'Estrange, as Surveyor or Overseer of the stationers, the power to stop 'these intolerable liberties of the press', with the right to search and seize.[20] Yet it should be pointed out that the mere existence of such blanket ordinances and their reiteration showed that censorship – like the control of the judiciary – was far from complete.

Nor was England subjected to more restrictions than the rest of Europe in this respect and at this date. As with all other aspects of an absolute rule, she still lagged behind.

The first real effects of these policies were felt in the King's handling of the so-called Rye House Plot of the spring of 1683. The Whigs as a whole were quiescent after the disbanding of the Oxford Parliament – it is notable that only a few ardent members of the Green Ribbon Club played any part in events after 1681. The autumn of 1682 went without the flickering fires and raucous cries of the great Pope-burnings of recent years: such political conflagrations were now banned. The streets were patrolled to make the ban effective.[21]

The Whig leaders however could not bring themselves to regard the question of the succession as solved. In the late July of 1681 William of Orange had paid a visit to London. But the Whigs as a whole were still not converted to the concept of

William as sole candidate for the Protestant succession. For his part, the King deliberately contributed to the confusion. He prevented William from dining with the Whig faction in the City by the simple means of inviting him to dinner at Windsor on the same date.

The increased cordiality between the King of England and the Prince of Orange was gloomily noted by the Whigs; nor was William's attitude to his uncle of York sufficiently hostile to be satisfactory. Thus the taint of Stuart authoritarianism had not been removed from William in the Whig view. William, for his part, was not in a mood to be particularly accommodating. He calculated that a man who stood to become an English King one day (through his wife) had no motive for becoming a Whig pawn in advance.

So the most active Whigs continued to concentrate on Monmouth, fearing the painted devil of William. This support, in particular the growing embroilment of Shaftesbury, took place despite ominous signs of the King's official disfavour towards his son. These only thickened between the summer of 1681 and the spring of 1683.

The dashing Duke – he could no longer truly be counted as young, being now older than his father had been at his Restoration – had not ceased to trail his coat in the last few years; he had learned nothing from his father's public fury. When Monmouth ostentatiously stood bail for Shaftesbury, that increased the King's ire to the point where, with equal ostentation, he gave offices previously occupied by Monmouth to his half-brothers Richmond and Grafton. Then there was the matter of the Chancellorship of Cambridge University. Monmouth was removed from this in April 1682, by royal injunction, and his portrait burnt.

Yet throughout 1682 Monmouth continued to fly high. He tried, for example, to eliminate Halifax from his father's counsels by accusing him of prejudice against him, and, failing in that, challenged Halifax to a duel. The King coldly sided with Halifax. Monmouth was treated as a pariah by the Court. Then Monmouth resorted to his previous habit of making a progress in the country, with all the panache of the true-born prince he believed himself to be. The progress turned out no better than the challenge to Halifax, for on 20 September Monmouth was arrested at Stafford, allegedly disturbing the public peace, and brought to London. He was then banned altogether from appearing at Court.

It was some time in the summer of 1682 that the Rye House Plot was hatched. A certain confusion of aim existed from the first, and persisted in the matured plot. There were those, like Shaftesbury, who believed in a series of risings in the country – as did Monmouth. But there were also those who were republicans, like Algernon Sidney – as Monmouth was of course not. The matter of assassination was particularly clouded in mystery. Afterwards Monmouth swore that he had never agreed to any plot which necessitated the killing of his father – 'I wish I may die this moment I am writing if ever it entered into my head' – he had on the contrary worked to distract the conspirators from this heinous course by concentrating on the possibility of risings.[22] It seems only fair to accept Monmouth's word: he was weak and vain but not without affection for the father who had done much for him.

On 28 September the fateful election of Tory sheriffs in the City of London convinced Shaftesbury that he was once more in serious danger from the King, and this time he might find it more difficult to wriggle out of a tight corner. It was a development which had been predicted in advance of the election in 'Advice to the City', a famous burlesque by Thomas D'Urfey, set to music by Signor Opidar. Its Tory sentiments so enchanted the King that he sang it with D'Urfey himself at Windsor, leaning familiarly on his shoulder and holding a corner of the paper. The opening lines were enough to commend themselves:

> Remember ye Whiggs what was formerly done,
> Remember your mischiefs in forty and one [1641] ...
> When cap was aloft and low was the crown
> The rabble got up and nobles went down. ...

The chorus was equally rousing:

> Then London be wise and baffle their power
> And let them play the old game no more.
> Hang, hang up the sheriffs, those barons in power,
> Those popular thieves, those rats of the tower....

As for 'Tony' – Anthony Lord Shaftesbury – the rabbles' 'speaker', the song went on: 'He knows if we prosper that he must run....'[23] And so it proved. 'Tony' did run. He went into hiding for a few weeks and then fled to convenient Holland. In Holland the sickness which had so long threatened but not sweetened Shaftesbury at last overcame him: he died in January 1683. If he had personally advocated a rising in England, he certainly left it without making any practical plans concerning troops and money.

Shaftesbury had a notion of the after-life which is uncharacteristically romantic to our ears: he believed that the souls of men entered stars after death and animated them. If so, then the star animated by the soul of Shaftesbury was sure to be brilliant; one feels that it might also cause trouble in the galaxy. In England, the tangled webs left behind by Shaftesbury found public expression in the Rye House Plot.

The Plot took its name from the Hoddesdon, Hertfordshire home of one Richard Rumbold, who long before had acted as a guard at the execution of Charles I. The Rye House (its previous owner, whose widow Rumbold married, had been a maltster) was conveniently sited from an assassin's point of view, for it lay at a peculiarly narrow point on the Newmarket road. The bones of this particular plot seem to have consisted of a plan to 'lop' both King and Duke of York on their way to or from their sporting retreat. It went wrong, as such brilliant ideas often do, as a result of a fortuitous accident: a fire made the royal brothers leave Newmarket early.[24] The alleged plot, having been put off, was then betrayed.

So far there might seem nothing earth-shaking in an unsuccessful move towards a double assassination – for, as we have seen, the King's life was regarded as generally under threat, like that of any modern head of state, and the Catholic Duke of York was certainly not without enemies. The importance of the

Rye House Plot derived from the involvement of the Whig leaders. That gave an extra nightmare quality to the violent daydreams of certain old Cromwellians.

Both Lord Russell and Algernon Sidney were arrested; Lord Grey of Werke escaped. The latter was a zealous Exclusionist and an avowed supporter of Monmouth. His private life was as colourful as that of some of the Wits: he had eloped with his sister-in-law and was tried for the offence. William Russell, the Whig aristocrat who intrigued with the Catholic Louis XIV as and when it suited his own best interests, had seconded the Exclusion Bill in March 1681. Algernon Sidney, the proud self-confessed republican or 'Commonwealthsman', as he significantly termed himself, had only narrowly escaped condemnation as a regicide in 1660. After wanderings abroad he had just returned to England in time to plague the King with his joyous support of Exclusion in 1677.

A colleague whose implication in the plot deeply distressed the King was Essex, once his serious and respected minister. Essex committed suicide. The King exclaimed that he would not have demanded his death when he heard the news.

'I owed him a life!' he said, referring to the execution of Essex's father, the Royalist hero Arthur Capel, thirty years before.[25]

The existence of the plot was only discovered officially at the beginning of June. It was convenient timing. As with the alleged plots against the life of Queen Elizabeth, so deftly handled by Walsingham, the sovereign's life was wonderfully preserved without having been actually endangered. Popular sympathy was however in proportion to the peril averted rather than the ordeal endured. From Holland, William of Orange hastened to send his own favourite, Bentinck, with a message of congratulations to his uncles on their joint escape. It is highly unlikely that he had been implicated in the plot himself;[26] but he was personally embarrassed by the presence of certain of the escaped conspirators in Holland, and wished to make the point of his continued Stuart loyalties.

Of those actively participating, Monmouth assuredly fared the best. The King himself took the line that Monmouth's involvement was, like his personality, showy without being deep. In July a Grand Jury found against Monmouth and a reward was offered for his capture. However, nothing too energetic was done to secure this. Monmouth was allowed to skulk in hiding at the home of his mistress Henrietta Wentworth (she to whom he considered himself married in the eyes of God), while the other conspirators were subjected to trial. At the instigation of Halifax, the King was soon prepared to stretch out his arms to his errant son once more. Monmouth's wife, Duchess Anne, also wrote piteously in his favour: 'So I hope your Majesty will not refuse to accept any of that entire submission and great penitence from him, which your goodness would not perhaps deny to another man.'[27] In view of Monmouth's behaviour as a husband, it was indeed gracious behaviour on her part.

At first the King received Monmouth with displeasure: but to observers it was 'the displeasure of a parent who seeks the reformation of his child'. The trouble was that Monmouth did not give much genuine proof of this reformation. Although he wrote two penitent letters (probably drawn up by Halifax), he jibbed at any further confession concerning his associates.[28] Monmouth was also determined that his recantation should not be made public. The King however was disgusted that his generosity should be met by quibbling. Monmouth was not allowed to get away with his partial submission. Eventually he flounced off to the Continent, where William of Orange took the opportunity to stir the pot – and stir up family trouble – by entertaining him.

This new toughness towards Monmouth has been ascribed to the Duke of York.[29] Yet as indulged children learn to their cost, even the mildest parent may reach a turning-point. In his heart of hearts the King probably loved his spoiled son as much as ever. In 1682 a play by Nathaniel Lee, *The Duke of Guise*, had been banned because it was rated an attack on Monmouth: it was remarked at the time that 'though his Majesty's pleasure is to be dissatisfied and angry with the Duke of Monmouth yet he is not willing that others should abuse him out of natural affection for him'. Nevertheless, the King had been cut to the quick by Monmouth's defiant action in going bail for his avowed enemy Shaftesbury. Immediately afterwards, at the launching of a ship at Deptford, he was seen to be 'very serious and more concerned than the greatest business did usually make him'.[30]

By 1683 Charles II, sadly profiting by experience, had decided that there was no peace while Monmouth was around. That progress the previous year would have been interpreted as a rebellion in a jumpier age; the Tudors, for example, would have made short work of a claimant to the throne who gallivanted around the country accompanied by an armed retinue, showing himself gorgeously to the people. Money, the parent's panacea, was not withheld for ever. The next year Monmouth was granted an annuity of £6,000 a year. But a lawful return from the Continent was denied to him.

The truth was that both Monmouth's personality and his position were against him. One of James' biographers has suggested that he might have quoted to his brother about this time the words of Prince Hal to Henry IV:[31]

> My due from thee is this imperial crown,
> Which, as immediate from thy place and blood,
> Derives itself to me...

Had James done so, Charles II would have respected the sentiment. So long as Monmouth was allowed to parade or intrigue in England, he ever served as a magnet to draw towards him the forces of dissent; and he lacked within himself the strength to resist such temptations.

As it was, Monmouth left behind him an uncle triumphant in the shape of the Duke of York. For James himself was now popularly felt to be a wronged man: he stood for the old values of monarchy and strength. When some Scholars of St Paul's School (headed by Lord Dartmouth's son) thanked the Duke of York for getting them a 'Play Day' (by Colet's statutes only to be granted by the sovereign or an ecclesiastic), James genially told their 'very Master to be careful to teach them their duty to the Church and Crown'. The very existence of the Rye House conspirators proved these bulwarks were under attack.

The glory of the British line
Old Jimmy's come again!

So ran a song of the time. Burnet commented angrily on the 'indecent courting and magnifying' of the Duke of York which took place.[32] Demonstrations of joy began to greet his appearances, similar to those which greeted Monmouth, but in direct opposition to them.

The King seized the hour: 'It is plain that an Handle was taken from that Discovery – i.e., of the Plot, to let in the Duke of York,' wrote a contemporary.[33] A declaration of 28 July 1683 gave the King's official view of the recent plot and his escape: 'Divine Providence which hath preserved us through the whole course of our life, hath at this time, in an extraordinary manner, showed itself in the wonderful and gracious deliverance of us, and our dearest brother, and all our loyal subjects, from this horrid and damnable conspiracy.' On 9 September a public Thanksgiving Day was held for the King's lucky escape. But Divine Providence had done even better than the King admitted. Once the uncovering of plots had cast the English nation into a state of neurotic panic on the subject of Popery. Now, as the State Papers plenteously reveal, plots were used to justify measures of repression. Monmouth may have been treated with mercy: Lord Russell and Algernon Sidney were not.

It is doubtful whether these conspirators had actually done much more than talk among themselves – albeit treasonable talk. Both Russell and Sidney admitted that they had declared it was lawful to resist the King on occasion, while denying they had converted words into deeds. But in their different ways they represented the elements most resented by the King in the Whig faction.

Russell's trial in July, presided over by Pemberton, did at least conform to the rules of justice at the time: Roger North in his autobiography cited it as an example of the fairness then to be found in English courts. Russell was executed, despite the intercession of his family and Louise Duchess of Portsmouth (who was paid to do so); pleas were even addressed to Louis XIV, via Barrillon, to save him – but in vain. When George

Legge gave a list of reasons for leniency, the King replied tersely: 'All that is true, but it is as true that if I do not take his life he will soon have mine.' The King was also said to have cast 'a sarcastical eye' towards the trial of Lord Stafford when Russell was condemned to a simple beheading; far more barbarous penalties had been demanded for Stafford and only commuted on the King's edict. Charles listened to Bishop Burnet's account of Russell's death in silence.[34]

The same fairness was not exhibited towards Sidney in November. In the interval between the two trials Saunders had been replaced by Jeffreys as Chief Justice of the King's Bench, as part of the reorganization of the judiciary. (Jeffreys had merely prosecuted Russell, not presided.) Jeffreys interrupted Sidney in a shocking manner; while his loaded summing-up brought no credit either to him or the royal system which had introduced him to the office. Sidney died on 7 December; according to the Duke of York, he met his end 'very stoutly and like a true republican' – the ungrudging admiration of one iron man for another.[35] Sidney protested the illegality of his trial, but declared that all the same he was prepared to die for the 'old cause' – the Commonwealth – fighting for which he had spent his youth.

The situation in Europe did not remain as stable as the English, otherwise engaged, might have hoped. Charles II had more than ever a strong motive for desiring European peace. The aggressive martial policies of Louis XIV continued to threaten the United Provinces – that he could bear; but the potential threat to his own French set-up was another matter. If Louis showed himself all-invading, there would be demands for military action on the part of England which Charles might find it very difficult to refuse. At the same time such military action (which no French subsidy could cover) would necessitate the recall of Parliament.

That was not a consummation to be wished by Charles II, nor for that matter by Louis XIV. But at least the French King's known distaste for an English Parliament and English military action offered the English King a possible way out of his predicament. Charles II could hold Louis XIV's advances in check by the threat of calling a Parliament. The English King was back in the world of the diplomatic see-saw on which he had balanced so successfully in the 1670s; in both cases the existence of a secret French subsidy added to the complexity of the situation.

The blockade of Luxembourg by Louis XIV in late 1681 provided an instance of Charles II's poise. Charles spoke firmly to Barrillon. He would be most reluctant to call a Parliament – 'they are devils who want my ruin' – but might yet be obliged to do so, 'if an expedient is not found over the Luxembourg affair'. 'Please tell the king my brother,' he begged Barrillon, 'to relieve me of my embarrassment.'[36]

It is doubtful whether Charles would in fact have called a Parliament. Too many things militated against it. Yet by the spring of 1682 Louis XIV had lifted the blockade of Luxembourg and was requesting Charles II to arbitrate between the various warring nations. It is true that Spain (England's ally, according to the most recent treaty negotiated by Sunderland) refused to accept Charles' arbitration. He was obliged to draw back. Still, Charles had not lost his balance on the European see-saw. Neither one King – Louis XIV – nor five hundred – the English Parliament – had managed to upset it.

What would now be termed the life-style of King Louis XIV continued to impress Charles II, as it impressed all Europe. We have seen how Charles' royal guards were an imitation of his cousin's. The King had laid out his parks and gardens in the grand French manner displayed by Le Nôtre. Now, on 23 March 1683, the foundation stone for a new royal palace was laid in England.

Nothing on a similar scale had been planned for years: the work at Greenwich begun at the start of the reign had never been completed and life at Newmarket had been conducted on altogether a more modest scale. The palace at Winchester owed its origin directly to Charles II's admiration for splendiferous Versailles and in design it resembled the work of Le Vaux there.[37] Its geographical site in southern England also fitted in with the concept 'of another way of ruling'.

The love affair with Newmarket, begun in the halcyon sixties, had faded. The trouble was that Newmarket lay in an area already dotted with the great palaces of the Whig lords. There was no way that the King could cut a more imposing figure than his own nobility, since all the available land had already been commandeered. The fire in his Newmarket lodgings which had enabled him to elude the Rye House assassination gave him an excuse to look elsewhere; the connection of this conspiracy and the Newmarket route was in any case an uncomfortable one. The King's eye fell on Winchester, which lay in the balmy south in Hampshire: an area where – on the whole – men and magnates were Royalists. More romantically, Winchester was on the way to that coast and those coastal towns, including Portsmouth, which nursed the Navy. Like many an enthusiast since, the King could go yachting off the Isle of Wight. The King expected to be able to see the fleet at Spithead from his projected palace; what fairer prospect?

The dwelling, designed by Sir Christopher Wren, was to be surrounded by a park and connected to the town's historic cathedral by a 'stately street'. It would lie east and west. There were to be 160 rooms, surmounted by a lofty cupola which would be visible from the sea. The grand staircase was to be ornamented with marble columns, a gift to the King from the Duke of Tuscany. Then there were to be a central portico and two wings, as well as a raised terrace all the way round, such as dignified Windsor Castle. As for the park, here a thirty-foot cascade was proposed; the King hoped to repeat his success with ornamental water in St James's Park. A river through the park was intended to be navigable by small vessels. The park itself, an eight-mile circuit, would open into the forest, suitable for stag-hunting. Back at the palace, stables, kennels and mews would house the equipment of the chase.[38]

In September 1682 Evelyn described the King as 'mightily pleased' by his plans; building began the following May. He intended Winchester, wrote Evelyn, to be the seat of 'autumnal field diversions' (as Newmarket had once been).[39] Long before the structure became habitable, the Court flocked down to the grave and charming cathedral town. They devoured it for lodgings, as once they had raided Oxford, producing an atmosphere of revelry reminiscent of Comus' rout. The houses of the

Cathedral clergy were not immune. During the King's early visits he lodged with the Bishop of the town, to the extent that a polite enquiry was made whether he intended to make the Bishop's house his inn.

A King was one thing but a mistress was another. When a new Bishop was needed for Winchester, it was made clear to the incoming incumbent that his duties included lodging his sovereign. But Thomas Ken was furious at the sacrilege of being asked to house Nell Gwynn. He considered it sacrilege on the not unreasonable grounds that 'a woman of ill-repute ought not to be endured in the house of a clergyman,' adding, 'least of all that of the King's chaplain'. Ken's fervour did him no harm. Later, when the bishopric of Bath and Wells fell empty, Charles recalled the incident – 'God's fish! the little black fellow who would not give poor Nelly a night's lodging' – and laughingly approved Ken's appointment. As for Nell Gwynn, she found a niche at the deanery, overruling further protests.[40]

In the last year of the King's life virtually the whole of September was spent at Winchester. Considerable expenses were also run up for furniture for the future for both King and Queen; for example, green damask chairs and stools embroidered in gold and white silk were ordered for Catharine, green remaining a favourite colour. The main expense was of course the structure itself. Only a shell had been completed when the King died – outside walls and a roof – but various payments had been authorized, although, in the general fashion of the time, not necessarily paid. The £90,000 found in the King's strong-box after his death was probably intended for this purpose. It was indeed expense rather than distaste for the new palace which caused James to halt building immediately on his brother's death. He probably intended to return to it at a leisure moment in his reign: but such a moment never arrived.

So Winchester Palace lingered on, the subject of vague royal plans from time to time. Queen Anne contemplated it as a residence for her consort Prince George of Denmark; in the end the financial demands of her foreign wars took precedence. French prisoners-of-war were incarcerated there in the middle of the eighteenth century, and in the Napoleonic wars the quondam palace was used as a barracks. At the end of the nineteenth century it finally burnt down. It was a melancholy end for a project which had once been intended to rival Versailles; at least the Versailles imitation of Ludwig of Bavaria, Herrenchiemsee, survives on its island, more substantial if equally melancholy.

The true memorial to Winchester Palace lies in the eager conversation of Charles II with Lord Bruce on one of the last evenings of his life. The King spoke with enthusiasm of the 'favourite castle' he was building, and how he would arrange for Bruce to be in waiting there. 'I shall be so happy this week as to have my house covered with lead,' he exclaimed.[41] As the King's body was wrapped in its lead coffin within the week, it was a prophecy – of the ambiguous sort beloved of the Greek oracle – that came grimly true.

In the last years of Charles II, his restless mind did not cease to turn over new schemes, explore new horizons. Less power-obsessed, more fruitful than Winchester Palace was another foundation – that of the Royal Hospital, Chelsea, in 1682.[42] This home for veteran soldiers, or for those incapacitated by wounds, was created directly on the model of the Kilmainham Hospital, Dublin, recommended by Sir Stephen Fox to the King. The site of Chelsea College, which had been founded by James I for controversialists against Catholicism and had then been granted to the Royal Society, was purchased for £1,300. Fox put up the money. Yet even here the influence of Louis XIV was felt: Monmouth, describing to his father the Hôtel des Invalides, a similar form of hostel built in 1670 in Paris, had also ignited his imagination.[43] In-Pensioners, as the residents were termed, were to be organized on military lines, and occupy a single quadrangle known as Figure Court. (The Royal Hospital today is considerably expanded, although Figure Court still exists.)

The Royal Hospital was not opened until 1692, by which date Charles II had been seven years in his house of lead. It fell into the kind of financial difficulties which might be expected and the money granted in maintenance proved hard to come by. Nevertheless, Founder's Day was regularly celebrated on 29

May – Oak Apple Day and the King's Birthday – in honourable acknowledgement of his part in it all.*

Not only the welfare of his Army and the well-being of his fleet were dear to the King's heart. He had other far-flung interests. In general, the reign of Charles II saw a remarkable accession of distant lands to the English flag. The great Hudson's Bay Company was founded in 1670. Not only in North America, but in the West Indies and West Africa, this was an age of territorial expansion and, above all, commercial energy. Along with his concern for soldiers and sailors, this nascent feeling for 'empire' was something which Charles II had in common with his great predecessor Cromwell. So unalike in so many ways, the two men shared a vague missionary feeling for the benefits of British rule extended, which was in its own fashion a kind of patriotism. In the case of Charles II, his curiosity drove him on, even if he did not understand the economic implications of colonial aggrandizement.

In India, for example, it was the great trading companies which were the sovereigns, not Charles II. The latter was quite content to hand over Queen Catharine's dowry of Bombay, which it had taken several years to possess owing to local opposition, to the East India Company. In April 1681 Charles II granted a vast tract of land, now Pennsylvania, to William Penn the Quaker – no doubt a far more congenial activity than his disbanding of the Oxford Parliament, which took place about the same time, particularly as it was in discharge of a Crown debt. He liked to hear details of life in the Carolinas, where busy colonists were enjoying a more fruitful kind of exile than he had known. Life in Tangier, because of its military importance, was something he could probably understand more readily; he took the eventual evacuation of the fortress hard.

At home in July 1683 there took place a royal event which might even, had Providence decreed, have granted one final

---

* The actual date changed; first it was too close to the birthday of George III on 4 June; then, in the 1920s, it was too close to the Chelsea Flower Show, celebrated in its grounds. Founder's Day and its Parade is now held on the Thursday of the first week in June.

satisfaction: a peaceful future for the monarchy. This was the marriage of James' daughter Anne to Prince George of Denmark. In this same year Bishop Burnet had made 'a melancholy speculation' on the withering of the Protestant succession in 'this family that [once] put forth so fair and promising a blossom'.[44] It was true that at the time of Anne's marriage the legitimate succession, Protestant or Catholic, was problematic. As had happened once before to the royal family of Stuart in Scotland, the harvest of descendants of James I had suddenly become a very meagre one; this despite the fruitful marriages of Charles I and Elizabeth of Bohemia, with six and thirteen surviving children respectively.

The two Catholic daughters of Madame were as yet childless: Marie Louise was married without children and Anne Marie, from whom Madame's line descends, did not marry until the following year. The Catholic Mary Beatrice Duchess of York had not yet succeeded in producing offspring who survived childhood. As for the Protestants, Mary of Orange had been married for six years and showed no signs of producing any heirs. The vast family of Elizabeth of Bohemia had proved itself as yet astonishingly infertile: the Elector Palatine was childless, while one sister had succeeded Madame as the next Duchesse d'Orléans, which put her within the unsuitable French Catholic orbit. Prince Rupert had died a bachelor at the end of the previous year.

The hand of the eligible Anne had been sought within England itself, notably by the Earl of Mulgrave. The King angrily snubbed his pretensions. An outside claimant was the Prince of Hanover, the son of Anne's youngest Palatine cousin the Electress Sophia (from his line, ironically enough, was to spring Anne's own successor). George of Denmark was widely rated to be a French-inspired choice, because the King of Denmark fell within the diplomatic network controlled by Louis XIV. In the Cambridge University *epithalamiun* celebrating the match, Matthew Prior referred to it gloriously as the mating of Venus and Mars. Given the protagonists, that was perhaps going a little far.

Nevertheless, very soon this amiable Protestant pair did

produce a child. Little significance was attached to the fact that this first baby died: it was merely one of the commonplace griefs of the time. The important point was that Princess Anne had proved herself fertile. Other children would surely follow. No one could foresee that the unfortunate woman would be condemned to bear seventeen children, not one of whom survived childhood.

As the last year of the life of King Charles II dawned, from the point of view of the monarchy there was no longer any reason to fear and much reason to hope.

CHAPTER TWENTY-SIX

The Dregs of Life

No one would live past years again,
Yet all hope pleasure in what yet remains,
And from the dregs of life think to receive
What the first spritely running could not give....

John Dryden

The last year of the King's life was exteriorly a tranquil one. His country was at peace and he took care that it should remain so. A soft sunlight of prosperity illumined the perilous landscape of his finances: however transient these shafts, they were enough to light him to the end of his reign. No major domestic embroilment ruffled the calm of these autumnal days – neither the angry debates of a Parliament nor the demands of a Pumpkin Plot nor official cries of anguish on the subject of the succession.

The French subsidy, which had been phased over three years, came to an end in theory (although the money had not yet been paid in full).[1] In any case the King remained openly, even gaily pro-French. He sent a message of congratulation to Louis XIV on his acquisition of Luxembourg. The Truce of Ratisbon in the summer of 1684 confirmed the French monarch not only in that precious possession but also Strasbourg. Without English help, there was no way that the United Provinces could play an aggressive part in keeping the French wolf at bay: the checking of this all-conquering animal would have to wait for another day, another reign.

The foreign policy of Charles II gave him no trouble at all during the last year of his life because, while it was emotionally pro-French, that meant being practically neutral.

Two matters could however have plagued him, had he allowed them to do so. One was the continued incarceration of Danby in the Tower of London, five years after he had been consigned there (without a formal trial). The other was the return of Parliament, which had now been dissolved for over three years; this was a significant period, although the Act of 1664 left it conveniently to the King to decide to call Parliament; there was no machinery to compel him to do so. One matter bothered the King, the other his opponents. As it fell out, one was resolved successfully, the other not. In both cases the result was only to further the King's mastery over the political scene.

The freeing of Danby on bail was not quite such a simple matter as the alterations in the character of the judiciary, stressed earlier, might have promised. Indeed, the anxiety of the judges concerned not to act in any way outside their own consciences illustrates an important point about them. Merely believing in the sanctity of the royal prerogative did not make the judges corrupt: it was a question of political conviction leading (generally) to docility, rather than a built-in pliability.

Danby in the Tower became quite desperate early in 1684, when there was a change of judges on the Court of the King's Bench. Holloway and Wallcott, the newcomers, asked for a longer time to consider the matter of giving Danby his freedom. On learning from his daughter-in-law, Lady Scroop, that the King had 'good intentions' towards him, Danby wrote back to Charles in alarm, 'But I would find that was not sufficient....' As to the new judges' plea for more time: 'If your Majesty will please yourself to let these two Judges know your mind and not let them be left to be informed by others I shall have relief this term.' Otherwise Danby feared to wait for the next legal term, and then any judge would once again ask for more time and so forth and so on. 'The way to my liberty is very obvious,' cried Danby.[2] He meant through the exercise of the royal will.

The judges did free Danby. The supposition is that the King had a private word in the ear of Holloway and Wallcott. Certainly Charles swore to Danby's son, as the latter duly reported back to his father, 'If the judges would not bail you ... by god he would free you himself.'³ But it did not come to that. The judges, including Jeffreys, satisfied their consciences and Danby was bailed against an enormous surety of £20,000 to appear in the House of Lords in the next session to answer the charges against him. Four peers put up £5,000 each. The very day of his release Danby appeared before the King and, on kissing hands, bewailed his long imprisonment. The King shrugged off the complaint: he replied that it was against his will and left it at that. At least Danby was free to commence his ascent back into public service and would, it seems, have formed part of a new administration in 1685 had not such a development been cut off by the King's death.⁴

The question of Parliament was equally resolved, but negatively. Within the King's own councils, Halifax at least believed that the spirit of the Triennial Act should be respected. But in March the King told Barrillon that he had 'no thought' of summoning a Parliament. In case the point should be missed by those further from the centre of power than the Byzantine Barrillon, Sunderland sent a circular letter on the King's behalf to the Lords Lieutenant and others. There were rumours that there was to be a new Parliament: but his subjects were to be disabused immediately of the notion, 'he [the King] having as yet no such intention'. As to the idea that there were or might be tumultuous petitions from the country for a Parliament (remember those odious Whiggish petitions which had made the time of the Popish Plot additionally uncomfortable): the King 'cannot but utterly dislike and condemn any such attempt'. He regarded such petitions as 'seditious practices inconsistent with the peace and quiet of the kingdom'.⁵

By October, as a result, the Whigs were reported to be quite cowed: 'I never knew the Whigs in London so wary of managing their discourse and of their company. If three or four be together on the Exchange talking of news or what each has to communicate, if two or more of their own party join them, part of the rest walk away....'⁶

In May 1684 the Duke of York took his place in the Privy Council once more. It was the final step in his restoration. He had been absent for eleven years. Now the King was confident enough to introduce him without fear of trouble. At about the same time Titus Oates was arrested at a coffee-house in London on a charge of *scandalum magnatum* against the Duke of York for calling him a traitor. Tried briefly by Jeffreys, he was sentenced to a token fine of £100,000 – token because of course there was no question of his paying it; thus Oates was consigned to prison and irons were put upon him. This preliminary fall of Oates (far worse things were to happen to him once James ascended the throne) marked a reaction against him which had begun just about the time that James' own star began to rise. From 1681 onwards Oates was no longer the secure and boastful rascal he had once been; in August 1682 he had lost his government pension.

James, triumphant, was restored to his former post as Lord High Admiral in all but name: the King continued to sign documents since the provisions of the Test Act were still officially in force, but the moving spirit was that of James.

It was a fortunate restoration for the Navy itself. The Navy, once a favourite child, had suffered signally not only from the departure of James in 1673 but also from that of Samuel Pepys in 1679. Pepys, that mastermind of creative organization, had acted as secretary to the Lord Commissioners after the fall of James, when the Admiralty was put to commission. He was driven from office and into the Tower of London – repository for the unlucky as well as the damned in this period – by intrigues based on his connection with the Catholic Duke of York.

Thereafter the King had been both too poor and too busy to remedy the situation. Those sums of money which were voted by Parliament were inefficiently administered. Matters drifted downwards until only twenty-four ships were actually at sea, and some of the new ships had never managed to leave the harbour.[7] Now the brothers were united to invigorate the Navy as it deserved: and Pepys, rescued, drew up a scheme for its reformation (put into commission in 1685 and finished in 1688).

Appropriately enough, to the last year of Charles' reign also belongs his support of Captain Grenville Collins, the royal hydrographer. A survey of the coasts of Great Britain was to be undertaken, for which the King recommended subscriptions and practical help, especially from naval officers and traders. The result, which the King predicted correctly would be 'of great use for the safety of navigation', was printed in 1693, and emerged as Collins' *Great Britain's Coasting Pilot.*[8] It was good that, where the Navy and navigation were concerned, the reign ended as it had begun, on a high note of investment for the future.

The rebirth of the Duke of York as a public (as opposed to private) figure of influence was also at the bottom of the government changes which occurred in August 1684. Slightly mysterious because their effects were so soon blighted by the King's death, these changes were clear in one thing: they worked to James' advantage by diminishing the power of Rochester and enhancing that of James' ally Sunderland.[9]

Having left Scotland with some feeling of accomplishment, James now turned his attention to Ireland. The plain truth was that Ireland had prospered under Charles II – if only its riches had not been drained out of the country to meet the needs of the King and Court. Some of its riches, although siphoned off, had not even got that far. Lord Ranelagh, the Lord Treasurer, was finally dismissed for peculation and the collection of taxes handed over to Revenue Commissioners under Lord Longford, a talented financier. James' aim, a laudable one by the standards of Ireland today, if not of England then, was to introduce more Catholics into the administration there.

The palace revolution at Whitehall could be made to fit into the overall Irish plan. Rochester was kicked upstairs, losing his post as First Lord of the Treasury for that of the Lord President of the Council. 'The King hath given me a great deal of ease and a great deal of honour,' commented Rochester wryly. Charles himself was careful to note that 'he did not make these Alterations out of any Dissatisfaction'.[10] But the hand of Rochester's open critic, Halifax, can be detected. Halifax, while his attitude to such major topics as Parliament and foreign policy was ignored, could still be made useful. It was however Sunderland, not Halifax, who ultimately benefited. The coveted post at the Treasury went to Sunderland's ally Godolphin.

Rochester was also promised a more lucrative position, that of the Lord Lieutenancy of Ireland, occupied over a long period of time, if intermittently, by the great Ormonde. There Rochester had the prospect of making himself both rich and secure. Once again Sunderland stepped in, and, acting in alliance with the Duke of York, saw to it that Rochester would not enjoy the independent viceregal style of an Ormonde. As Ormonde's son reported, matters were to be very differently organized in Ireland and therefore Rochester, 'who fears no odium', had been selected for that purpose. Ormonde himself had no great regrets at losing the Lord Lieutenancy under the new deal: for now the power of making army appointments was to be stripped away from the Lord Lieutenant. All such decisions and appointments were to be made in London. 'From this difficulty, I thank God and the King I am delivered,' commented Ormonde vigorously.[11]

Rochester never took up his emasculated appointment, the King's death bringing about yet another revolution in the political situation. But the whole handling of affairs both in London and Dublin demonstrated the new control of the York–Sunderland axis. It is unlikely that Halifax himself would have survived long at the centre and the King's reign been further extended.[12]

Where the succession was concerned, neither Monmouth nor William of Orange had now the muscle to bar the smooth ascent of the Duke of York towards his legitimate goal. In the autumn the King felt particular indignation all over again at the news of William's 'extraordinary caressing' of Monmouth in Holland. Charles forbade his own envoy to visit William for the time being; furthermore, the royal anger was to be conveyed both to the Dutch States and to William's ministers. In vain William's own ambassador in London protested his master's innocence of any conspiracy. The King's response was forthright.

'It is as if a man going to a brothel should ask me to believe and accept the excuse that he had done no wrong because he had only gone in to convert people …,' exclaimed Charles in derision. The Ambassador was left rather feebly responding that although anyone entering a brothel must be 'suspect', yet his general character should also be taken into account, and if he was a man of 'probity and honour', the King should be prepared to listen to his explanation.[13] The Ambassador should perhaps have realized that where the English succession and the Whig opposition were concerned, Charles considered neither his nephew nor his son men of probity or honour.

There was a wistful notion entertained by Monmouth's admirers after the King's death – still occasionally resurrected even now – that some time during the last autumn Monmouth was actually promised the succession.[14] Monmouth himself spoke wildly on the subject after his father's death, when there was no-one to contradict him. It is true that the forbidden favourite did slip into England from Holland at the end of November. He was accompanied by Henrietta Wentworth. The Duke of York, for one, when he got wind of the foray, comforted himself with the thought that Monmouth was after a settlement of his mistress's estates upon himself. As for a reconciliation, 'there is no real danger of it,' James wrote firmly up to Scotland, 'H.M. having no inclination to receive his [Monmouth's] deceiving submissions again....'[15]

In one sense, the Duke of York was wrong. There was probably some kind of limited reconciliation, although the King in his secretive way left no record of the encounter and did not even confirm to his brother that it had taken place. An enthusiastic letter written to Monmouth from Halifax on 3 February spoke of his 'business', which he had heard was 'almost as well as done' but must be 'so sudden as not to leave room for 39 [code for the Duke of York]'s party to counterplot'.[16]

Yet given the King's knowledge of Monmouth's character and given what had only just transpired in Holland, it is unlikely that this reconciliation amounted to more than the mere prospect of Monmouth returning to England. The conditions would probably have been stringent and, as after the Rye House Plot, humiliating. The Duke of York was therefore right in his further assumption that no 'real danger' to his own cause was presented by Monmouth's clandestine journey. Had the reconciliation genuinely produced a violent change in the King's feelings he would hardly have kept his mouth shut on the subject. As we shall see, he maintained this silence even on his death-bed. Once again in his enthusiasm Monmouth was the victim of his own over-optimistic and self-deceiving nature. The tranquillity of the King's public life was not disturbed at last by the maverick sortie of his erstwhile favourite son.

So far as we can tell, the interior man was tranquil too. Of all people in the world, King Charles II was in a position to test the truth of Dryden's dictum on the subject of old age:

> No one would live past years again,
> Yet all hope pleasure in what yet remains,
> And from the dregs of life think to receive
> What the first spritely running could not give....

Much of Charles' 'spritely running' had been spent literally eluding his own and his father's enemies in the crippling period of exile: no one could have wished to relive those bitter years again. The more recent past, including the long war of attrition with Parliament, brought its own memories of danger and suffering. Yet from the 'dregs' of his own life it was true that there were pleasures still to be tasted.

This was no Henry VIII, a monstrous figure bloated with disease. The King's upright appearance impressed observers. A portrait of him as Founder of the Royal Society, commissioned by Christ's Hospital, was painted by M. Laroon in 1684. With a background of ships, and an appropriate foreground of a globe and other aids to navigation, it shows a strong man unbowed. His energy continued to startle and confound even those who had known it to their cost for years. It is true that he was having trouble with a sore on his leg as well as painful gout; the long walks were reluctantly cut down. His keenness was now channelled into his laboratory, where he would devote himself to his experiments for hours at a time in the same obsessional manner. Besides, the King believed the delay in the walks was only temporary. Soon he would be striding out once more, outdistancing courtiers and subjects alike, pausing only for the demands of the ducks. In the last winter of his life, he was described by Bishop Burnet as looking 'better than he had done for many years'.[17]

Unlike that of Henry VIII, the character of Charles II was not permanently marred by savagery, even if he had displayed something verging on it, in recent years. One effect of England's public calm was to enable Charles II to regain that unruffled air with which he preferred to confront the world at large. The plotting was over; the trials were through; Shaftesbury was dead; the Whigs were cowed. His ministers were there to conduct the country along the guide-lines he had evolved; his brother was there to provide the vim and vigour of the policy and if necessary to take the brunt of the unpopularity. A typical anecdote was related by the playwright John Crowne, who was in negotiation with the King over that adaptation of a Spanish play referred to in Chapter 18. Crowne swore that he overheard the King say to the Duke of York, 'Brother, you may travel, if you will, I am resolved to make myself easy for the rest of my life.' There are other variants of the same story: we must accept that the King harped upon the theme as his life drew to its close. To Sir Richard Bulstrode, the English Resident in Brussels, he spoke warmly of the people of Flanders, but as for himself: 'I am weary of travelling, and am resolved to go abroad no more. But when I am dead and gone, I know what my brother may do: I am much afraid that when he comes to wear the crown he will be obliged to travel again. And yet I will take care to leave my kingdoms to him in peace....'[18] Part of the King's 'easiness' consisted in radiating a fatherly benevolence, now that he had brought about peace at home by defeating those who had sought to defeat him.

The winter of 1683 was one of the most severe ever recorded; the King, who had himself known vividly what it was like to be cold and hungry, gave particular orders for the relief of the poor. His subjects' welfare in distress was indeed an interest he maintained throughout his reign. His efforts after the Fire of London have been remarked; in 1675 he gave the town of Northampton, badly damaged by its own Great Fire, one thousand tons of wood from his estates – thirty-six years later the Mayor and Corporation showed their appreciation by erecting a statue to him, still to be seen today, above the portico of All Saints' Church.

In 1683 there was at least one benefit to be derived from the ice and snow. The new sport of skating flourished. Nahum Tate wrote of the popular enthusiasm in his elaborate way:

> Ourselves without the aid of Tide or Gale
> On Keels of polish't steel securely sail....

Yes, the King too was securely sailing. And the ice beneath his feet was no longer thin and cracking. The vast statue erected to him at the Royal Exchange was one symbol of the powerful stability of the monarchy. Less tangible but equally real was the affection felt for the sovereign by his subjects. Halifax, weighing up his last period from a critical standpoint, had to admit that 'in his autumnal fortune' there still remained 'a stock of warmth in men's hearts for him'.[19] This warmth was reciprocated.

King Charles II, wrote Bishop Burnet, was the greatest instance in history of the various revolutions of which any one man was capable. His deathbed, fittingly, was to be the scene of yet one more. Played out over nearly a week, a fugue for alternating voices of hope and despair, it also involved his secret conversion to a proscribed Faith.[20]

The drama began quite suddenly on a Sunday night. It was 1 February 1685. The day itself had passed placidly enough. The King's leg still bothered him. He told Sir Richard Mason that he did not feel well, but believed that it would pass. He could not take his favourite constitutional; instead, he went for a drive with his attendant Thomas Lord Bruce, whose period of waiting had begun the previous Monday and was due to end on the morrow. It is thus to Bruce that we owe many of the most affecting details of his master's last days, still vivid in his memory when he wrote his memoirs many years later.* At supper the

* These and various other sources for the King's death-bed are considered and collated in Raymond Crawfurd, *The Last Days of Charles II*, 1909. But Crawfurd's list of sources is not exhaustive: amongst others an interesting account by Anne Margaret, wife of Sir Richard Mason, second Clerk Comptroller of the Household, printed in *Household Words*, 9 (1854), as by 'a wife of a person about the Court at Whitehall', is omitted by Crawfurd.

King ate his customary hearty meal, but it included something out of the ordinary, a couple of goose eggs. Afterwards Bruce sought both natural and supernatural explanations of the King's collapse. On the one hand, he blamed the eggs, on the other hand, he divined in the sudden extinction of a vast wax candle held by a page, 'where no wind was to be found', a fearful omen of what followed.

At the time the King merely carried out his usual practice after supper and loped off to the apartments of Louise to see who might have been supping there. These were the rooms whose indiscreet opulence both enchanted and shocked John Evelyn. Here Louise held her own not-so-mimic court. More rounded than ever, the King's 'Fubbs' was also more cherished since an illness in November which had held the Court in a state of well publicized public distress. On this occasion a high game of basset was being played, which also shocked Evelyn. His eyes widened at the sight of £2,000 in gold on the table, with about twenty courtiers and 'other dissolute persons' surrounding it – all this on a Sunday to boot! For Evelyn the tale lost no moral in the telling: 'Six days after was all in the dust,' he wrote with doleful glee.[21]

It seems more relevant to the life of King Charles II that he spent the last active night of his life in his own version of peaceful domesticity. Evelyn also professed himself appalled to see the King 'toying' with 'Cleveland' and 'Mazarin' (Barbara and Hortense respectively, both returned to England and restored to friendly favour), as well as his hostess 'Portsmouth'. A French boy was singing love songs in the background. These songs may have been recent imports from the Court of France, but as for the great ladies they, if anything, represented love's old sweet song. Not one of them could be remotely considered young and between them one way and another they could number nearly fifty years in the King's service. The evening was therefore marked as much by the King's fidelity to old friends as by profligacy.

Afterwards there were plenty of people to bear witness that they had never seen the King in a better mood. Bruce duly conducted his master to bed: it was at this point that the wax candle was so ominously extinguished (although it is surely straining credulity to suggest that *no* draught could be responsible in a corridor in February – in the seventeenth century). The King put on his nightgown. Bruce, as Gentleman-in-waiting, and Harry Killigrew, as Groom of the Bedchamber, were to share his room according to custom. The King lay down to sleep.

That night the vast, sprawling Palace of Whitehall was restless. There were the endless striking clocks, none of which kept time with each other, chiming through the small hours. There was the flickering, shooting light of the Scotch coal in the enormous grate, lighting up rich tapestries and dusty corners. There were the King's indulged dogs, a whole pack of them in the very bedroom and even in the bed, the bitches and their whelps whimpering and shifting. Bruce, the Lord-in-waiting, could not sleep. None of these sounds, however disturbing, was unusual. Besides, Bruce was going off duty the next day – he could sleep then.

What was both unusual and disquieting was the fact that the King himself tossed and turned. Normally he was a very heavy sleeper when he finally got to bed (worn out no doubt by his various versions of physical exercise). He even muttered occasionally in his sleep, as Calpurnia cried out before the death of Caesar, something Lord Bruce had never known him do before. Robert Howard, another Groom, hearing of this, commented, 'Lord! that is an ill mark, and contrary to his custom.'

When the King did awake, he looked quite different. His normally olive complexion was 'pale as ashes'. He went immediately, still earing only his nightgown, into his Privy Closet just off the bedroom. When Howard went to join him, he found the King completely silent. Buckling on his garters, Howard took a worried look at his face and exclaimed, 'Sir, how do you do?' The King merely blew out his cheeks and 'puffed' as he did when he was vexed.

In the meantime, the royal doctors were actually waiting in the antechamber to the bedroom to dress the tiresome sore on his leg. As time passed and still the King did not emerge from his closet, the worried Bruce searched for William Chiffinch, the King's Keeper of the Closet (and confidant), to take his master something thicker to wear than a mere nightgown. Etiquette forbade anyone other than Chiffinch to enter the closet unbidden. In the end it was Chiffinch, who had carried out so many more cheerful errands in the past, who conducted the King out of the closet back into the bedroom.

The King's speech was obviously by this time seriously impaired, if not worse. The Earl of Craven, proffering him a paper on which were written the passwords (for the guards) for the new month, could get no response. The King could only occasionally manage a few disjointed words, such as 'All-All' when trying to discuss the death of Lord Allington.[22] At one point he began to mutter in French: in what shadows of the past was his mind lurking?

But the King did manage a little sherry and China Orange. And because no one dared to take it upon themselves to interrupt his routine – although it must have been obvious that he was dangerously sick – his barber Follier now proceeded to shave his master as usual.

The King was sitting as was his wont, with his knees against the window, and Follier was just fixing the linen round his neck, when the King gave vent to the most extraordinary and piercing noise. Afterwards described by one as 'the dreadfullest shriek' and by another as an 'exclamation as one that dies suddenly', it was clearly audible outside the chamber.[23] Then the King sank back into Bruce's arms, unconscious. It was exactly eight o'clock in the morning. It could no longer be denied that something was horribly, even catastrophically, wrong.

The responsibility for making the first decision about treatment fell upon Bruce, the senior gentleman present. By this time one of the doctors, Sir Edmund King, had arrived in the bed-chamber and had witnessed the incident. Bleeding was the obvious remedy of the time. And bleed the King this doctor now proceeded to do in style, while a panic-stricken message was sent off to the Duke of York and the rest of the Privy Council were summoned as hastily as possible. By the time a Privy Council of sorts had gathered together in the outer room at midday, Charles had had sixteen ounces of blood removed via a vein in his arm, a task for which the doctor was afterwards paid £1,000.[24]

Soon other doctors came flocking in as the news of the King's collapse reached them. A series of remedies were frantically applied. The King's head was shorn. Cantharides was used as a blistering agent. A further eight ounces of blood was removed. And as a result of these steps – or despite them – the King did actually recover. Two hours later his speech had come back.

He found the Duke of York beside him. The Duke was once more in command of the situation, as he had been in 1679, but it was a token of the general disarray that he had forgotten to put on both his shoes and was still wearing one slipper. One of the first things the King did, with his speech returned, was to ask for the Queen. He also explained what had happened to him earlier: how he had felt ghastly on rising and had immediately gone to his closet to take some of the so-called King's Drops, made up in his own laboratory out of extract of bone after a formula of Dr Jonathan Goddard. Leaving his closet, the last thing he could remember was feeling intensely giddy. The King was now laid on his bed.

All round the relief was incredible. The official newsletter of the day, referring to 'the fit' which had seized the King, was also able to pronounce him out of danger. It was to be, surely, a repetition of those illnesses of 1679 onwards – sharp but short-lived.

Immediate precautions had been taken following the King's seizure. Horse guards and foot guards were posted everywhere in Whitehall. Sentries were reinforced. Above all, the ports were stopped. No passengers or ships were allowed in or out. Even in his agony – and he wept unashamedly beside his brother – the Duke of York was quite clear that for the time being no message should reach the Duke of Monmouth, or for that matter the Prince of Orange, lest they try to turn the situation to their advantage. A few days later outgoing traffic was allowed to continue, but incoming was still banned. Only Barrillon, as usual receiving most favoured treatment, was allowed to transmit a solitary letter to Louis XIV. Similar precautions had followed the death of Oliver Cromwell (in order that Charles Stuart should not seize the day).

In the country the Lords Lieutenant were asked to keep themselves in readiness against a crisis. The Lord Mayor and other dignitaries of the now docile City of London were quick to show where *their* sympathies lay by sending a message of loyalty to the Duke of York. As for the common people, those whose affections the King had never lost throughout his autumnal fortune, they too demonstrated their sympathies by grieving openly: 'They cried as they walked the streets, and great sadness in all faces, and great crowds at all the gates.'[25]

In the general relief, the doctors at least did not let up on the application of their remedies. It was actually in the presence of his physicians – twelve of them by this time – that next morning, Tuesday, 3 February, the King was seized with another 'fit' or convulsion. Immediately and with renewed frenzy the remedies were stepped up and new ones were imported.

Lord Macaulay described Charles II on his death-bed as being tortured like an Indian at the stake. The comparison is apt, except that one doubts whether any tormentor of Indians ever had quite such a battery of instruments at his command as the seventeenth-century royal doctors. It has been estimated that a total of fifty-eight drugs were administered over five days, many of whose names are as exotic to us as their effects were painful to the King.

There was white hellebore root (a sneezing powder to clear his nose) and plasters of combined spurge and Burgundy pitch (these were applied to his feet), as well as plasters of cantharides on his head. The ingredients of the enemas which were applied frequently were rock salt and syrup of buckthorn. As an emetic, an orange infusion of metals, made in white wine, was employed. White vitriol was dissolved in paeony water; other remedies varied from the homely, such as the distillation of cowslip flowers, to the more striking spirit of sal ammoniac. An anti-spasmodic julep of black cherry water, oriental bezoar stone from the stomach of an East goat and spirits of human skull were amongst other cures named.

The poor King's body was purged and bled and cauterized

and clystered and blistered. Red-hot irons were put to his shaven skull and his naked feet. His urine became scalding through the lavish use of cantharides. Cupping-glasses and all the many weird resources of medicine at the time were applied. They all had one thing in common: they were extremely painful to the patient.

These prodigious efforts were much admired at the time. Colonel Thomas Fairfax, an Irish officer visiting London, hastened to write to Dublin of the employment of 'all the means that the art of man thought proper for the King's distemper'.[26] The doctor's report afterwards spoke of 'every kind of treatment attempted by Physicians of the greatest loyalty and skill'. The doctors did not exaggerate the universality of their treatments; their loyalty was doubtless incomparable; but they did somewhat gloss over their own incompetence. The King's mouth and tongue became 'much inflamed' with scalding medicines and where his teeth had been forced apart during convulsions. Not all the doctors were as skilled at blooding as Edmund King. James Pearse, Charles' Surgeon in Ordinary, and Surgeon General to the Navy and Land forces, could not find the jugular vein successfully, a desperate experience for the patient. Another doctor, Thomas Hobbs, who lived in nearby Fleet Street and was Surgeon to the Household and the King's troops of the Horse Guards, had to finish the job: for the efficiency he was later rewarded by inclusion in Dryden's poem on the King's death, 'Threnodia Augustalis'.[27]

The need to keep up the patient's strength through all this was however fully recognized: from time to time the King was given draughts of emulsion, light broth and liquid posset. At the same time the purges and emetics continued remorselessly to drain his resistance from him. Once again the comparison with torture arises, as when the tormenters are determined that their victim shall not finally elude them through death, and therefore fortify them.

Once again the King rallied. By the Wednesday morning he was distinctly better. He was however forbidden to speak. With a gleam of the old wit he observed that the edict would have killed Harry Killigrew, a notorious chatterbox, but 'he would obey it'. Dryden celebrated the wave of relief in the world at large:

> Friends to congratulate their friends made haste;
> And long inveterate foes saluted as they passed....

As usual with illnesses which may prove fatal, people behaved both well and badly. Burnet afterwards tried to create scandal by suggesting that Louise took care of Charles throughout as 'a wife of a husband'. In fact, the reverse was true. The ladies of the Court reacted entirely according to type. Louise, the ready weeper, swooned and had to be carried out for air. Nelly 'roared to a disturbance and was led out and lay roaring behind the door'.[28]

The Queen was overcome with pure grief and had to be carried back to her apartments in a state of collapse, or, as the poet more picturesquely put it,

> Which was nearest the Grave could scarce be seen
> The dying Monarch, or the living Queen....

But Princess Anne, who was pregnant again, was not allowed into her uncle's chamber because he looked so dreadful, with his eyeballs rolled back, that it was feared a miscarriage might ensue.[29]

Louise, once she recovered her energies, showed that practical streak in her nature of which she was never long devoid. According to Lady Mason's story, she sent her boxes of goods packing to the French Ambassador's house, where they would be safely stowed if things looked ugly. It was a wise precaution for a Catholic foreigner who had once been in danger of being arraigned as a common prostitute (and who, furthermore, had a lot of worldly goods to lose). Less appealing is the second half of the story that has Louise drawing off two great diamond rings from the King's fingers. Interrupted by the Duke of York, she is supposed to have blushed. At which James begged her courteously to proceed: 'No, Madam, they are as safe in your hands as mine. I will not take them till I see how they go.'

But the rings, according to Lady Mason's account, vanished from view for ever.[30] It is however unlikely that this ghoulish incident ever took place (although one can believe that Duchess Louise packed her bags) for sheer lack of opportunity.

In truth, one of the main features of the death-bed of King Charles II was its total lack of privacy. When a rather more serious matter was at stake than the future of a couple of rings – the future of the King's immortal soul – it would prove extraordinarily difficult to secure a moment's relief from the throng surrounding him. Just as the number of medicines proliferated, so did the interested observers. When the room came to be cleared on Thursday, it contained seventy-five assorted lords and Privy Councillors, surgeons and servants. By this time the company also included no fewer than five bishops.

Thomas Ken, the King's former chaplain, now Bishop of Bath and Wells, was the first of these to arrive. He appeared on the Wednesday morning, when the King was thought to be rallying. He was present on the Wednesday afternoon, when the King suffered another major convulsion and the hopes aroused by each small recovery were finally dashed. From the first, 'little Ken', as the King had familiarly termed him in the past, made his presence felt; the man who had refused Nelly her place at Winchester was not likely to flinch now from his duty. Ken had last administered Communion to the King at Christmas. He now pressed the King to receive it again. Charles however steadfastly declined to do so, giving two contradictory reasons: first, there was no particular hurry, and secondly, he was too feeble to receive it. He was silent too when Ken asked him to declare himself a member of the Church of England, either because his voice was weak or because some deeper emotion was already stirring within his failing body.

Towards the evening of Wednesday the King's condition worsened. He broke out in a cold sweat. He also suffered from intermittent bouts of fever. That night six of the chorus of physicians watched by his bed as well as Lord Chesterfield, Lord Keeper Guilford and two others deputed by the Privy Council. The bulletin issued on Thursday morning was sanguine: the Privy Council 'conceive His Majesty to be in a condition of safety, and that he will in a few days be freed from his distemper'. But this of course referred to the apparent progress of Wednesday. The church bells began to ring, bonfires were readied, when the dramatic news began to leak out that the King was sinking. Silence stole over the city as vigils of continuous prayer in the royal chapels replaced the joyful cacophony of the bells.

Exactly what was wrong with the King? At four o'clock on Thursday afternoon, in the language of the doctors, there was 'some exacerbation or paroxysmal increase'. In other words, the convulsions were mounting. Great bouts of fever were shaking his body. Ironically enough, the same doctors who were so busy at the cure were still very much in the dark as to what they were curing. Their energies were great; but then so was their ignorance. Guilford angrily pointed out that, when finally taxed on the nature of the King's illness, they behaved in the Spanish way over difficult cases: *'Hazer il bove,* that is stared and said nothing.'

After the King's death the official verdict was apoplexy. It would be translated today more familiarly as a stroke. Apoplexy was a portmanteau word, much used in the seventeenth century and not necessarily narrowly defined: Lord Chesterfield called it 'a sort of apoplexy'. It is easy to believe that the King, like many middle-aged men, was suffering from high blood-pressure, followed by a stroke, brain damage and finally cardiac arrest. However, that verdict presents certain difficulties.

If the King had a stroke, then it is remarkable that he was never paralysed – paralysis down one side would have been expected. He also recovered his speech totally, while he never lost his reason. This point is not a purely academic one: for if the King had had a stroke, it could be argued that he was incapable of making a positive decision in favour of the Catholic faith. Yet it is clear from the account of Father Huddleston and others that his mind was quite clear, if his body was weak. The intermittent fevers or 'fits of ague' to which the doctors bear witness are equally puzzling if the King had had a stroke.

We may discount the usual titillating rumours of poison which surrounded the death-bed of Charles II, as with most other notable characters in the seventeenth century, including his grandfather and Oliver Cromwell. Monmouth, predictably, later accused the Duke of York of poisoning his brother. Other popular scapegoats were the servants of the Duchess of Portsmouth (presumably because they were Catholics and foreigners). One rumour had the King being killed by inhaling poisoned snuff. James Welwood, ardently advancing this view in the memoirs written later at the command of Queen Mary, had to admit, as a physician himself, that there were no outward signs of poisoning. But he sidestepped this neatly, in a manner worthy of twentieth-century spy fiction: 'It must be acknowledged that there are poisons ... of so subtle a nature that they leave no concluding marks upon the bodies of those they kill.'[31]

The fact that Peruvian bark of *cinchona* (the so-called Jesuit's powder) was now once again, as in 1679, used to treat the King's fever excited another suggestion in the nineteenth century. The Principal of the Calcutta Medical College formed the opinion that the King died of malaria, from his habit of feeding the ducks in St James's Park.* But the malaria *P. (plasmodium) vivax*, from which a great many people suffered in Europe in the seventeenth century, was not a lethal disease and should not be confused with the malaria *P. falciparum*, which swept away so many Europeans in India in the nineteenth.[32] One is glad to acquit the ducks and St James's Park.

Another enterprising theory has been recently advanced that the King poisoned himself slowly through his constant experiments, trying a process for the fixing of mercury; gradually he developed erethisma. Uraemia attendant on kidney failure is one of the common sequents of mercury poisoning. Thus the massive blood-letting caused a temporary recovery by removing the circulating toxins from the King's system: the nephritic damage was however irreparable. It is a tempting thesis, but further exploration is needed, since it is outlined in a very short article, in which the medical and historical evidence cited is far from exhaustive. As the authors themselves conclude, 'Further work

---

* See Norman Chevers, M.D., *An Enquiry into the Circumstances of the Death of King Charles the Second of England*, Calcutta 1861 (not mentioned in Crawfurd).

will no doubt be necessary....'* For example, the King's increased irritability as time went on is given as one proof of mercury poisoning: but that could be attributed to a number of causes, including quite simply advancing years.

At the present time the theory of Raymond Crawford, elaborately set out in 1909, still seems the most plausible: the King was suffering from chronic granular kidney disease (a form of Bright's disease) with uraemic convulsions. During the winter he had been plagued by gout. The fatal use of cantharides, to promote blistering on the first night of his illness, must have done much to rob the King's kidneys of their vestige of functional activity. The autopsy fitted exactly with what would now be expected of 'gouty kidney' coupled with uraemia. It would nevertheless not be fair to describe King Charles, as Macaulay did, as the victim of his doctors. The physicians did substantially increase his sufferings, while failing to alleviate the cause. But they did not kill him. The disease would have done so in any case.

In the end however most medical historical investigation, however fascinating, has a double disadvantage. First, there is never a body, let alone a patient, and the bones of Charles II have never, rightly, been troubled. Secondly, the medical language of the time, on which reliance has to be placed, is not precise by our standards. There can be no certainties. King Charles II was ageing and had endured some recent severe attacks of illness. Perhaps in the end the best verdict on the King's death was given in a poem by Abraham Cowley, addressed to his leading doctor, Sir Charles Scarburgh:

> Let Nature and Art do what they please,
> When all is done, Life's an Incurable Disease.

* See M. L. Wolbarsht, Naval Medical Research Institute, Bethesda, Maryland, and D. S. Sax, Psychiatric Institute, University Hospital, Baltimore, Maryland: 'Charles II, A Royal Martyr', in *Notes and Records of the Royal Society of London*, vol. 16, no. 2, November 1961. As they themselves point out in an Appendix to the article, Pascal's death 'was almost certainly not due' to mercury poisoning; as for Faraday's death, 'it would be difficult to say mercury was the specific cause....' Yet both Pascal and Faraday's experiments far outstripped those of Charles II.

The men of science proving useless, the men of God were given their turn. The Archbishop of Canterbury and the Bishops of London, Durham and Ely were now ranked round the King's bed, joining Bishop Ken. The King however paid no attention to these princes of the Church, perhaps because their nebulous and rather unattractive voices did not reach him. Ken, who had a voice 'like to a nightingale for the sweetness of it', fared better. He read the Prayers for the Sick out of the Book of Common Prayer.

In the meantime, a dangerous and different drama was being played out behind the scenes. It is not clear who made the original suggestion that the King should receive a Catholic priest. One obvious candidate was the Queen. As early as Monday Catharine had said to the Catholic Duchess of York: 'Sister, I beg you to tell the Duke that he, who knows as well as I do the King's convictions about the Catholic religion, should do what he can to take advantage of any opportunity that offers.' Mary Beatrice went to her husband. The Duke of York replied, 'I know, and I am thinking of nothing else.' But he took no action.[33]

The Duke's cautious attitude illustrates the extreme delicacy of the situation. The fact was that the King could well recover (and indeed subsequently did so, albeit temporarily). Then, although the Queen referred to the King's 'convictions' about the Catholic religion, a sentiment echoed by Louise, who described him as a Catholic 'at the bottom of his heart', neither lady pretended that these convictions had as yet been given public expression. Indeed, the nervousness of the King's intimate circle is yet another argument against the proposition that the King was already an established Catholic. It has been postulated throughout this book that the King never at any point underwent an official conversion – neither in his youth in exile, nor in 1669, nor in 1684 when he was rumoured at the French Court to have become a Catholic, nor at any other date. This whole death-bed episode, attested by so many witnesses, makes little sense if such a conversion had already taken place.

All the Catholics surrounding the King – all in their way branded by their religion – were well aware of the care with which he himself had avoided suffering similar damage. Catharine was in a particularly difficult position: a woman who had valued discretion throughout her time in England, she well knew that she was closely watched. The King had not asked for a Catholic priest. Catholicism was a proscribed religion; not only were its priests under heavy sentence, but many of them had recently been executed. Were his family now to involve Charles in something desperate and ruinous, for which a convalescent King would castigate them?*

Nevertheless, the question remained: given that the King intended to live as a 'public' Protestant, did he intend to die as a private one? The fateful move to introduce a Catholic priest was only made when the King was clearly dying, and then in fear and trembling. Catharine was not involved: her approach to Mary Beatrice on Monday, passing the responsibility to the Duke of York, was as far as she dared go.

The two people who did finally broach the matter were both in their different ways more reckless. Louise Duchess of Portsmouth received a visit from Barrillon in her apartments. He found her in the midst of her general grief, extremely agitated on the subject of the King's religion. She bewailed the fact that he was surrounded by Protestant bishops since, in her precisely limited observation, 'at the bottom of his heart the King is a Catholic'. Was there any possibility of a priest being produced? She herself could no longer enter his room 'with any decency' since the Queen was nearly always present. Barrillon, with his usual freedom of movement, could go to the Duke of York.

---

* There is of course the mysterious matter of the two papers 'containing about a quarter of a sheet on both sides' shown by James, then King, to Pepys about six months after his brother's death. These papers gave arguments in support of the Church of Rome. But it is not clear if they were in Charles II's own handwriting, annotated by him, or merely copies certified by James. Nor is it clear if these arguments were supposed to be Charles II's own composition or the arguments of others proposed by him. Most of the evidence concerning these papers is second if not third hand. (Pepys never wrote about the matter himself but reported it to Evelyn. Burnet heard about it from Thomas Tenison, but his account differs from that of Evelyn. Halifax would say no more than that the King 'might do it'.)[34] All one can reliably conclude is that Charles II continued to show an interest in the tenets of Catholicism.

The Queen being absent – she was being 'blooded' herself to alleviate her distressed condition – Barrillon delivered Louise's message.

A Capuchin monk, Padre Mansueti, one of the chaplains to the Duchess of York who came over to England with her, was also prompted to go to the Duke of York with the same message. He had been entertaining a Benedictine monk, Dom Gibbon, at dinner, when the news came that the King was sinking; Gibbon spurred on Mansueti to act.*

To Barrillon, James was said to have responded immediately with a characteristic declaration: 'I would rather risk everything than not do my duty on this occasion.' He told Barrillon he was aware that there was no time to lose. To Mansueti he was said to have been equally accommodating. It may be questioned whether these pleas were necessary: whether James the straight-forward believer would really have let his brother die as a Protestant. The answer seems to be that it was not until he knew his brother to be dying that he dared countermand his known policy, and then only when encouraged by Barrillon and, on another level, one of his priestly entourage. So close and secret had Charles kept his inner soul.

The introduction of a Catholic priest into the royal chamber remained a challenging task. For one thing, there were the Protestant bishops, innocent vultures unaware of the embarrassment their presence was causing: how could they be politely ejected? Even if that were accomplished, the problem of discovering a Catholic priest at short notice and smuggling him into Whitehall was even more horrendous in the fierce light of publicity which shone down upon the whole palace.

First of all, the King's consent still had to be gained. Only the Duke of York had the opportunity to do so. As discreetly as possible he bent down and whispered in his brother's ear. The King answered. From time to time James had to repeat his words, so low did he speak. The King himself was barely audible,

* See *A True Relation of the late King's Death*, by P. M. Dated early march 1685. Printed in full in J. G. Muddiman, 'The Death of Charles II', *The Month*, 1932. (Not mentioned in Crawfurd, cited above.)

except to those closest to him, who included Barrillon. But the King's basic answer remained the same: 'Yes, with all my heart.'

The King had agreed.

On Barrillon now devolved the duty of actually finding a priest. All parties concerned agreed that time was short. But there was an absurd complication. Those priests most readily available were the Queen's chaplains; for they were in a room divided from the King's only by the entrance to the Privy Stairs, used by Chiffinch and others to conduct visitors discreetly to him. The Queen's priests were not in on the secret – there seems to have been a general, if unacknowledged, conspiracy to keep the Queen's household clear of it for her own sake as well as the King's. That was less serious than the fact that they only spoke Portuguese, a language the King had never mastered.

The chaplains of the Duchess of York, on the other hand, spoke Italian, a language in which he was comparatively fluent. But these priests were both well known and extremely unpopular: they would be immediately recognized for what they were if they attempted to enter the King's chamber, with fatal results. And the Duke of York's apartments lay on the wrong side of the King's: entry from one to the other could be vetted by the watchful.

It was the Portuguese Count of Castelmelhor who pointed out the language barrier of the Queen's household. Barrillon and James between them therefore decided to tackle the house of the Venetian Resident, where they would find an Italian priest. Before they set off, Castelmelhor did look into the Queen's room. And there, by a merciful dispensation, he discovered Father Huddleston.

It had been a long road from Worcester for both parties. Mary Beatrice afterwards described Father Huddleston to the nuns at Chaillot as *'un homme très simple'*. She even regretted that a more suitable 'subject' could not have been found 'to help this great Prince make a good death'. She had presumably managed to avoid taking in (language barrier again) her brother-in-law's tales of escape and derring-do, which involved the good priest. Otherwise she must surely have realized that no more appropriate missionary could have been discovered.

Besides, if Father Huddleston had preserved a certain simplicity in the quarter of a century which had passed since Worcester, it was appropriate holy simplicity rather than something more rustic. Rewarded by the gratitude of the King after the Restoration, he had formed part of the household of two Queens, Henrietta Maria and Catharine; he was thus hardly a stranger to Court circles.

Disguised in a wig and a cassock, Father Huddleston was led from the Queen's suite of rooms to a closet just off the King's chamber which had a private communicating door. Here he waited. There was a further problem. Father Huddleston had not been bearing the Blessed Sacrament with him on his visit to the Queen's rooms (although he did have a viaticum of holy oil). So one of the Portuguese priests, Father Bento de Lemoz, had to be despatched outside the palace on the vital mission to secure a Host. In the meantime, the Duke of York cleared the King's room in soldierly fashion by simply announcing in a loud voice, 'Gentlemen, the King wishes everybody to retire except the Earls of Bath and Feversham.' The former, a fervent Royalist, was the Groom of the Stole; the latter, a Frenchman naturalized English, the Queen's chamberlain. But both gentlemen were Protestants, which helped to pacify the Bishops. Their continued attendance, which was contrary to the King's own wishes, was also due to James' concern that his dying brother's conversion should be seen to be voluntary; he did not want to be the sole witness to such a momentous event. When the room was ready, Chiffinch, who had brought so many clandestine night visitors to his master in the past, brought in one more, a man of God.

Charles II cried out with pleasure at the sight of Huddleston. The various accounts of the conversion scene vary in detail, but the King's general reaction to Huddleston was clear: 'You that saved my body are now come to save my soul.' He was certainly well aware of the providential element in the presence so close at hand of 'this good father, whom, I see, O good Lord, that Thou hast created for my good'.

Father Huddleston put a series of questions to the King. Did he wish to die in the Faith and the Communion of the Holy Roman Catholic Church? Did he wish to make a full confession of all his sins? To all these questions, Charles answered firmly, in a low but distinct voice. His resolution was clear. Then he made his general confession. Amongst the things for which he declared himself 'most heartily sorry' was the fact that 'he had deferr'd his Reconciliation so long' – these words on the lips of a dying man, reported by Father Huddleston without contradiction, being yet another proof, if proof were needed, that the King was not already a secret Catholic.* The King's confession ended in an act of contrition: 'Into Thy Hands, Sweet Jesus, I commend my soul. Mercy, Sweet Jesus, Mercy.' The priest gave him absolution.

Huddleston's last question concerned the Blessed Sacrament: 'Will you receive it?'

The King replied, 'If I were worthy of it, Amen.'

But since the Host had not yet arrived, Father Huddleston asked the King's leave to anoint him with the holy oil, in the Sacrament of Extreme Unction. To which the King agreed 'with all my heart'. When the Portuguese priest returned with the Host – probably from the chapel at Somerset House – Huddleston went to the side door and received it. The King, with a touching flash of the old spirit, tried to rise. As he struggled, he said, 'At least let me meet my heavenly Lord in a better posture than in my bed.' Father Huddleston calmed him: Almighty God, who saw into his heart, would accept his good intention.

So the King received the Catholic Communion and afterwards Huddleston sat quietly by him, reading the Catholic prayers for the dying in a low voice. It was by Charles' own request that Huddleston recited once again the Act of Contrition, ending 'Mercy, Sweet Jesus, Mercy.' Then the priest put a crucifix into the King's hands, saying that it only remained to him to meditate on the death and passion of 'Our dear Saviour Jesus Christ'. Father Huddleston recited more prayers as the King held the crucifix: 'Beseech Him with all humility, that His most precious

---

* Barrillon was told by the Duke of York afterwards that Father Huddleston 'made the King formally promise to declare himself openly a Catholic if he recovered his health'. But Father Huddleston does not mention this in his own detailed account.''

Blood may not be shed in vain for you ... and when it shall please Him to take you out of this transitory world, to grant you a joyful resurrection, and an eternal crown of glory in the next.'

Then Father Huddleston left as he had come, through the secret door. The whole momentous episode had lasted three-quarters of an hour.

The King's progress out of the transitory world, although sure, was slow. The stubborn way his body clung to life even gave hope to those Catholics in the know that his conversion might have wrought a miraculous cure. The King himself summed it up with his ineffable politeness: he told the gentlemen surrounding his bed that he was sorry to trouble them by taking so long a-dying, and he asked their pardon.[36]*

Throughout the long night of Thursday, 5 February, Charles remained conscious. The physicians, allowed back into the torture-chamber, set to work with their remedies again with even greater energy. At one point the King referred to his continuing ordeal. He told his attendants, 'I have suffered very much and more than any of you can imagine.' Once, listening to those innumerable palace clocks striking, he asked the time. They told him and he said, 'My business will shortly be done.' But his stoicism continued to excite the admiration of all those about him. It was an exemplary death-bed, as might have been expected of one who had learnt early to confront the unknown with courage and hope.

There were a series of farewells. Catharine came. Charles greeted her lovingly. But her distress, both at the King's tenderness and at his suffering, was too great. Tears overcame her. She was carried back to her own apartments, half-fainting. She sent back a message to her husband to beg his pardon if she had ever offended him.

'Alas! poor woman,' said the King. 'She beg my pardon! I beg hers with all my heart.'

* A saying given its unforgettable expression in Macaulay's *History of England*: 'He had been, he said, a most unconscionable time dying; but he hoped they would excuse it.'[37] But the word 'unconscionable' is not in the original source.

To James too, linked to him by every shared memory of boyhood and now at last by Faith, the King showed much tenderness. James, kneeling, could not hold back his own tears. Charles begged his pardon too, for the hardships which he had inflicted upon him from time to time. At some point in the long midnight hours he handed him the keys of his cabinet and begged God to give him a prosperous reign. The Duchess of York remained openly weeping at her husband's side.

The King also spoke of his children. He recommended his little family most touchingly to his brother, naming each one meticulously. When he stumbled on the name Burford – as Nelly's handsome, spirited boy was still known, despite his new dukedom of St Albans – the King put the boy 'into his [James'] hand'. He asked James to take particular care of Burford's education, 'for he will be spoiled else'.

But the King did not name Monmouth. And James, repeating the list back to him, did not mention the forbidden name either.

The ladies, those other members of his extended family circle, were not forgotten. In a phrase sometimes supposed to be apocryphal but in fact attested by three sources, the King adjured the Duke of York 'to be well to Portsmouth' and 'not let poor Nelly starve' – even in his last hours the vital social distinction between the two ladies was preserved.[38]

One by one his children came and knelt down by the King's bed and received his blessing. At which the throng of people once more surrounding the royal bed, and crowding into the chamber, cried out that the King was their common father. So all present in fact knelt down for his blessing. It was of course an Anglican blessing. But when Bishop Ken repeatedly urged the King to take the Sacrament, Charles declined it. He would only say that he had thought of his approaching end, and hoped that he had made his peace with God. Ken was unaware what this characteristically courteous evasion meant.

At six o'clock in the morning the King asked for the curtains to be drawn back. He wanted, he said, to watch the dawn for the last time. He was still conscious enough to ask that the eight-day clock in his room should be wound up, because it was the appointed day. An hour later he became breathless and struggled to sit up. Once again the doctors bled him, taking twelve ounces, and gave him heart tonics. At half-past eight his speech began to fail once more. This time it did not return. By ten o'clock he was in a coma.

The rising sun over the Thames was probably the last sight he took in. It was an appropriate one for this man who had so loved the early morning on its misty waters.

King Charles ii died at noon. It was now high water on the river and the time of the full moon. The day was Friday, 6 February 1685, and he was in his fifty-fifth year.

CHAPTER TWENTY-SEVEN

His Royal Ashes

~~~~~

'Let his royal ashes then lie soft upon him, and cover
him from harsh and unkind censures.'

Halifax, *Character of King Charles II*

After the death of King Charles II the ordinary people
walked about 'like ghosts'. Roger North wrote that
'almost every living soul cried before and at his Decease,
as for the loss of the best Friend in the World'.[1] Others felt
that they had lost a father, that feeling spontaneously expressed
at the King's death-bed when all present, not only his children,
had knelt for his paternal blessing.

The universal application was given its first expression when
the King's body lay in state in the Painted Chamber at Whitehall
for several days. As was the custom of the time, his wax effigy,
standing upright over the catafalque, dominated the scene. It
was dressed in robes of crimson velvet trimmed with ermine,
and surmounted with an imperial crown of tin gilt, all specially
ordered for the occasion by the Lord Chamberlain. Such effigies,
taken from the death-mask, often have a haunted look: the lines
on the face of Charles II are deep, the face is slightly twisted,
the expression very sad. Still to be seen exhibited in the precincts
of Westminster Abbey, it commemorates the cruel sufferings of
his death-bed.

Queen Catharine, as befitted a devout woman who had once
been a Portuguese Infanta, understood how to conduct her
official position as widow with stately grief. She received the

Ambassadors and other great persons who came to offer their condolences on a vast black bed of mourning. Her whole chamber, from the ceiling to the floor, was hung with black, and lit by innumerable tapers. The callers came thronging and their sympathy was not purely formal: no-one doubted the sincerity of the Queen's own passion for the King, and besides, she had won universal respect.

One does however detect a firm, even righteous hand, in the way the funeral and other mourning arrangements kept the mistresses at last in their place. The royal concubines were allowed to wear black themselves in their official capacity as ladies-in-waiting, but could not put their households into mourning, a privilege reserved for royal persons. There were other nice distinctions preserved, such as that between the cambric doled out to the Queen's entourage, while the rest made do with mere muslin. It was not for nothing that the Lord Chamberlain commanded from the Treasury yards of black and white satin for eight escutcheons showing the royal arms of England and Portugal.[2]

The funeral itself took place on the night of 14 February. The King's body was enclosed in a lead coffin – that 'house of lead' which had been prophesied – bearing a solid silver plate with an inscription which began: '*Depositum Augustissimi et Serenissimi Principis Caroli Secundi....*' In its last line, '*Regnique sui tricesimo septimo*' ('in the thirty-seventh year of his reign'), the inscription dated the King's accession once again from his father's execution.

Then the body of Charles II was laid to rest in a vault beneath the Henry VII Chapel in Westminster Abbey. There it remains to this day.* Many of the King's natural children were later buried near him: Charles Earl of Plymouth had already been placed there in his early grave.

Careful provision was made for discreet display – banners of

---

* According to Dean Stanley, that great Victorian guardian of the Abbey, the vault was accidentally disclosed in 1867 in the process of laying down the apparatus for warming the Chapel. The lead coffin was very much corroded and had collapsed; the King's remains were visible. In 1977, when the vault was again opened, the remains, as described by Dean Stanley, were still visible.[3]

black taffeta with strings and tassels of black silk – and appropriate sad sound – black-coated trumpeters, kettle-drummers, and a fife. Despite this care, despite the fact that the body was carried under a velvet canopy from the Painted Chamber to Westminster Abbey in a procession headed by the Archbishop of Canterbury and Norroy, King of Arms, and attended by James II, Mary of Modena, various other royalties, nobles and their servants, the rumour has arisen that, in the words of John Evelyn, 'the King was very obscurely buried'.[4]

This has sometimes been ascribed to the religious embarrassment caused by the King's last-minute conversion. The new monarch, it is suggested, did not wish his brother's body to be buried according to the Anglican rite and did not dare employ the Catholic one. This is also the explanation sometimes given for the fact that James himself stayed away from the burial. The truth is rather less dramatic. Royal interments at the time were traditionally held privately at night, as for example that of the Duke of Gloucester in 1660 and of Prince Rupert in 1682. It was according to custom that the nearest relative stayed away, the role of Chief Mourner devolving upon an officially designated person: in the case of Charles II it fell upon the stalwart shoulders of his nephew-in-law, Prince George of Denmark. He was 'supported' by the Dukes of Somerset and Beaufort, and 'assisted' by sixteen earls – hardly a meagre representation.[5]

An exception was the state funeral of Cromwell, the Lord Protector, in 1658. Like a coronation, this august ceremony had its own rhythm: it took place three months after his death (both impressing and disgusting Evelyn). The actual burial might even be separate from the State ceremony: Cromwell's corpse was secretly interred about a fortnight before this took place, because the embalming had failed. Such a magnificent piece of pageantry was mounted with the explicit intention of demonstrating the strength of the regime – in the case of the Cromwellian Protectorate, to bolster its prestige abroad against a young man then known as Charles Stuart. The money spent was crippling: not much less than £50,000.[6]

Where the late King Charles II was concerned, no such demonstration was felt to be necessary. A staid succession was, surely, to be followed by a steady reign. Above all, there was the question of paying for such pageantry: the monies voted by Parliament for the late King all came to an end with his death, while Charles himself had left large debts. James II, faced with a financial crisis and the daunting prospect of a Parliament to solve it, was in no mood for unnecessarily lavish expenditure. The shade of Charles II, no stranger to State penury and its ramifications, would certainly have agreed.

The outbreak of verse on the King's death (including an ode by the Quaker Penn, a tribute to the King's tolerant spirit, and Otway's long poem on Windsor Castle, a tribute to his artistic enthusiasm) showed a genuine spirit of lamentation.

> Sad was the morn, the Sadder Week began...

was Aphra Behn's contribution. Two other slightly bathetic starts were as follows:

> No more, he's gone, with Angel's wings he fled...

and:

> O God! Some pity, and I am turned to stone...

All however stressed the state of serenity in which King Charles left his realm. One, by Edmund Arwaker, will serve for many:

> The best of Christians as the best of Kings:
> By him such Blessings to his Realms were given;
> He seemed created for his People's good...[7]

So, in a mellow atmosphere of regret the King was buried. It seemed that the peace which he so much desired for his country had fallen upon it, even as he himself was laid to peace in his grave.

It was not to be. Only a few months later those characters dismissed from the stage by the final curtain of one play, found themselves engaged in quite a different drama. There was to be no happy ending to the reign of King James II.

Monmouth died at the executioner's axe after his foolish and bloody rebellion, only a few months after his father's death. Three years later James himself was fighting off the political onslaught of William of Orange and his own daughter Mary; the birth of the long-dreaded Catholic Prince to Mary Beatrice in June 1688 had brought disaster in its wake. By 1689 Titus Oates, savagely whipped after trial for perjury in May 1685, was being received by William, now King of England: Oates remained a weather-vane for the direction of the English political wind. As a counter-poise it is good to relate that Father Huddleston lived on to the ripe old age of ninety – protected in the household of Queen Catharine at Somerset House.

Another mercurial figure, whose story had been even more closely entwined with that of Charles II, did not survive to see the new Protestant reign. Buckingham had divided himself from the opposition in the King's last years, unable to remain in accord with Shaftesbury, and had thus been received back into Charles' favour. On the accession of James, he retired to his great Yorkshire estates, which his friend Etherege complained was like the hero leaving the play at the beginning of the fourth act. But Buckingham's health was failing, through prolonged dissipation, as it was generally thought. He died two years after his master and childhood friend; but it was somehow characteristic of the man that his burial at least – like that of Charles himself in the Henry VII chapel at Westminster Abbey – was a most splendid affair. As for the younger politicians, Sunderland, Rochester, Godolphin and the like, for the most part they stepped willingly onto the new stage to act out all the intricate if not heroic dramas of politics in the ages of William and Mary, and Anne.

The mistresses did not fare so well. Most of their latter ends would have satisfied a Puritan moralist. Nell Gwynn died – of a stroke – two years after her royal Charles. She was only thirty-five. The King's death had plucked from her at the last minute the coveted title of Countess of Greenwich. She also endured the common struggle of the late King's pensionaries to secure those payments she had been promised. At one point she addressed James in language strangely reminiscent of another ill-treated royal servant, Cardinal Wolsey, a character with whom she cannot otherwise be said to have had much in common (perhaps one may attribute the Shakespearean echo to Nelly's theatrical education): 'Had I suffered for my God as I have done for your brother and you, I should not have needed either of your kindness or justice to me,' she told the new King.

In general, James did his best by the mistresses and their children, hampered in his turn by lack of money, but recognizing the duty of their upkeep. He did make the point very firmly to Louise Duchess of Portsmouth that her debts must be paid: but the ladies, like their late protector, remained a byword for negligence. To quote Nelly once more: 'The King's Mistresses are accounted ill Paymasters....'[8]

Barbara Duchess of Cleveland was made of more lasting stuff. She may have lived to regret her own durability. For at the age of sixty-five she married a much younger man, a notorious rake known as Beau Fielding, who treated her abominably; what was more, the marriage itself proved to be bigamous. As for Louise, she survived (in France) to the then remarkable age of eighty-five – the yacht *Fubbs* named in her honour lasted even longer: it was not broken up until 1770.[9] She died, wrote Saint Simon, 'very old, very penitent and very poor'. The Louise who held luxurious court at Whitehall beneath Evelyn's fascinated gaze would have deplored all three states, but particularly the last.

Catharine of Braganza survived too. It was characteristic of her tenderness that she pleaded with James II for the life of Monmouth, who was certainly too desperate to appreciate the irony of his supplication to the childless Queen: 'Being in this unfortunate condition, and having none left but your Majesty that I think may have some compassion for me; and that, for the last King's sake ...' In her first widowhood Catharine withdrew to Hammersmith and spent her time amongst the nuns in a convent she had founded there. Later she moved to Somerset House, the palace which belonged by right to a Queen Dowager (Henrietta Maria had also occupied it). She was present at the controversial birth of James II's son, the so-called

Warming-pan Baby, and acted as the child's godmother; she subsequently bore witness that no act of substitution had taken place. Catharine was still in England at the Revolution of 1688, her return to Portugal having been delayed by a lawsuit against her former Chamberlain. She finally sailed back to Portugal in March 1692, after thirty years spent in England, during which, as Evelyn said: 'She deported herself so decently upon all occasions ... which made her universally beloved.'[10]

Even then her public life was not over. Catharine's last years were spent acting as Regent of Portugal for her sick brother Pedro. Her efforts were rewarded in at least one direction: in 1703 she was able to see an alliance with England, the so-called Methuen Treaty, which she advocated, carried through. Catharine of Braganza died at the end of 1705, twenty years after the husband she had loved, served, and in all but one vital respect over which she had no control, satisfied. In her case a magnificent state funeral in Portugal testified to the general esteem in which this practical and pious lady was held.

King Charles II had inherited a country war-torn and poor, divided, restless and suspicious. He left behind him a country outwardly at harmony. He was personally beloved from his early days, when the crowds saluted their Black Boy come again, to those last years, when he still basked in national affection. One mourning sermon of the time – 'A Loyal Tear Dropt on the Vault of the High and Mighty Prince Charles II', dedicated to the Bishop of Winton, Prelate of the Garter, by a Hampshire vicar – referred repeatedly and with evident sincerity to the late King's 'Clemency and Tenderness'. These were enduring – and endearing – qualities. When Evelyn wrote of his sovereign as having 'many Virtues and many great Imperfections' he did not specify the contents of either category. The balance of the character of Charles II, where vice and virtue are concerned, was in fact a very human one which could not fail to appeal to many of his subjects and fellow-sinners. Here was a man who knew all about Sloth and Lust, but was singularly free from Pride, Greed, Avarice, Anger and Envy. As for the Virtues, he was touched in some measure by them all, from Charity downwards, including Temperance while in exile, and Prudence at home.

The admonition of Halifax at the very end of his *Character of King Charles II* (written some time after 1688) expresses the final mood of that time: 'Let his royal ashes then lie soft upon him, and cover him from harsh and unkind censures; which though they should not be unjust can never clear themselves of being indecent.' For all Halifax's criticisms of his master, Halifax and his contemporaries understood that they had good reason to be grateful to him.

But his royal ashes have not in fact lain particularly softly upon the King. History is inevitably a long avenue of hindsight: and the basic law by which men are judged according to what follows after them, whereas they act in accordance with what has come before, is illustrated to the full in the life of Charles II. The 'Glorious' Revolution of 1688 casts its shadow backwards without difficulty across his career, whereas the obscurities and murkiness left behind by the English Civil War are too often ignored.

The historiography of his reign, a fascinating subject in its own right, is however not the concern of the present volume.* Here it is more appropriate to judge the character of King Charles II in the light of those challenges he actually faced. The first of these – and indeed the key challenge throughout most of his career – was the challenge to the position of the monarchy. Where Charles was concerned, it proved a triple contest.

First, as Prince of Wales, he had to endure the strange and unexpected ordeal of civil unrest, followed by war. If Charles was by nature a straightforward, affectionate, essentially normal creature, his early upbringing confirmed that tendency. Loved by his parents, endowed with a happy family life, and many brothers and sisters, he found it natural to display exactly that kind of open and gracious character most suited to his position. He made the transition to a martial young prince, courageous

---

* The best introductions to it are J. P. Kenyon, 'Review Article: The Reign of Charles II', *Cambridge Historical Journal*, vol. XIII, 1957, and K. H. D. Haley, *Charles II*, Historical Association Pamphlet, 1966.

and determined, without much apparent difficulty, but then it was not on the surface a very difficult one to make. If royal princes had not been conducting the arts of war recently, there was a strong chivalric tradition that the Prince of Wales must be equipped to do so. Charles in Western England, the Scilly Islands and Jersey did as well as, or even better than, he could have been expected to do. The scars – for there must have been scars, as his whole secure world was reft asunder and his father murdered – did not as yet show.

The obvious ordeal began a few years before he inherited the crown. The ordeal, none the less burdensome for being nominal, came in the shape of months, then years and finally over a decade of expectation, despair, inertia all mixed – with a great deal of the last. It is surely impossible to over-estimate the effect of the exile upon his character. Charles ii was like a soldier captured in his first youth, who spends the crucial span of his development as a prisoner-of-war. He was never in command of his own destiny at a time when he should have been flexing his muscles both as a man and a ruler.

In public the King survived all this admirably, putting out more flags. The second challenge to the monarchy, one more often faced in the twentieth century than in the seventeenth, that of enduring a protracted period of exile and then emerging *capax imperator*, was one which Charles ii met better than most. He kept his nerve. He kept up his spirits. Like another more ferocious leader, Satan, he ever took the line in public: 'What though the field be lost? All is not lost ...' He also emerged in 1660 untainted. He had preserved himself against the 'slur of the Catholic religion', on the one hand, the rather different slur of a bad character on the other.

It was hardly surprising that ever after there was something different, pessimistic about him in private, a knowledge that this world is to be regarded with a cynical eye if one is not to be betrayed by it. The exile also bred other characteristics. They do not sound attractive on paper, although they were not without their uses in the tricky post-Restoration era. To dissimulate successfully was one essential lesson Charles had to learn – for there is no evidence that he was a born deceiver. Like vacillation, another quality which stole upon him in the exiled years, it was alien to the young Hotspur he once was. Nor, it seems, did he convince himself of the rightness of deception, even if he came to understand the necessity. Late in life – discussing his championship of the Queen – he told Burnet that he regarded falsehood and cruelty as 'the greatest of crimes in the sight of God'.[11] Cruelty at least he eschewed, as all his contemporaries testified.

Laziness, or at any rate a desire to concentrate on the pleasurable over the dutiful, was, on the other hand, more inherent. Everyone after the Restoration commented on the King's apparent sloth, from Madame his sister downwards. It should therefore be noted that the King was never actually let down by this laziness (except in so far as the low estimate of his contemporaries let him down). On the contrary, he was quite often successfully served by his powers of delay, or by what is sometimes termed a 'Negative Capability' – for which Queen Elizabeth I, another procrastinator, has been much praised. When the true moment of crisis came for the monarchy the King acted with despatch. The sovereign who disposed of the Oxford Parliament in 1681 was neither lazy nor irresolute.

The extent to which King Charles II overcame the third challenge to the monarchy, that embodied in the reign itself, is more debatable. Certainly by his last year the King had so shored up the hereditary monarchy that it gave every appearance of being secure, unthreatened in its traditional powers. The theory behind all his moves was the same: the traditional authority of the Crown, eroded in the past, was being properly upheld once more. This theoretical emphasis on the traditional is characteristic of the period, which takes its very name from an act of Restoration. It poses a problem concerning King Charles II himself. Given that many of these moves were practical encroachments, how far did he evolve a new theory of monarchy?

Here his reputation for indifference, even cynicism, was probably fully justified. Neither he, nor indeed his opponents, in the main the Whigs, had overcome the basic problem lurking at the heart of a hereditary office – and still for that matter lurking there today, if in a less extreme form. Within living memory the engine of our constitutional monarchy has juddered at the hands of Edward VIII, needing a George VI to steady its forward progress. The central role of the monarch calls at least for an actor suited to the part, if a great actor is not available. But such casting can never be ensured by the hereditary couch. It was significant that both Tory and Whig philosophies depended upon a good king to make them work. Faced with such a need, it cannot be argued that Charles II ever came to grips with the problem of his own successor.

Pragmatic rather than lazy, he took the whole succession question only as it came along. This he dealt with in the short term, but never in the long. A mixture of deference to his much-betrayed Queen, and allegiance to the principle of legitimate monarchy embodied by his brother, kept him from the more ruthless settlement implied by a divorce on the one hand, legitimization of a bastard on the other. One emotion was a private weakness (where a less sympathetic man might have been stronger); the other fell into the Whigs' own trap of confusing the succession with the powers of the Crown. Because they spent so much energy in denouncing Catholic James, as though the constitution depended on it, the King too began to believe the two were synonymous.

Of course a far-seeing king can still leave behind him an unintentional legacy of succession troubles. It is peculiar to the case of Charles II that he seems to have been under little illusion about the consequences of his brother succeeding. The frame of mind of Charles II in his very last phase reminds one of Dryden's paraphrase of Horace:

> Happy the Man, and happy he alone,
> He, who can call today his own:
> He who, secure within, can say,
> Tomorrow do thy worst, for I have lived today.
> Be fair, or foul, or rain, or shine,
> The joys I have possessed, in spite of fate, are mine.

That kind of noble resolution, admirable in a private individual, is more complicated in a king with responsibilities to the next reign. Yet one has to face the fact that Charles II regarded his brother's succession not only as inevitable – but in a curious way right. Here, perhaps, the deep melancholy of the once-exiled King, the ex-prisoner-of-war, came into play.

In other ways, in a confused and transitional period, Charles II was a highly estimable king. Not every prince in a position to do so has practised the virtue of gratitude so thoroughly. The determined healing of the first ten years should be balanced against the more rigorous absolutism of the last five. The healing was policy. The absolutism, as King Charles saw it, was forced upon him. Indeed, so hand-to-mouth was the absolutism of this last period, so little was it based on a cunning philosophy, that the King has been criticized for not pursuing such policies rigorously enough.

The kind of propaganda exercise indulged in by Louis XIV, with every breath he drew every day of his life, was unthinkable to Charles II. The arts, for example, were there for enjoyment: a simple and even laudable view, but not one that has been shared by every monarch in history. The bewigged and padded creatures of his stage, the saucy mistresses in their boys' clothing, the graceful wielders of his garlanded violins, the shepherds and satyrs of his masques: none of these conspired to glorify the monarchy; if they did so, it was purely by accident. Dryden as Poet Laureate was given no great direction for his verse.[12] Satire – often of the monarchy itself – was a far more potent theme in the reign of Charles II than propaganda.

It would be going too far to say that the King enjoyed the satirical attacks on himself, his friends and his mistresses. Very few notable figures have enjoyed being satirized. But temperamentally the King was inclined to shrug his shoulders at personal lampoons (otherwise his friendship with Rochester, to say nothing of Buckingham, would have rapidly withered). Here again one is inclined to seek the explanation in the years of exile, as well as in Charles' natural affability. Charles II could hardly say with Charles I that a king and a subject were two quite different things – or, if he had said so, he could hardly have believed it. He came of a long line of kings, but he himself had once been Charles Stuart, the wanderer. Like Lear, he had experienced the storm on the heath. He had also watched how easily might could be turned into royalty in the case of Cromwell.

The lack of sheer interest in regal formality displayed by Charles was another topic of general comment among his contemporaries. Mulgrave, who knew Charles well, wrote of him as having a 'natural aversion' to it: 'He could not on premeditation act the part of a King for a moment, which carried him to the other extreme ... of letting all distinction and ceremony fall to the ground as useless and foppish.' He preferred, as Bruce tells us, to take off his hat to 'the meanest' as he strode through the royal galleries or the parks.[13]

Charles II would surely have found the propagandist pranks of his father and grandfather, virtually deifying themselves through the medium of art, deeply embarrassing. One can imagine the wisecracks with which he might have distanced himself from such practices. To that extent he was a highly modern monarch, if not a highly modern dictator. Such unconcern, attractive to contemplate from afar, was not the stuff of which a strong absolute monarchy, the magnet of the country, was made.

Two great institutions, one ancient and the other comparatively new, the English Church and the City of London, might have been moulded into pillars of support had Charles II had the Nietzschean will to do so. This will he singularly lacked. He took the situation as he found it, got on with it as best he could. Where the Church was concerned, he preferred toleration to repression, an admirable view, but against his time: one must never forget that Charles' personal tolerance, so attractive to us, was considered a liability by his contemporaries – be it for the Catholics or the Jews. As for the City of London, his attitude never extended much beyond a preference for low-interest loans, which was hardly surprising. All the interests of Charles II in scientific experiment and the way things worked went to make him a great pragmatist, not a political philosopher.

It was perfectly appropriate that he lived in an age when political theories were so chaotic. It left him free to follow his natural bent, which was to ignore such matters. He wished to incarnate that kind of monarch described by Dryden, 'who is just and moderate in his nature', and provides 'a government which has all the advantages of a liberty beyond a commonwealth, and all the marks of kingly sovereignty, without the danger of a tyranny'.[14] To many people who remembered the Commonwealth, it was a republic which 'gave that mock appearance of a liberty where all who have no part in government are slaves'. As these memories faded, so the unifying and unrestrained role of the King was no longer necessary. No-one, including the King, yet knew what was to be put in its place.

Ut was not that Charles II was ill served. In their different ways men such as Clarendon, Arlington and Danby, and on a lower level Williamson – and Pepys – were highly talented at home; in Scotland Lauderdale displayed strength and some national feeling; in Ireland one can go much further in praise of Ormonde and even Essex. Talented as they were, these men were, like their King, floundering in an age of change. The role of Parliament? The role of the *people*? Because the era of the Civil War ha ended in such a complete theoretical 'Restoration', such questions were still unresolved.

There is one charge which is constantly levelled against Charles II – lack of patriotism, based on his acceptance of secret French subsidies. But it is a charge which must lead directly to a question: what *was* the nature of patriotism then? No one can deny that Charles himself loved England (and things English) with a passion. He also equated the happiness of England with stable monarchical government. In a memorable phrase he told Lord Bruce: 'I would have everyone live under his own vine and fig-tree. Give me my just prerogative and I will never ask for more.' That was very far from being an outrageous view at the time: most of his subjects shared it for most of his reign and in 1660 virtually all of them did.

The next step, the employment of the French funds in order to do without the boa-constrictor's embrace of Parliament, is more controversial. The acceptance of such subsidies then was not of course the national scandal it would be today: let us remember not only the bribes administered by William of Orange to English MPs but also the guileful manner in which the Whig leaders, those showy enemies of absolutism, allowed themselves to receive similar payments from the absolute Louis XIV. Nevertheless, had Charles II intended to use these funds to change the religion of the country to Catholicism against its will it would be impossible to defend him as a patriot. But Charles II never even changed his own religion until it was too late to matter, let alone took any step to change that of the country as a whole.

His conception of the French money was as a support in his struggles with his Parliamentary enemies; without this support he feared, rightly or wrongly, that he would go the way of his father. And that, he sincerely believed, would lead to the perdition of his country once again. The receipt of foreign subsidies, far from being in contrast to such overtly (by our standards) patriotic actions as the maintenance of the Navy, the extension of the Empire, was part of the same process. One may therefore criticize Charles II for his Machiavellian policies, but not for lack of patriotism.

There is a comparison to be made with another popular charge: that Charles II was the political plaything of his mistresses. In fact, their opinions tended to echo his own predilections of the time rather than the other way round. One may criticize him for extravagance towards these ladies, or indeed for having mistresses in the first place – but not for succumbing to their political influence.

There must be 'condescensions from the throne, like kind showers from heaven', wrote Halifax. Of these condescensions, not to be confused with stiffer formalities, Charles II was a master. Dryden spoke of him awakening the English from the 'natural reservedness' of their dull and heavy spirits on his Restoration.[15] The enthusiasm with which his presence galvanized so many sides of English life was not assumed.

Both sport and the arts brought him towards his people. It was easy for him to discern the human being behind the office. He dined with the jockeys not only because of his passion for racing, but because he found jockeys good company. In the same way actors, and of course actresses, were for the first time treated with proper respect in English society during his reign, because of the King's love of the theatre. His love of a pretty face extended to a general respect for women: the position of women in the second half of the seventeenth century was in many ways preferable to their position in the nineteenth. Was it a complete coincidence that the climate of the Restoration led to a remarkable flowering of female playwrights not paralleled till our own day? Charles II was fascinated by science and patronized the Royal Society. Delight in his Navy and his Army extended to care for the welfare of his sailors and soldiers. His connection with Purcell has been mentioned, spreading out from his love of the new instrumental music brought from France which flourished during his era. Gardens and paths sprang up, as the King laid out and sauntered through his own.

Witty and kind, grateful, generous, tolerant, and essentially lovable, he was rightly mourned by his people, walking in the streets 'like ghosts' after his death, their faces suffused with tears. He had been their spirited young prince, their Black Boy, 'born the divided world to reconcile', in Waller's phrase, whose restoration brought about the return of ease. As a father to them in later years, he had incarnated so much of what they pined for in a ruler. Cynical and dissimulating, it can be argued that Charles II was not a king for all seasons. But he was the right king for that strange, demanding season in which he lived.

He was not a Merry Monarch – never has a popular catch-phrase been so deceiving. The age itself might be merry in many of its jollier public aspects: but the man who presided over it was in contrast marked by melancholy at the very heart. More important to his people was the fact that he understood one deep need of their nature. 'If he loved too much to lie upon his own down bed of ease,' wrote Halifax, 'his subjects had the pleasure during his reign of lolling and stretching upon theirs.' Many a monarch has had a worse epitaph than giving back peace to a torn nation.

Let his royal ashes lie soft upon King Charles II.

References

These have been kept to the minimum (except for Mss and where a point is controversial) on the grounds that the general reader will not want to know them, and the experts on the period already do. Authors and/or titles are given in the most convenient abbreviated form; full details will be found in the list of Reference Books alphabetically according to the first letter of the abbreviation used. '*Letters*' indicates *The Letters of King Charles II*, edited by Sir Arthur Bryant. 'Burnet' is a reference to the edition of O. Airy; 'Evelyn' to the edition of W. Bray, unless otherwise stated; 'Halifax' to the *Complete Works*, edited by J. P. Kenyon; 'Pepys' followed by a date is a reference to Pepys' *Diary*, edited by R. C. Latham and W. Matthews.

Chapter 19: Subsisting Together?

1 *Letters*, p. 261.
2 Dalrymple, II (A), p. 80.
3 *Ailesbury*, I, p. 92; Oldmixon, p. 553; Clark, *Edward Backwell*, p. 53.
4 Feaveryear, p. 103.
5 Printed in Kenyon, *Stuart Constitution*, pp. 407–408.
6 C. S. P. Venetian 1671–2, p. 187; Havighurst, Pt I, pp. 72–4.
7 Haley, *Shaftesbury*, pp. 297–9.
8 *Letters*, p. 246; C. S. P. Domestic 1671, p. 220.
9 C. S. P. Venetian 1671–2, p. 244.
10 *Letters*, pp. 257, 259.
11 Renier, p. 49.
12 R. A. SP, Add. 1/18.
13 *Letters*, p. 258; Renier, p. 52.
14 Hatton Correspondence, I, p. 98.

15 Delpech, pp. 42–3.

16 Delpech, p. 82.

17 Hatton Correspondence, I, p. 76.

18 Ogg, I, p. 77.

19 Fea, *James II*, p. 95 (Diary of Lady Cowper, 10 March 1716).

20 Reresby, p. 24; Wilson, *Court Wits*, p. 119; Cunningham, II, p. 33.

21 Evelyn, I, p. 63; R. A. Wardrobe 79104 verso.

22 *King's Works*, p. 278; Evelyn, II, pp. 102, 107.

23 *Letters*, p. 255.

24 Petty, p. 8; Ogg, II, p. 400, note 3.

25 Bagwell, III, p. 112, note 1.

26 Bagwell, III, p. 115 and note 1; C. S. P. Domestic 1673, pp. 596–7, 12.

27 R. A. Wardrobe 85669.

28 *Letters*, pp. 260–62.

29 C. S. P. Domestic 1673, p. 126.

30 Essex Papers, I, p. 181.

Chapter 20: The Knot in the Comb

1 Miller, *Popery*, pp. 9–12; but see Kenyon, *Plot*, pp. 24–5 and note, for the much higher figure of 260,000.

2 Kenyon, *Plot*, p. 27; Childs, pp. 28–9.

3 Evelyn, II, p. 71.

4 Childs, pp. 219, 230, refers to 'little evidence' but cites no evidence.

5 Haley, *William and the Opposition, passim*.

6 Turner, *James II*, p. 109.

7 Miller, *James II*, pp. 71–3.

8 Pepys, 16 June 1665.

9 Hyde Correspondence, I, p. 45; Fraser, *Mary, Queen of Scots*, p. 123.

10 Foxcroft, *Burnet*, p. 143; Margoliouth, II, p. 338.

11 Miller, *James II*, p. 73.

12 Browning, *Danby*, I, p. 107.

13 Burnet, I, p. 470 *et seq.*

14 Haley, *Shaftesbury*, p. 346; Cunningham, II, p. 73.

15 Jones, *First Whigs*, p. 216.

16 *Letters*, p. 55; Hartmann, *King My Brother*, p. 134; *Letters*, p. 231.

17 Josten, *Ashmole*, I, p. 189; IV, pp. 1347–8.

18 Josten, *Ashmole*, I, p. 234 and note 4; IV, pp. 1350–1 and note 1, 1362.

19 *Letters*, p. 275; *Motteville*, II, p. 80.

20 *Letters*, p. 276.

21 C. S. P. Venetian 1673–5, p. 233.

22 Browning, *Danby*, I, p. 129 *et seq.*; Browning, *Parties and Party Organization*.

23 Chandaman, p. 235 *et seq.*

24 Chandaman, p. 271.

25 Bryant, *Charles II*, p. 192; See Shaw, *Treasury Books*, Introduction, for the view that the King was kept intolerably short by Parliament; recently upset by Chandaman.

26 Williamson, *Investigation*, pp. 182–4.

27 Millar, *Queen's Pictures*, p. 69.
28 Evelyn, II, pp. 53–5; *King's Works*, p. 28.
29 Millar, *Queen's Pictures*, p. 81.
30 Girouard, p. 130.
31 *King's Works* (*Windsor Castle*), pp. 313–41, *passim*.
32 North, p. 132.
33 Bryant, *Charles II*, p. 196 note.
34 Hamilton, *William's Mary*, p. 24; Strickland, V, p. 623.
35 R. A. Wardrobe 85774.
36 R. A. Wardrobe 85774.
37 Parry, p. 203 *et seq.*
38 Latham, *Pepys*, VIII, p. 73 and note 3.
39 Browning, *Danby*, I, pp. 147, 168.
40 *Letters*, p. 280.
41 *Letters*, pp. 281–2.
42 *Letters*, p. 282.
43 Browning, *Danby*, I, pp. 190–91.

Chapter 21: Peace For His Own Time

1 *Reresby*, p. 40; Halifax, p. 54.
2 Jones, *Green Ribbon Club*; Haley, *Shaftesbury*, p. 530.
3 Dalrymple, II, p. 117.
4 Chandaman, p. 35.
5 Dasent, p. 249.
6 Girouard, p. 130; Ailesbury, I, p. 95.
7 Halifax, p. 251.
8 Osborn Files, 50.17.
9 *Letters*, p. 221.
10 Hartmann, *Duchess*, p. 149 *et seq.*
11 *Mazarine's Memoires*.
12 C. A. 120, folio 227.
13 C. A. 123C, fol. 109 (Courtin).
14 Renier, p. 61.
15 Chapman, p. 240.
16 Browning, *Danby*, I, p. 214.
17 Burnet, II, p. 118.
18 North, p. 153; Havighurst, Pt 2, pp. 230–31.
19 Browning, *Danby*, I, p. 226; II, pp. 66–9.
20 Margoliouth, II, p. 355.
21 Robb, I, p. 88.
22 *Lake*, I, p. 9.
23 Robb, I, p. 98; *Letters*, p. 290.
24 Pepys, 1 May 1662; Hatton Correspondence, I, p. 151.
25 Oldmixon, p. 605; Robb, I, p. 101; Burnet, II, p. 132.
26 *Letters*, pp. 288–90.
27 Sitwell, p. 19.
28 Browning, *Danby*, I, p. 268; Haley, *Shaftesbury*, p. 415.
29 Clarke, *James II*, I, p. 259.
30 Clark, *Later Stuarts*, p. 90.
31 Browning, *Danby*, I, p. 282.
32 *Letters*, p. 295; Childs, p. 219.
33 R. A. Wardrobe 79612 verso.

Chapter 22: Against Exclusion

1 Kenyon, *Plot*, p. 51; for the course of these events see Kenyon, *Plot*, *passim*.
2 But see Kenyon, *Plot*, p. 53, for view that Charles believed there was some substance in the plot.
3 Kenyon, *Plot*, pp. 46–7 (F. J. Warner, *History of the English Catholics*).
4 Kenyon, *Plot*, pp. 34–7.

5 Evelyn, II, p. 131.
6 Kenyon, *Plot*, p. 114; *Letters*, p. 304.
7 Blencowe, I, p. 86.
8 Halifax, p. 203; Kenyon, *Plot*, p. 77.
9 *Letters*, pp. 329–30.
10 Jones, *First Whigs*, p. 23.
11 Jones, *Green Ribbon Club*; Evelyn, II, p. 152.
12 *Reresby*, p. 29; Elmes, p. 287.
13 *Letters*, p. 301.
14 Childs, p. 228.
15 Hatton Correspondence, I, p. 157; Miller, *Popery*, pp. 159, 184.
16 Kenyon, *Plot*, p. 93.
17 Haley, *Shaftesbury*, pp. 483–5.
18 Burnet, II, p. 180; Falkus, p. 101.
19 Grammont, p. 121.
20 Hatton Correspondence, I, p. 168; Harris, II, App., p. 393.
21 Browning, *Danby*, I, 309 and note 1.
22 Hatton Correspondence, I, p. 175; Summers, *Restoration Theatre*, p. 80.
23 Wilson, *Nell Gwynn*, p. 179 *et seq.*
24 Wilson, *Court Wits*, p. 119 *et seq.* (Rochester, *The Royal Angler*; Buckingham, *The Cabin Boy*).
25 Blencowe, I, p. 2.
26 *Letters*, p. 304.
27 *Lords' Journals*, p. 348 (31 Car. II, 1679).
28 Oldmixon, p. 578; Wheatley, I, p. 451.
29 Renier, p. 85.
30 Ogg, II, p. 585.
31 Clarke, *James II*, I, p. 555; Browning, *Danby*, I, p. 319.
32 Kenyon, *Sunderland*, p. 25.
33 Sitwell, p. 60.
34 Sitwell, p. 66.
35 Brett, p. 55.
36 Chapman, *Villiers*, p. 229 (Buckingham's *Commonplace Book*); *Ailesbury*, I, pp. 75–7.
37 Burnet, II, p. 353; Kenyon, *Plot*, p. 90.
38 Robb, I, p. 141.
39 Evelyn, II, p. 228.
40 Burnet, II, p. 216.
41 Mackenzie, *Lauderdale*, pp. 459–60.
42 Burghclere, *Ormonde*, II, p. 260.
43 Essex Papers, 28 March 1674 (Essex to Harbord).
44 Pierpont Morgan, R. of E. box IX, pt 3, fol. 96.
45 *Appeal from the Country to the City*, 1679.
46 *Reresby*, p. 66.

Chapter 23: A King at Chess

1 Jones, *First Whigs*, p. 63 *et seq.*
2 Burnet, II, p. 251, note 1.
3 Burnet, II, p. 213.
4 See Nutting, *The Most Wholesome Law.*
5 Haley, *Shaftesbury*, p. 536; Kenyon, *Sunderland*, p. 27; Blencowe, I, p. 36.
6 Hatton Correspondence, I, p. 196.
7 See Kenyon, *Acquittal of Wakeman*; but see Havighurst,

pt 2, p. 234, for view that collusion possible.

8 Kenyon, *Acquittal of Wakeman*.

9 Mason, *Account of the death*.

10 Haley, *Shaftesbury*, p. 466; Western, *Monarchy and Revolution*, p. 35; Clarke, *James II*, II, p. 5; but see Turner, *James II*, p. 102, note 2, for Mary of Modena's contrary view.

11 See Siegel and Poynter, *Talbor and Cinchona*.

12 Kenyon, *Sunderland*, p. 30; Blencowe, I, pp. 99, 147; R. A. Wardrobe 79693.

13 Hatton Correspondence, I, p. 206.

14 Lauderdale Papers, III, p. 211–12; Halifax, p. 61.

15 Jones, *Green Ribbon Club*; Chapman, *Villiers*, pp. 257–9; *Domestick Intelligence*, 18 November 1679.

16 Kenyon, *Plot*, pp. 189–90.

17 *Letters to a Person of Honour concerning the King's disavowing Monmouth's mother*.

18 *Letter to a Person of Honour concerning the Black Box*.

19 Pierpont Morgan, R. of G. box VIII, pt 2, fols 52, 53.

20 Halifax, p. 319.

21 Kenyon, *Sunderland*, pp. 41–2.

22 See Sacret, *Municipal Corporations*.

23 North, p. 121; Furley, *Whig Exclusionists, passim*.

24 Miller, *James II*, p. 109; *James II's Memoirs, 1821*, p. 283,

25 Dalrymple, II, p. 282.

26 Halifax, p. 325.

27 Clark, *Later Stuarts*, p. 102.

28 *Letters*, p. 313.

29 *Letters*, p. 314.

30 Grey, *Debates of the House of Commons*, VIII, p. 11.

31 Kenyon, *Sunderland*, pp. 51, 66.

32 Burnett, I, p. 493.

33 de Beer, *House of Lords in 1680*.

34 Foxcroft, *Halifax*, pp. 246–7, 252–5.

35 Tate, *Poems by several hands*, p. 93.

Chapter 24: Bolder and Older

1 *Reresby*, pp. 110, 103.

2 Ashley, *Charles II*, p. 275, 342, note 22.

3 Welwood, p. 138.

4 Haley, *Shaftesbury*, p. 584.

5 *Letters*, p. 316.

6 Kenyon, *Plot*, p. 203.

7 *Stafford's Brief and Impartial Account*.

8 *Ailesbury*, I, p. 95.

9 Nicoll, I, p. 434.

10 Haley, *Shaftesbury*, p. 621; Pollock, *Plot*, pp. 390–91.

11 C. S. P. Domestic 1680–81, p. 178.

12 Summers, *Playhouse*, p. 129.

13 Childs, p. 229.

14 Dryden, VII, p. 5–7; Tate, *Poems by Several Hands*, p. 127.

15 *Letters*, p. 317, wrongly dated 20 March; H. M. C. Ormonde, V, p. 619.

16 *Ailesbury*, I, p. 57; Turberville, Pt I.

17 *Debates in the House of Commons,* 21 March 1680.

18 *Letters,* p. 319.

19 *Ailesbury,* I, p. 58.

20 Bryant, *Pepys,* II, p. 351, note.

21 Chandaman, p. 135; Ashley, *Charles II,* p. 278.

22 *Letters,* pp. 319–22.

23 Ogg, II, p. 620, note 1; Blencowe, I, p. 212.

24 Howell, *State Trials,* VIII, p. 246.

25 Howell, *State Trials,* VIII, pp. 591, 595, 602.

26 Hatton Correspondence, II, p. 10.

27 Kenyon, *Sunderland,* p. 66.

28 Haley, *Shaftesbury,* p. 667.

29 Airy, *Charles II,* p. 261.

30 Burnet, II, p. 176, note 3.

31 Foxcroft, *Burnet,* p. 136; *Ailesbury,* I, p. 86; *Reresby,* p. 133.

32 R. A. Wardrobe 86382; Pierpont Morgan, R. of E. box IX, Pt 2.

33 Sergeant, p. 209.

34 See Dillon, *Some familiar Letters, passim.*

35 Evelyn, II, p. 195; Hatton Correspondence, I, p. 96; *Letters,* p. 327; Dasent, p. 70; Dillon, *Some familiar Letters,* p. 188; Evelyn, II, p. 199.

36 Withycombe, *English Christian Names*; Hoskins, II, p. 352.

37 Dillon, *Some familiar Letters,* pp. 159–62.

38 Evelyn, II, p. 199; H. M. C., 7th Rept, App., Pt 1, p. 373.

39 Halifax, p. 252.

Chapter 25: Another Way of Ruling

1 *Reresby,* p. 175; *Ailesbury,* I, p. 21.

2 Chandaman, p. 135.

3 R. A. SP Add. 1/69.

4 R. A. Wardrobe 79904 verso, 79781, 79785.

5 C. S. P. Domestic October 1683–April 1684, p. 365.

6 As did James himself; Clarke, *James II,* I, p. 746.

7 Turner, *James II,* pp. 213–15.

8 Dillon, *Some familiar Letters,* p. 160.

9 *Reresby,* p. 177; Clarke, *James II,* I, p. 746.

10 Western, *Monarchy and Revolution,* p. 10 *et seq.*

11 Dillon, *Some familiar Letters,* p. 181.

12 North, p. 251; Burnet, II, p. 180.

13 Havighurst, Pt 2, p. 247.

14 North, p. 141.

15 Havighurst, Pt 2, p. 246.

16 *Reresby,* p. 170.

17 C. S. P. Domestic May 1684–February 1685, pp. 216, 94, 20, 85, 292, 151–6.

18 Airy, *Charles II,* p. 266; C. S. P. Domestic May 1684–February 1685, p. *vii et seq.*

19 Burnet, II, p. 384, note 1.

20 C. S. P. Domestic May 1684–February 1685, p. 187.

21 Jones, *Green Ribbon Club.*

22 Haley, *Shaftesbury,* p. 707 *et seq.*; Wyndham, p. 105.

23 D'Urfey, I, pp. 246–9.

24 Burnet, II, p. 363.

25 Airy, *Essex*, D. N. B., where it is called 'flippant and cruel' – but more probably sincere.

26 Robb, I, p. 183.

27 C. S. P. Domestic October 1683–April 1684, p. 35.

28 C. S. P. Domestic October 1683–April 1684, p. 36; Kenyon, *Sunderland*, p. 95.

29 Miller, *James II*, p. 116.

30 Duffy, p. 216.

31 Turner, *James II*, p. 229.

32 C. S. P. Domestic May 1684– February 1685, p. 248; Burnet, II, p. 287.

33 North, p. 233.

34 Airy, *Charles II*, p. 385.

35 Havighurst, Pt 2, p. 246; H. M. C., 15th Rept, App., VIII, p. 200.

36 Ashley, *Charles II*, p. 289.

37 *King's Works*, p. 305.

38 *King's Works*, p. 308.

39 Evelyn, II, p. 186.

40 Plumptre, p. 158.

41 *Ailesbury*, I, p. 87.

42 Ascoli, pp. 40–75.

43 de Beer, *Charles II Fundator*, p. 44.

44 Foxcroft, *Burnet*, p. 75.

Chapter 26: The Dregs of Life

1 Chandaman, pp. 134–5.

2 H. M. C., 14th Rept, App., Pt IX, p. 400.

3 Havighurst, Pt 2, pp. 248–9 and note 16.

4 Browning, *Danby*, I, p. 363.

5 Ogg, II, p. 654; C. S. P. Domestic May 1684–

February 1685, pp. 22–3, 39.

6 C. S. P. Domestic May 1684– February 1685, p. 187.

7 Clark, *Later Stuarts*, p. 110.

8 C. S. P. Domestic May 1684– February 1685, p. 187.

9 Kenyon, *Sunderland*, pp. 99– 100.

10 Bagwell, III, p. 146.

11 Carte, *Ormonde*, II, App., p. 128.

12 Kenyon, *Sunderland*, pp. 108– 109.

13 C. S. P. Domestic May 1684– February 1685, p. 168.

14 Foxcroft, *Halifax*, I, pp. 420– 33; Browning, *Danby*, I, pp. 362–3.

15 H. M. C., 15th Rept, App., Pt VIII, I, p. 212.

16 Oldmixon, p. 691; Foxcroft, *Trimmer*, p. 209.

17 Burnet, II, p. 455.

18 Ogg, II, p. 453, note 1; Crowne, Foreword to *Sir Courtly Nice*; Bryant, *Charles II*, p. 283; *James II*, 1821, p. 177.

19 Tate, *Poems*, 1684, p. 69; Halifax, p. 98.

20 Burnet, II, p. 466; for sources in general, see Crawfurd, *Last Days*, Intro. pp. 1–11, and Narrative; references not given in Crawfurd listed below.

21 Evelyn, II, p. 210.

22 Mason, *Account of the death*.

23 Mason, *Account of the death*.

24 Morris, *Dryden, Hobbs, Tonson*.

25 Mason, *Account of the death*.

26 Mason, *Account of the death*.

27 Morris, *Dryden, Hobbs, Tonson*.

28 Mason, *Account of the death.*
29 Tate, *Poems by Several Hands*, p. 425; Mason, *Account of the death.*
30 Mason, *Account of the death.*
31 Welwood, p. 147.
32 Fraser, *Cromwell*, p. 671.
33 Muddiman, *Death of Charles II.*
34 Evelyn, II, pp. 237–8; de Beer, *Evelyn*, IV, pp. 476–9; *Copies of Two Papers, 1686*; Burnet, II, pp. 472–3; Halifax, p. 250.
35 Huddleston, *Brief Account*; Dalrymple, II, pp. 94–9 for Barrillon's despatch.
36 Ellis, 1st series, III, p. 333.
37 Macaulay, *History of England, 1866*, I, p. 342.
38 Mason, *Account of the death*; Evelyn, II, p. 206; Burnet, II, p. 461.

Chapter 27: His Royal Ashes

1 North, p. 253.
2 Wilson, *Nell Gwynn*, p. 218; C. S. P. Domestic February– December 1685, p. 8.
3 Stanley, pp. 499–500; details confirmed to author, 1978.
4 Evelyn, II, pp. 210–211.
5 Turner, *James II*, p. 244; Latham, *Pepys*, I, p. 249, note; C. S. P. Domestic February– December 1685, p. 8.
6 Fraser, *Cromwell*, pp. 680–85.
7 *The Quaker's Elegy*; Arwaker, *The Vision.*
8 Wilson, *Nell Gwynn*, p. 241; C. S. P. Domestic February– December 1685, p. 8.
9 Heaton, *Yachting*, p. 50.
10 Strickland, v, p. 682; Evelyn, II, p. 209.
11 Burnet, II, p. 180.
12 Plumb, *Growth of Political Stability*, p. 15.
13 Buckingham, *Short Character of Charles II*, p. 8; *Ailesbury*, I, p. 95.
14 Dryden, *Preface to All For Love.*
15 Halifax, p. 55; *Dryden Essays (Defence of the Epilogue).*

Reference Books

This list is not a bibliography, impracticable for reasons of space. It is merely intended to give details of works cited in brief in the references. For a full bibliography of the period the reader is referred to Godfrey Davis (1st edition) and Mary Frear Keeler (2nd edition) *Bibliography of British History, Stuart period 1603–1714* (Oxford, 1970). As a supplement: J. P. Kenyon, *Stuart England* (1978) includes a critical bibliography, and J. R. Jones, *Country and Court 1658–1714* (1978) appends a bibliographical essay, surveying recently published work on the period.

Abbott, W. C., *The Long Parliament of Charles II*, English Historical Review, Vol. 21, 1906.

Abbott, W. C., *Writings and Speeches of Oliver Cromwell*, 4 Vols, Cambridge, Massachusetts, 1937–47.

Aberdare, Lord, *The Story of Tennis*, 1959.

An Abstract of Provisions made in the Office of the Great Wardrobe for the use and Service of His Majestie King Charles the Second as well against his Royal Proceeding through the City of London the 22nd April 1661. As also for his Royall Coronation the day following, Royal Archives.

An Account of the Preservation of King Charles II, after the Battle of Worcester Drawn up by Himself to which are added His Letters to Several Persons, Glasgow, 1766.

Memoirs of Thomas, Earl of Ailesbury written by himself, 2 Vols, Roxburghe Club, 1890.

Airy, Osmund, *Charles II*, 1901.

Alden, John, *The Muses Mourn; A Checklist of Verse Occasioned by the Death of Charles II*, Charlottesville, Virginia, 1958.

Almack, Edward (ed.), *The Cavalier Soldier's Vade-Mecum*, 1900.

Correspondence of Sir Robert Kerr, 1st Earl of Ancram, and his son William, 3rd Earl of Lothian, Vols I and II, Edinburgh, 1871.

Anderson, Henry, *A Loyal Tear Dropt on the Vault of the High and Mighty Prince Charles II, Of Glorious and Happy Memory*, 1685.

Annals of Pittenweem, 1526–1793, ed. D. Cook, Anstruther, 1867.

An Appeal from the Country to the City by Junius Brutus, 1679.

The Armouries of the Tower of London, I, Ordnance, H. L. Blackmore, H.M.S.O., 1976.

Arwaker, Edmund M. A., *The Vision: A Pindarick Ode Occasion'd by the Death of Our Late Gracious Sovereign King Charles II*, 1685.

Ascoli, David, *A Village in Chelsea: An informal account of the Royal Hospital*, 1974.

Ashley, Maurice, *Charles II: Man and Statesman*, 1971.

Ashley, Maurice, *General Monck*, 1977.

Bagwell, Richard, *Ireland under the Stuarts*, 3 Vols, 1908 (reprinted 1963).

Baker, Sir Richard, *A Chronicle of the Kings of England ... with a continuation of the chronicle in this fourth edition to the coronation of his sacred majesty King Charles II*, 1665.

Balleine, G. R., *All for the King: The Life Story of Sir George Carteret (1609–1680)*, Société Jersiaise, St Helier, 1976.

Barbour, Violet, *Henry Bennet, Earl of Arlington*, 1914.

Baschet, A., *Transcripts of the despatches of French Ambassadors in London*, Public Record Office.

Beer, E. S. de, *The Diary of John Evelyn*, 6 Vols, Oxford, 1955.

Beer, E. S. de, *The House of Lords in the Parliament of 1680*, Bulletin of the Institute of Historical Research, Vol. xx, No. 59, November 1943.

Beer, E. S. de, *King Charles II, Fundator et Patronus*, Notes and Records of the Royal Society of London, ed. Sir Harold Hartley, Vol. 15, 1960.

Beer, E. S. de, *King Charles II's own fashion: An episode in English–French Relations* 1666–1670, Journal of the Warburg Institute, Vol. 2, 1938–9.

Beer, E. S. de, *Members of the Court Party in the House of Commons 1670–1678*, Bulletin of the Institute of Historical Research, Vol. XI, 1933–4.

Behrens, B., *The Whig Theory of the Constitution in the Reign of Charles II*, Cambridge Historical Journal, Vol. VII, 1941.

Bell, W. G., *The Great Fire of London in 1666*, 3rd edition, 1923.

Bell, W. G., *The Great Fire of London*, 1957.

Benson, Donald R., *Halifax and the Trimmers*, Huntingdon Library Quarterly, Vol. XXVII, February 1964.

Birch, Thomas, *The History of the Royal Society of London*, etc., Vol. I, 1761.

Blencowe, R. W. (ed. with notes), *Diary of the times of Charles II, by the Honourable Henry Sidney*, etc., 2 Vols, 1843.

Blount, Thomas, *Boscobel: or the Compleat History of His Sacred Majesties Most Miraculous Preservation after the Battle of Worcester, 3 Sept 1651*, 1660.

Boddington Commonplace Book.

Boscobel House and White Ladies Priory, Department of the Environment, H.M.S.O., 1965 (reprinted 1975).

Bosher, R. S., *The Making of the Restoration Settlement*, 1951.

Bowle, John, *Charles the First*, 1975.

Brett, A. C. A., *Charles II and his Court*, 1910.

Brett-James, G. N., *Growth of Stuart London*, 1935.

A Briefe Relation, 2 October 1649–22 October 1650.

Browning, Andrew, *Thomas Osborne, Earl of Danby and Duke of Leeds, 1632–1712*, 3 Vols, Glasgow, 1951.

Browning, Andrew, *Parties and Party Organization in the Reign of Charles II*, Transactions of the Royal Historical Society, 4th Series, Vol. XXX, 1948.

Bryant, Arthur, *King Charles II*, 1931 (revised edition, 1955, to which references are given).

Bryant, Arthur, *Samuel Pepys*; (I) *The Man in the Making*, new edition, 1947.

Bryant, Arthur, *Samuel Pepys*; (II) *The Years of Peril*, 1935.

Buckingham, John, Duke of, *A Short Character of King Charles II, King of England*, 6th edition, 1725.

Buckingham, John, Duke of, *Works*, 2 Vols, The Hague, 1726.

Burghclere, Winifred, Lady, *George Villiers, 2nd Duke of Buckingham, 1628–1687*, 1903.

Burghclere, Winifred, Lady, *The Life of James, 1st Duke of Ormonde, 1610–1688*, 2 Vols, 1912.

Burnet's History of my own time, new edition by Osmund Airy, 2 Vols, Oxford, 1897, 1900.

Calendar of the Clarendon State Papers, Vol. IV, 1657–60, and Vol. V, 1660–1726, F. J. Routledge, 1932.

(C. S. P. Domestic) Calendar of State Papers Domestic.

(C. S. P. Venetian) Calendar of State Papers Venetian.

Cardwell, Edward, *Documentary Annals of the Reformed Church of England*, Oxford, 1839.

Carlingford Papers, Osborn Collection.

Carlyle, E. I., *Clarendon and the Privy Council*, English Historical Review, Vol. 27, 1912.

Carte, Thomas, *A Collection of Original Letters and Papers ... Found among the Duke of Ormonde's Papers*, 2 Vols, 1739.

Carte, Thomas, *Life of James, Duke of Ormonde*, 3 Vols, 1735–6.

Cary, H., *Memorials of the Great Civil War in England, 1646–1652*, edited from original letters in the Bodleian Library, 2 Vols, 1842.

Chandaman, C. D., *The English Public Revenue, 1660–1688*, Oxford, 1975.

Chapman, Hester W., *Great Villiers; A Study of George Villiers, Second Duke of Buckingham, 1628–1687*, 1949.

Chapman, Hester, W., *The Tragedy of Charles II*, 1964.

Chevers, Norman, *An Enquiry into the Circumstances of the Death of King Charles the Second of England*, Calcutta, 1911.

Childs, John, *The Army of Charles II*, 1976.

Church, Richard, *Royal Parks of London*, H.M.S.O., 1956.

The History of the Rebellion and Civil Wars in England by Edward, Earl of Clarendon, ed. W. Dunn Macray, 6 Vols, Oxford, 1888.

The Life of Edward Earl of Clarendon ... in which is included a Continuation of his History of the Grand Rebellion, written by Himself, 3 Vols, new edition, Oxford, 1827.

Clarendon Mss, Bodleian Library, Oxford.

Clark, Dorothy K., *Edward Backwell as a Royal Agent*, Economic History Review, Vol. XI, 1938.

Clark, Sir George, *The Later Stuarts 1660–1714*, 2nd edition, Oxford, 1955.

Clarke, Rev. J. S. (ed.), *The Life of James the Second, King of England*, etc., 2 Vols, 1816.

Commons Journals, Vols VII–IX.

Cook, Aurelian, *Titus Britannicus: An Essay of History Royal in the Life and Reign of his Late Sacred Majesty Charles II of Ever Blessed and Immortal Memory*, 19 March 1685.

Copies of Two Papers Written by the late King Charles II, Together with a Copy of a Paper Written by the late Duchess of York, Henry Hills, 1686.

(C. A.), *Correspondence Politique, Angleterre*, Ministère des Affaires Etrangères, Paris.

Cowan, Edward J., *Montrose: For Covenant and King*, 1977.

Crawfurd, Raymond, *The Last Days of Charles II*, Oxford, 1909.

Crist, Timothy (ed. with Introd. and Notes), *Charles II to Lord Taaffe, Letters in Exile*, 1974.

Croft-Murray, Edward, *Isaac Fuller's Paintings of Charles II's Escape after the Battle of Worcester*, Society of Antiquaries, Oxford, 1971.

Crowne, John, *Sir Courtly Nice or It Cannot Be; A Comedy*, 1685.

Cunningham, Peter (related and collected by), *The Story of Nell Gwynn: and the Saying of Charles II*, 2 Vols, New York, 1883.

Dalrymple, Sir John, *Memoirs of Great Britain and Ireland*, 2 Vols, 1773.

Dasent, Arthur Irwin, *The Private Life of Charles the Second*, 1927.

Davies, Godfrey, *The Restoration of Charles II 1658–1660*, 1955.

Davis, Ralph, *The Rise of the English Shipping Industry in the Seventeenth and Eighteenth Centuries*, 1962.

The Debates in the House of Commons, Assembled at Oxford, 21 March 1680.

Debates of the House of Commons from the year 1667 to the year 1694, ed. Anchitel Grey, 1769.

Deedes, Cecil (ed.), *Royal and Loyal Sufferers*: 1903, includes: (1) Wase's *Electra* 1649; (2) *An Exact Narrative and Relation of his Sacred Majesties Escape from Worcester on the 3rd of September 1651*, etc.; (3) *Eikon Basilike or the True Portraiture of His Sacred Majestie Charles the II*, etc., *1630–1660*, by R. F., Esq., an eye-witness.

A Defence of the Papers Written by the late King of Blessed Memory and Duchess of York, Against the Answer Made to Them, by command H. Hills, 1686.

Delpech, Jeanine, *Life and Times of the Duchess of Portsmouth,* 1953.

Dillon, William, and Arthur, Harold, (transcribed and ed.), *Some familiar Letters of Charles II and James, Duke of York, addressed to their daughter and niece, the Countess of Lichfield,* Archaeologia, second series, Vol. VIII, Society of Antiquaries of London, 1902.

Domestick Intelligence.

Domiduca Oxoniensis: sive musae academicae gratulato ob auspicatissimum serenissimae principis Catharinae lusitanae regi suo desponsatae in Angliam appulsum, Oxoniae, 1662.

Donaldson, Gordon, *Scotland: James V to James VII,* Edinburgh, 1965.

Douglas, W. S., *Cromwell's Scotch Campaigns 1650–51,* 1898.

Downes, J. F., *The Strawberry Roan,* unpublished MS.

Works of John Dryden, ed. Sir Walter Scott, Vol. VII, 1808.

Dryden, John, *Essays,* ed. W. P. Kerr.

Duffy, Maureen, *The Passionate Shepherdess; Aphra Behn 1640–1689,* 1977.

D'Urfey, Thomas, *Wit and Mirth or Pills to Purge Melancholy,* Vol. I, 1719.

The Earl of Manchester's Speech to His Majesty in the name of the Peers, At his Arrival at Whitehall 29th May 1660. With his Majesties Gracious Answer, printed by John Macock and Francis Tyton, 1660.

Earle, John, *Microcosmography,* Pt I, 'The Child', 1628.

Earle, Peter, *James II,* 1972.

Eikon Basilike or the True Portraiture of His Sacred Majestie Charles the II, Beginning from his Birth 1630 into this present year 1660. Wherein is interwoven a Compleat History of the High-Born Dukes of York and Gloucester, in 3 books by R. F., Esq., an eye-witness, 1660. See Deedes, Cecil (ed.), *Royal and Loyal Sufferers,* 1903.

Ellis, Sir Henry, *Original Letters Illustrative of English History,* 1st and 2nd Series, Vols 3 and 4, 1824, 1827.

Elmes, James, *Sir Christopher Wren and his Times,* 1852.

Essex Papers (1672–7), ed. O. Airy and C. E. Pike, Camden Society, 1890, 1913.

Diary and Correspondence of John Evelyn, F. R. S., ed. William Bray, 4 Vols, 1850.

An Exact Narrative and Relation of his Sacred Majesties Escape from Worcester on the *3rd September 1651*, etc., see Deedes, Cecil (ed.), *Royal and Loyal Sufferers*, 1903.

Fagel, Henry, *A Foreigner at the Court of Charles II*, 1661, Osborn Collection.

Falkus, Christopher, *The Life and Times of Charles II*, 1972.

The Memoirs of Ann, Lady Fanshawe, ed. E. J. Fanshawe, 1907.

Fayette, Madame de la, *The Secret History of Henrietta, Princess of England*, translated by J. M. Shelmerdine, 1929.

Fea, Allan, *After Worcester Fight*, 1904.

Fea, Allan, *The Flight of the King*, 1897.

Fea, Allan, *James II and his Wives*, 1908.

Feaveryear, A. E., *The Pound Sterling, A History of English Money*, Oxford, 1931.

Feiling, Keith, *British Foreign Policy, 1660–1672*, new impression, 1968.

Feiling, Keith, *A History of the Tory Party, 1649–1714*, Oxford, 1924.

Feiling, Keith, *Henrietta Stuart, Duchess of Orleans, and the Origins of the Treaty of Dover*, English Historical Review, Vol. 47, 1932.

Feiling, Keith, *Two Speeches of Charles II*, English Historical Review, Vol. 45, 1930.

Feiling, Keith, *Two Unprinted Letters of Henrietta Stuart, Duchess of Orleans*, English Historical Review, Vol. 43, 1928.

Fitzmaurice, Lord Edmond, *The Life of Sir William Petty 1623–1687*, 1897.

Foley, Mss, Jesuit Archives, Farm Street, London.

The forme and order of the Coronation of Charles the Second ... As it was acted and done at Scone, Jan. 1st 1651, Aberdeen, 1651.

Forwood, Mary Gwendoline, Lady, *The Cavalier King Charles Spaniel*.

Foxcroft, H. C. (ed.), *A supplement to Burnet's History of my own time*, Oxford, 1902.

Foxcroft, H. C., *A Character of the Trimmer*, 1946.

Foxcroft, H. C., *Life and Letters of Sir George Savile, Bart., first Marquis of Halifax*, with a new edition of his works, 2 Vols, 1898.

Fraser, Antonia, *Cromwell: Our Chief of Men*, 1973.

Fraser, Antonia, *Mary Queen of Scots*, 1969.

Furley, O. W., *The Whig Exclusionists: Pamphlet Literature in the Exclusion Campaign, 1679–81*, Cambridge Historical Journal, Vol. XIII.

Gardiner, S. R., *The Commonwealth and Protectorate*, 4 Vols, 1903.

Gardiner, S. R., *The Last Campaign of Montrose*, The Edinburgh Review, Vol. CLXXIX, 1894.

Gardiner, S. R. (ed. with Notes and Introduction), *Letters and Papers Illustrating the relations between Charles II and Scotland in 1650*, Edinburgh, 1894.

Geyl, Pieter, *Orange* and *Stuart 1641–72*, 1969.

Girouard, Mark, *Life in the English Country House*, 1978.

Grammont, Count, *Memoirs of the Court of Charles the Second*, also *The Personal History of Charles II* and *Boscobel Tracts* etc., ed. Sir Walter Scott, 1864.

Greene, Graham, *Lord Rochester's Monkey*, 1974.

Grey, A., *Debates of the House of Commons from 1667–1694*, 1769.

Guildhall Library Mss, London.

Habbakuk, Sir John, *Land Settlement and the Restoration of Charles II*, Transactions of the Royal Historical Society, 5th series, 28, 1978.

Haley, K. D. H., *Charles II*, Historical Association pamphlet, 1966.

Haley, K. D. H., *The First Earl of Shaftesbury*, Oxford, 1968.

Haley, K. D. H., *William of Orange and the English Opposition, 1672–4*, Oxford, 1953.

Halifax: Complete Works, ed. with an Introduction by J. P. Kenyon, 1969.

Hamilton, Elizabeth, *Henrietta Maria*, 1976.

Hamilton, Elizabeth, *William's Mary: A Biography of Mary II*, 1972.

Hamilton Papers, ed. S. R. Gardiner, Camden Society, 1880.

Harris, William, *An Historical and Critical Account of the Life of Charles II*, etc., 2 Vols, 1747.

Hart, W. H., *A Memorial of Nell Gwynne, the Actress, and Thomas Otway, the Dramatist*, 1868.

Hartmann, C. H., *La Belle Stuart*, 1924.

Hartmann, C. H., *Charles II and Madame*, 1934.

Hartmann, C. H., *Clifford of the Cabal: A Life of Thomas first Lord Clifford of Chudleigh, Lord High Treasurer of England 1630–1673*, 1937.

Hartmann, C. H., *The King My Brother*, 1954.

Hartmann, C. H., *The Vagabond Duchess*, 1926.

Correspondence of the Family of Hatton, 1601–1704, ed. E. M. Thompson, Camden Society, 2 Vols, 1878.

Havighurst, A. F., *The Judiciary and Politics in the Age of Charles II*, The Law Quarterly Review, Vol. 66, January and April 1950.

Hayward, John (ed.), *Collected Works of Rochester*, 1926.

Heaton, Peter, *Yachting: A History*, 1955.

Heraldic Visitations of Wales, ed. Sir Samuel Meyrick, 2 Vols, 1846.

Hillier, George, *A Narrative of the attempted Escapes of Charles I ... Including the letters of the King to Colonel Titus, now first deciphered and printed from the originals*, 1852.

Memoires by Sir John Hinton, Physician in ordinary to His Majestie's Person ... 1679.

His Majesties Gracious Message to all his loving Subjects in the Kingdom of Ireland upon their Exemplary Return to their Obedience, 30 March 1660.

(H. M. C.) Historical Manuscripts Commission, 1st Report.

(H. M. C.) Historical Manuscripts Commission, 6th Report.

(H. M. C.) Historical Manuscripts Commission, 7th Report, Part I, Report and Appendix, 1879.

(H. M. C.) Historical Manuscripts Commission, 10th Report, Appendix IV.

(H. M. C.) Historical Manuscripts Commission, 14th Report, Appendix, Part IX, *Mss The Earl of Lindsay*, 1895.

(H. M. C.) Historical Manuscripts Commission, 15th Report, Part VIII, *Mss of the Duke of Buccleuch and Queensberry*, Vol. I, 1897.

(H. M. C.) Historical Manuscripts Commission, *The Marquess of Ormonde*, new series, Vol. V.

Hore, J. P., *The History of Newmarket and the Annals of the Turf*, Vols II and III, 1886.

Hore, J. P. (compiled by), *The History of the Royal Buckhounds*, Newmarket, 1895.

Hoskins, S. Elliott, *Charles the Second in the Channel Islands*, 2 Vols, 1854.

Household Book: Minutes of the Board of Green Cloth during Charles II's residence in Scotland 1650–1, Scottish Record Office.

Howell, T. B., (compiled by), *1809 State Trials*, 8 Vols, London and Middlesex Archaeological Society, 1935.

Huddleston, John, *A Brief Account of Particulars occurring at the happy death of our late Sovereign Lord King Charles II, in regard to Religion ... Annexed to A Short and Plain Way to the Faith and Church by Richard Huddleston*, 1688.

Hughes, J. (ed.), *The Boscobel Tracts: relating to the Escape of Charles the Second after Worcester*, Edinburgh and London, 1830.

Correspondence of Henry Hyde, Earl of Clarendon, and of his brother Lawrence Hyde, Earl of Rochester, ed. S. W. Singer, 2 Vols, 1828.

Hutchinson, Lucy, *Memoirs of the Life of Colonel Hutchinson*, ed. James Satherland, repr. 1973.

The Diary of Alexander Jaffray, ed. J. Barclay, Aberdeen, 1856.

Memoirs of James II, 2 Vols, Colchester, 1821.

The Memoirs of James II: His Campaigns as Duke of York 1652–1660, trans. A. Lyton Sells from the Bouillon Manuscript, 1962.

Jones, J. R., *Country and Court: England 1658–1714*, 1978.

Jones, J. R., *The First Whigs: The Politics of the Exclusion Crisis, 1678–1683*, 1961.

Jones, J. R., *The Green Ribbon Club*, Durham University Journal, December 1956.

Josten, C. H. (ed. and with Introduction), *Elias Ashmole 1617–1692*, 5 Vols, Oxford, 1966.

Jusserand, J. J., *A French Ambassador at the Court of Charles II*, 1892.

Kenyon, John, *The Popish Plot*, 1972.

Kenyon, J. P., *The Acquittal of Sir George Wakeman 18 July 1679*, The Historical Journal, 1971.

Kenyon, J. P., *The Stuart Constitution, 1603–1688: Documents and Commentary*, Cambridge, 1966.

Kenyon, J. P., *Stuart England*, 1978.

Kenyon, J. P., *Robert Spence, Earl of Sunderland, 1641–1702*, 1958.

King Charles Preserved: An Account of his Escape after the Battle of Worcester dictated by the King himself to Samuel Pepys, Rodale Press, 1956.

The King's Coronation: Being an Exact Account of the Cavalcade, with a Description of the Triumphal Arches, and Speeches prepared by the City of London, etc., John Ogilby, 1685.

The History of the King's Works, Vol. v, 1660–1782, General Editor H. M. Colvin, H.M.S.O., 1976.

Kingston, H. P., *The Wanderings of Charles II in Staffordshire and Shropshire after the Worcester Fight*, Birmingham, 1933.

Diary of Dr Edward Lake, ed. G. P. Elliott, Camden Society Miscellany, I, 1847.

Latham, R. C., and Matthews, W. (eds), *The Diary of Samuel Pepys*, 9 Vols, 1970–76.

The Lauderdale Papers, ed. O. Airy, 3 Vols, Camden Society, 1884–5.

Lee, Maurice, Jr, *The Cabal*, Urbana, 1965.

Legg, L. G. W., *English Coronation Records*, 1901.

A Letter farther and more fully evidencing the King's stedfastenesse in the Protestant Religion, written by Monsieur de l'Angle, Minister of the Protestant Church at Rouen, to a friend in London, 1 June 1660.

A Letter to a Person of Honour Concerning the Black Box, 1680.

A Letter to a Person of Honour, concerning the King's disavowing the having been Married to the Duke of Monmouth's mother, Robert Ferguson, 1680.

The Letters, Speeches and Declarations of King Charles II (Letters) ed. Arthur Bryant, 1935.

Lindley, K. J. *The Part played by the Catholics in the English Civil War*, University of Manchester.

Lipscomb, F. W., *Heritage of Sea Power*, 1976.

Lives of the most Celebrated Beauties, 1715.

London's Roll of Fame 1885–1959, Introd. Irving B. Gare, 1960.

Longrigg, Roger, *A History of Horse-racing*, 1972.

Lords Journals, Vols IX–XIII.

Lower, Sir William, *A Relation In Form of Journal, Of The Voyage and Residence Which the most Excellent and most Mighty Prince Charles the II King of Great Britain*, etc., *hath made in Holland, from the 25th of May, to the 2nd of June 1660*, The Hague, 1660.

Lyon, C. J., *Personal History of King Charles the Second 1650–1651*, Edinburgh, 1851.

Mackenzie, W. C., *The Life and Times of John Maitland, Duke of Lauderdale 1616–1682*, 1923.

McKie, Douglas, *The Origins and Foundation of the Royal Society of London*, in *Notes and Records of The Royal Society of London*, ed. Sir Harold Hartley, Vol. 15, 1960.

MacLaurin, C., *Mere Mortals*, New York, 1925.

Macpherson, James, *Memoirs of King James II*, 1775.

Macray, W. D., (ed.), *Notes which passed at Meetings of the Privy Council between Charles II and the Earl of Clarendon 1660–1667*, Roxburghe Club, 1896.

Margoliouth, H. M. (ed.), *The Poems and Letters of Andrew Marvell*, 3rd edition revised by Pierre Legoirs, with E. E. Duncan-Jones, 2 Vols, Oxford, 1971.

Mason, Anne Margaret, Lady, *Account of the death of Charles II 'by a wife of a person about the Court at Whitehall'*, Household Words, 9, 1854.

Matthews, William (ed.), *Charles II's Escape from Worcester: A Collection of Narratives Assembled by Samuel Pepys*, Berkeley and Los Angeles, 1966.

Memoires of the Duchess of Mazarine: together with reasons for her coming into England, likewise a letter containing a true character ..., trans, P. Porter 1676.

Mercurius Britannicus.

Mercurius Politicus.

Millar, Oliver, *The Age of Charles I: Painting in England 1620–1649*, Tate Gallery, 1972.

Millar, Oliver, *The Queen's Pictures*, 1977.

Millar, Oliver, *Sir Peter Lely*, National Portrait Gallery, 1978.

Millar, Oliver, *The Tudor, Stuart and Early Georgian Pictures in the Collection of H. M. The Queen*, 1963.

Miller, John, *James II: A Study in Kingship*, Hove, 1977.

Miller, John, *Popery and Politics in England 1660–1688*, Cambridge, 1973.

Monarchy Revived: being the Personal History of Charles the Second from his earliest years to his Restoration to the throne, reprinted from 1661 edition, 1822.

Mémoires de Mademoiselle de Montpensier, ed. A. Cheruel, 4 Vols, Paris, 1892.

Morrah, Patrick, *Prince Rupert of the Rhine*, 1976.

Morris, G., *Dryden, Hobbs, Tonson and the Death of Charles II*, Notes and Queries, new series, Vol. 22, No. 12.

Morton Muniments, Scottish Record Office.

Memoirs of Madame de Motteville on Anne of Austria and her Court, trans. K. R. Wormsley, 3 Vols, 1902.

Muddiman, J. G., *The Death of Charles II*, The Month, 1932.

Nalson, John (taken by), *A true copy of the journal of the High Court of Justice for the Tryal of King Charles I*, 1683.

(Newbattle) *Inventory of Documents, State Papers and Letters belonging to the*

Marquess of Lothian and formerly preserved at Newbattle Abbey, Scottish Record Office.

The Life of William Cavendish Duke of Newcastle … by Margaret Duchess of Newcastle, ed. C. H. Firth, 1886.

The Nicholas Papers: Correspondence of Sir Edward Nicholas, Secretary of State, ed. Sir G. F. Warner, Camden Society, 4 Vols, 1886–1920.

Nicoll, Allardyce, *A History of English Drama 1660–1900*, Vol. I, *Restoration Drama*, 1952.

North, Roger, *The Life of the Right Honourable Francis North, Baron of Guilford*, etc., 1742.

Notes and Records of the Royal Society of London, ed. Sir Harold Hartley, Vol. 15, 1960.

Nuttall, G. F., and Chadwick, Owen (eds), *From Uniformity to Unity*, 1962.

Nutting, Helen, A., *The Most Wholesome Law – The Habeas Corpus Act of 1679*, American Historical Review, Vol. LXV, April 1960.

Ogg, David, *England in the Reign of Charles II*, 2nd edition, 1963.

Oldmixon, John, *The History of England during the Reigns of the Royal House of Stuart*, 1730.

Ollard, Richard, *The Escape of Charles II after the Battle of Worcester*, 1966.

Oman, Carola, *Henrietta Maria*, 1936.

Osborn Collection, Yale University.

Parry, C. Hubert H., *The Music of the Seventeenth Century*, 2nd edition, with revisions and an Introductory Note by Edward J. Dent, 1938.

The Diary of Samuel Pepys, ed. R. C. Latham and W. Matthews, 9 Vols, 1970–76.

Perrinchief, R., *The Royal Martyr: Life and Death of King Charles I*, 1676.

Petrie, Sir Charles (ed.), *Letters of King Charles I*.

Petty, Sir William, *Political Anatomy of Ireland*, 1691.

Pierpont Morgan Library Mss, New York.

Piper, David, *The Age of Charles II*, Royal Academy Catalogue, 1960.

Plumb, J. H., *The Growth of Political Stability in England 1675–1725*, 1967.

Plumb, J. H., and Weldon, Huw, *Royal Heritage: The Story of Britain's Royal Builders and Collectors*, 1977.

Plumptre, E. H., *The Life of Thomas Ken, D. D.*, 2 Vols, 1888.

Policy, no Policy, the Devil Himself Confuted, 1660.

Pollock, John, *The Popish Plot*, 1903.

Powys, Marion, *The Lace of King Charles II*, Bulletin of the Needle and Bobbin Club, Vol. XII, No. 2.

The Quakers Elegy on the Death of Charles Late King of England, 'written by W. P., a sincere Lover of Charles and James', 1685.

Rait, R. S., *Five Stuart Princesses*, 1908.

Ratcliff, E. C., *The Savoy Conference and the Revision of the Book of Common Prayer*, in Nuttall, G. F., and Chadwick, Owen (eds), *From Uniformity to Unity*, 1962.

Rawlinson Mss, Bodleian Library, Oxford.

Receuil des instructions données aux ambassadeurs de France, Vols XXIV–XXV, *Angleterre*, 1648–90, ed. J. J. Jusserand, Paris, 1929.

Renier, G. J., *William of Orange*, 1952.

The Memoirs of the Honourable Sir John Reresby, Bart, etc., 1735.

Robb, Nesca A., *William of Orange, 1650–1673; A Personal Portrait*, 2 Vols, 1962.

Robbins, Caroline, *The Repeal of the Triennial Act 1664*, Huntingdon Library Quarterly, Vol. XII, 1948.

Roberts, Clayton, *The impeachment of the Earl of Clarendon*, Cambridge Historical Journal, Vol. XIII, 1957.

Roth, Cecil, *History of the Jews in England*, 3rd edition, Oxford, 1964.

(R. A.) Royal Archives, Windsor Castle.

The Royal Pilgrimage of the Progresse and Travels of King Charles the Second, Through the most and greatest Courts of Europe, by an Eye Witness, 26 March 1660.

Rushworth, John, *The Tryal of Thomas Earl of Stafford, Lord Lieutenant of Ireland*, etc., 1680.

Sackville-West, V., *Daughter of France: The Life of Anne-Marie Louise d'Orléans, duchesse de Montpensier 1627–1693*, 1959.

Sacret, J. H., *The Restoration Government and Municipal Corporations*, Economic History Journal, April 1930.

St George, Sir Thomas, *Coronation of King Charles II*, Osborn Collection.

Samuel, Edgar R., *David Gabay's 1660 Letter from London*, Transactions of the Jewish Historical Society, xxv.

Scott, Eva, *The King in Exile: The Wanderings of Charles II from June 1646 to July 1654*, 1904.

Scott, Eva, *The Travels of the King: Charles II in Germany and Flanders, 1654–1660*, 1907.

Scott, Lord George, *Lucy Walter – Wife or Mistress?*, 1947.

(S. R. O.) Scottish Register Office, Edinburgh.

The Secret History of the Reigns of King Charles II and King James II, 1690.

Sergeant, Philip W., *My Lady Castlemaine*, 1912.

Shapiro, Barbara J., *John Wilkins, 1614–1672: An Intellectual Biography*, Berkeley and Los Angeles, 1969.

Shaw, W. A. (ed.), *Calendar of Treasury Books*, 1904–62.

Short but True Account of the Cruel and Terrible Fire through which almost the whole of the City of London became Ashes, Rotterdam, 25 September 1666.

Shrewsbury, J. F. D., *A History of Bubonic Plague in the British Isles*, Cambridge, 1970.

Siegel, Rudolph E., and Poynter, F. N. L., *Robert Talbor, Charles II and Cinchona: A contemporary document*, Medical History, Vol. 6, 1962.

Sitwell, Sir George, *The First Whig*, Scarborough, 1894.

Société Jersiaise, Bulletin Annuel, Vol. 3, 1890–96.

Société Jersiaise, Bulletin Annuel, *Some letters of Charles II to Jersey*, 1952.

A Brief and Impartial Account of the Birth and Quality, Imprisonment, etc., *Last Speech and Final End of William, late Lord Viscount Stafford*, 1681.

Stanley, Dean, *Memorials of Westminster Abbey*, 7th impression with Appendix, 1867.

Strickland, Agnes, *Lives of the Queens of England*, Vols IV and V, 1851.

Summers, Montague, *The Playhouse of Pepys*, 1935.

Summers, Montague, *The Restoration Theatre*, 1934.

Sykes, Marjorie, *Pleasures of the Park*, History Today, Vol. XXVIII, April 1978.

Taaffe Letters, Osborn Collection.

Memoirs of the Family of Taaffe, Vienna, 1856.

Tate, Nahum (collected by), *Poems by Several Hands and on Several Occasions*, 1685.

Tate, Nahum, *Poems written on Several Occasions*, 2nd edition, 1684.

Tate, Nuham, *The History of King Richard Second*, 1681.

Thirsk, Joan, *The Restoration Land Settlement*, Journal of Modern History, Vol. XXVI, 1954.

Thirsk, Joan, *The Sales of Royalist Land during the Interregnum*, Economic History Reviw, Vol. X, 1952.

(Thurloe) *A Collection of the State Papers of John Thurloe*, ed. Thomas Birch, 7 Vols, 1742.

Tozer, Basil, *The Horse in History*, 1908.

True and Good News from Brussels: Containing a Sovereigne Antidote agst the Poysons and Calumnies of the present time, 2 April 1660.

Tuke, Sir Samuel, *A Character of Charles the Second written by an Impartial Hand*, etc., 1660.

Turberville, A. S., *The House of Lords under Charles II*, Parts I and II, English Historical Review, Vols 44 and 45, 1929 and 1930.

Turner, F. C., *James II*, 1948.

Udal, J. S., *Dorsetshire Folk-Lore*, With a fore-say by the late William Barnes, Hertford, 1922.

Underdown, David, *Royalist Conspiracy in England 1649–1660*, New Haven, 1960.

Van Doren, Mark, *The Poetry of John Dryden*, Cambridge, 1931.

A very curious and well attested story concerning King Charles II, Osborn Collection.

Walker, James, *The Secret Service under Charles II and James II*, Transactions of the Royal Historical Society, 4th Series, Vol. XV, 1932.

Warwick, Sir Philip, *Memoires of the reign of King Charles I with a continuation to the happy restoration of King Charles II*, 1701.

Wase's *Electra*, 1649, see Deedes, Cecil (ed.), *Royal and Loyal Sufferers*, 1903.

Wedgwood, C. V., *The Trial of Charles I*, 1964.

Welwood, James, M. D., *Memoirs of the most Material Transactions in England for the last Hundred Years*, etc., 7th edition, 1749.

Western, J. R., *Monarchy and Revolution: The English State in the 1680s*, 1972.

Wheatley, H., *London Past and Present*, based on the *Handbook of London* by P. Cunningham, 1891.

Whiteman, Anne, *The Restoration of the Church of England*, in Nuttall, G. F., and Chadwick, Owen (eds), *From Uniformity to Unity*, 1962.

Willcock, John, *The Great Marquess, Life and Times of Archibald 8th Earl and 1st (and only) Marquess of Argyll*, 1903.

Williamson, Audrey, *The Mystery of the Princes: An investigation into a supposed murder*, Dursley, 1978.

Wilson, Charles, *Profit and Power: A study of England and the Dutch Wars*, 1957.

Wilson, J. H., *The Court Wits of the Restoration: An Introduction*, Princeton, 1948.

Wilson, J. H., *Nell Gwynn: Royal Mistress*, 1952.

Witcomb, D. T., *Charles II and the Cavalier House of Commons*, Manchester, 1966.

Withycombe, E. G., *Oxford Dictionary of English Christian Names*, 2nd edition, Oxford, 1949.

Wolbarsht, M. L., Naval Medical Research Institute, Bethesda, and Sax, D. S., Psychiatric Institute, University Hospital Baltimore, *Charles II, A Royal Martyr*, Notes and Records of the Royal Society of London, Vol. 16, No. 2, November 1961.

Wolf, Lucien, *The Jewry of the Restoration 1660–1664*, Transactions of the Jewish Historical Society.

Wyndham, Violet, *The Protestant Duke: A Life of Monmouth*, 1976.

Young, Peter, *Edgehill*, 1972.

Index